Senate Procedure
and Practice

Senate Procedure and Practice

Martin B. Gold

Foreword by Senator Bill Frist

ROWMAN & LITTLEFIELD PUBLISHERS, INC.
Lanham • Boulder • New York • Toronto • Oxford

ROWMAN & LITTLEFIELD PUBLISHERS, INC.

Published in the United States of America
by Rowman & Littlefield Publishers, Inc.
A wholly owned subsidiary of The Rowman & Littlefield Publishing Group, Inc.
4501 Forbes Boulevard, Suite 200, Lanham, Maryland 20706
www.rowmanlittlefield.com

PO Box 317
Oxford
OX2 9RU, UK

British Library Cataloguing in Publication Information Available

Library of Congress Cataloging-in-Publication Data

Gold, Martin, 1947–
  Senate procedure and practice / Martin B. Gold.
      p. cm.
  Includes bibliographical references and index.
  ISBN 0-7425-3451-0 (hardcover : alk. paper)—ISBN 0-7425-3452-9 (pbk. : alk.
paper)
  1. United States. Congress. Senate—Rules and practice. 2. Legislative
bodies—United States—Rules and practice. 3. Parliamentary practice—United
States. I. Title.
  KF4982.G65 2004
  328.73'05—dc22

                                                          2004001614

Printed in the United States of America

∞™ The paper used in this publication meets the minimum requirements of American
National Standard for Information Sciences—Permanence of Paper for Printed Library
Materials, ANSI/NISO Z39.48-1992.

Dedicated to the United States Senate

The Senate floor is one of the two most important places in one of the three most important buildings in America. Standing there, one cannot but feel like a patriot.

Contents

Foreword

United States Senate Majority Leader
William H. Frist, M.D.

The United States Senate is often referred to as the world's greatest deliberative body. And that is for good reason. The Senate Chamber—from its incep-
tion to its Golden Age to the present—has been the setting for some of the
most moving, decisive, and consequential debates in American history.

But why the Senate? Why the Senate and not its sister chamber, the House
of Representatives? Why the Senate—so unlike the upper chambers of many
other nations? Why the Senate—not for a few years or even decades—but
continuously over the entire course of the Republic?

The Senate is first and foremost a legislative body. It exists to pass legislation that may become law or to prevent legislation from becoming law. Beyond that, its responsibilities are to consent or deny consent to the ratification
of treaties, to provide advice and consent on presidential nominees, and to try
impeachments. It is by far the most powerful and influential upper chamber
anywhere in the world.

The Framers of the Constitution wanted the Senate to be an exceptional
legislative body. And by exceptional, I mean both unique in its structure and
superior as an institution. They believed this was essential for the Republic to
endure. As James Madison wrote in Federalist No. 63, "History informs us of
no long lived republic which had not a senate."

So the Framers provided for the following, among other things, in the Senate: equal representation of every state; terms extending six years, beyond
those of the House and the president; elections in which only one-third of
members would stand before the people every two years; and a minimum age
requirement to attract "enlightened citizens" into the service of the body.

These attributes lent to the Senate a unique character—a small, sta-
ble, stately, thoughtful, independent, experienced, deliberative body. With

equal legislative authority to the House of Representatives, it was hoped by the Framers that the senate would be a steady anchor in the sometimes raging seas of representative democracy.

This—along with its duties specified in the Constitution—was the Framers' design for the Senate. But it was just a design. The Senate required a structure from which it could operate. And that structure has for more than two hundred years taken the form of Senate procedure—standing rules, rule-making statutes, and precedents.

In the first Senate, in 1789, the Senate adopted twenty standing rules. Remarkably, sixteen of those rules still form the core of Senate procedure today. Since 1939, the Senate has adopted twenty-five rule-making statutes. And the presiding officer has established a quantity of precedents over the course of the Senate's history to fill nearly sixteen hundred pages in the seminal reference work—*Riddick's Senate Procedure*.

The Senate's rules, rule-making statutes, and precedents are nothing less than the institution's DNA: they have evolved over time; they are intertwined; they are complex; and those who unlock and understand and apply Senate procedure can hold tremendous sway over their colleagues and the course of the Senate's deliberations.

But, above all, together the Senate's rules and practices form a whole. It is a whole that faithfully reflects the Framers' design and ambition for the body. It is a whole that remains true to the Senate's two paramount values: unlimited debate and minority rights. And it is a whole that to this day calls extraordinary individuals from every state into the service of the nation.

Senator Daniel Webster, one-third of the great triumvirate that led the Senate during its Golden Age, said of his beloved institution and its colleagues, "This is a Senate of equals, of men of individual honor and personal character, and of absolute independence. We know no masters, we acknowledge no dictators. This is a hall for mutual consultation and discussion; not an arena for the exhibition of champions."

So how does the United States Senate work? Martin B. Gold, a longtime Senate staffer and a highly distinguished scholar, makes an extraordinary and extraordinarily successful effort to explain and illustrate not only how the Senate works, but, most importantly, why it has worked so well for more than two hundred years.

Indeed, to understand Senate procedure is to understand, in many respects, the greatness of America.

Preface

An Apples-to-Apples Comparison of the Senate and the House

In 1985, an extremely close election was held in Indiana for a seat in the United States House of Representatives. The Republican candidate, Richard McIntyre, was declared the victor by the state's election machinery and was given a certificate of election by Indiana's Republican governor. McIntyre's Democratic opponent, Frank McCloskey, subsequently challenged McIntyre's right to be seated. The House of Representatives agreed to consider the contest under article 1, section 5, of the Constitution, which grants to each chamber the right to judge the elections, returns, and qualifications of its own membership.

A special House committee reviewed the election, attempted to ascertain voter intent, and determined in a party-line vote that McCloskey had won. The Democratic majority then put a resolution before the House to seat McCloskey. Republicans strongly opposed the resolution but could not stop its passage on the floor, and McCloskey prevailed.

Ten years earlier, there was a similarly close Senate election in New Hampshire. The Republican, Louis Wyman, was declared the winner and was given a certificate of election by the state's Republican governor. John Durkin, the Democrat in the race, challenged Wyman's seating. Pending the outcome of the challenge, the Senate did not seat Wyman but referred the controversy to the Senate Committee on Rules and Administration.

The Rules Committee then conducted an exhaustive review of the election and decided in a party-line vote that Durkin had won. The Democratic majority brought to the Senate floor a resolution to seat Durkin. Republicans filibustered. Democrats offered a cloture motion to close debate. The motion failed. Cloture was attempted five more times, and on each occasion cloture failed. In the face of continuing futility, the majority leader took the resolution off the floor and proceeded to other business. The Senate passed a resolution to declare the New Hampshire seat vacant, and the matter was returned to the state for a new election, in which Durkin finally prevailed.

This apples-to-apples comparison of the two chambers illustrates a point central to understanding the Senate. Unlike the House, the Senate is not a majoritarian institution. In most cases, the majority governs comfortably in the House. In the Senate, the minority has a distinct voice, and the majority often struggles to govern at all.

The Senate is a place where political minorities and individual members hold great power, resting on authority drawn from Senate rules and more than two hundred years of related precedents and traditions. This fundamental truth provides a necessary context for understanding the subject matter of this book.

At the start of the new millennium, the Senate retains many of its ancient rules and traditions. For the most part, it has not been an institution built for efficiency. Though modernized some over two centuries, its procedures continue to reflect the great deliberative body envisioned by the Founding Fathers. Because the Senate remains faithful to their legacy, the Constitution's framework of checks and balances between the branches and within the legislative branch itself continues to thrive.

Acknowledgments

I have been privileged during my years of service to the Senate to work for three great Senators. Senator Mark O. Hatfield of Oregon lent fatherly support to an enthusiastic young man who was not an Oregonian but who had an interest in politics and government. Because of the opportunities and teaching he provided, my career at the Senate was launched and came to prosper. Senator Howard H. Baker Jr. of Tennessee first brought me to work for the Senate Republican leadership. Watching Senator Baker, I learned something useful every day. When I left his staff in 1982 for the private sector, I told him that there was an exception to every axiom. In that case, the axiom was that no man is a hero to his own valet. In 2003, Senator William H. Frist of Tennessee, the new majority leader, requested me to return to Capitol Hill. I was honored that he asked and thrilled at the chance to work again inside the Senate institution. Senator Frist understands the importance of educating senators, staffers, and others about the principles and nuances of Senate procedure. Due to his encouragement and example, the project to publish this book was launched. These senators have been mentors. I am deeply indebted to them for their trust and confidence.

The office of the Senate Parliamentarian is a vital part of Senate operations. In that office work dedicated and talented professionals. Alan Frumin, Elizabeth MacDonough, Peter Robinson, and Preeti Tolani have been patient counselors as I labored on this book and on numerous other projects involving parliamentary expertise. They serve the Senate with real distinction.

Christine Dodd, now legislative director for Senator Lamar Alexander of Tennessee, has been greatly helpful to me. She read through this text with a discerning eye. Her thoughtful perspectives and recommendations were important in creating this book.

My wife, Celeste, has assisted me on this project for a long while. Her original contribution was to the 1998 edition of a manual I authored on Senate procedure. She worked closely with me on a 2001 revision and strongly helped and supported me as those earlier manuals became the foundation for this book. Around her, one does not rest on old achievements. She encourages me to push beyond myself to reach greater heights. That is what a best friend should do.

Chapter One

Senate Procedure and Practice

This text is designed to proffer an introduction to Senate procedure. It reflects the core rules and precedents that govern the Senate's floor work. Very often these procedures are modified or waived by unanimous consent. The Senate is a twenty-first-century body operating with a core of eighteenth-century rules. Being able to structure consent orders to expedite business is essential to being able to function in a modern Senate environment. Accordingly, a caveat runs throughout these pages, even where not explicitly stated, that procedures are frequently adjusted by unanimous consent agreements to respond to particular needs. An extended discussion of the prevalence and importance of such agreements is set out later in this book. Absent unanimous consent, the processes reviewed here will apply.

THE PILLARS OF SENATE PROCEDURE

Senate procedure rests on three pillars:

1. The Standing Rules of the Senate, adopted pursuant to the Senate's right under article 1, section 5, of the Constitution to make rules governing its own proceedings
2. Special procedures found in rule-making statutes, also written under the Senate's rule-making power
3. Precedents that interpret the Standing Rules, interpret provisions in rule-making statutes, and interpret other precedents

TWO DISTINGUISHING CHARACTERISTICS OF
THE UNITED STATES SENATE

Senate procedure also embraces two characteristics that distinguish the Senate from other parliamentary bodies in the world:

1. Debate rules are fundamentally unrestricted.
2. Amendment opportunities are fundamentally unrestricted.

The United States Senate is the most influential upper chamber on Earth. Unlike many upper chambers that have limited authority, the Senate has equal legislative jurisdiction with the House and is empowered to address two areas the House does not: nominations and treaties. The Senate's authority is grounded in the Constitution[1] and is enhanced by the rules and precedents through which the body elects to govern itself.

THE FIRST PILLAR: THE TEXT OF THE STANDING RULES

There are forty-three Standing Rules of the Senate, ten of which are a code of ethics. All but the ethics rules are printed in the appendix. The genesis of certain rules can be found in the twenty rules of the first Senate in 1789, sixteen of which have substantially carried over until the present day. At pertinent points in this book, the original 1789 rules are recited so that the foundations of current rules and procedures can be plainly traced. Certain rules and practices have specific constitutional derivations, such as Rule VI, relating to quorums, and the Rule XXX procedures by which the Senate considers treaties.

The rules and their history reflect the stability and uniqueness of the Senate. They represent strong fibers in the fabric that binds the institution together.

Senate rules grant substantial power to individual members, minority coalitions, and the minority party. Individuals with knowledge of procedure—and willingness to employ it—can wield influence far beyond their single vote. For example, Senator Robert Byrd (D-WV) is a giant in the field of parliamentary history and law. No senator has had a greater impact on Senate rules and precedents. Other senators have been less proficient or skilled in this field, but they are still effective in maximizing their power by using the rules. The case of Senator Howard Metzenbaum (D-OH) is particularly illustrative.

Metzenbaum was appointed to the Senate in 1973. He lost in a primary election to Senator John Glenn (D-OH) in 1974 but came back to win the general election in 1976. He did not run for reelection in 1994. It became traditional for Metzenbaum to station himself on the floor during the final weeks of a session, threatening to object to this bill or that amendment. At the end of the session, a story would appear in the *Washington Post* about how much legislation Metzenbaum had killed. Also a significant story is how many mea- sures Metzenbaum caused to be modified as he leveraged modifications through the threat of objection or filibuster, changes he might have been un- likely to secure through the amendment process. No senator today operates quite as Metzenbaum did, at least on a consistent basis, but every senator can do so, and these rights are jealously protected. A disciplined and organized minority can sometimes derail by filibuster a measure or matter favored by a majority of senators. An individual senator can play the role of "spoiler" in the many situations in which unanimous consent is a practical prerequisite for floor action.

Unlike the House of Representatives, which adopts new rules at the begin- ning of each Congress, the rules of the Senate continue from one Congress to its successor and remain in force until amended. The Standing Rules provide that "the rules of the Senate shall continue from one Congress to the next Congress unless they are changed as provided in these rules."[2]

On more than a half dozen occasions between 1953 and 1975, groups of senators proposed to enact rules changes without regard to the procedures set out in the Standing Rules, basing their arguments on the inherent rule-making power of a new Senate, free of procedural constraints imposed by prior Con- gresses. The story of their efforts is told in the pages of this book. Their ini- tiatives strongly influenced modifications that were made to the rules, but every such change ultimately came about through traditional methods.

Changes to the Standing Rules have not been frequent. Before changes can be proposed, Rule V requires a one-day notice in writing.[3] Amendments to the text of the Standing Rules customarily are adopted by simple majority pas- sage of a Senate resolution. However, such a measure is debatable and sub- ject to a special cloture requirement. Normally, a vote of three-fifths of all senators duly chosen and sworn, or sixty senators, is sufficient to invoke clo- ture. To end debate on a rules change resolution requires an affirmative vote of two-thirds of all senators present and voting, a level unchanged since the cloture rule amendment of 1959.[4]

Recodification of the rules has occurred only seven times in Senate history, the first being in 1806 and the most recent occurring in 1979 under the lead- ership of Senator Robert Byrd. When Senator Byrd proposed the 1979 ad- justments, the rules had not been recodified since 1884.[5]

Implementation of the rules often is circumscribed by unanimous consent orders. Under consent orders, senators voluntarily agree to forgo or adjust some aspect of their rights. A single objection bars agreement and forces re- liance on Senate rules and precedents. An objection can be manifested on the floor by a senator exercising his own rights or by his party leadership acting on his behalf, and often the objection need not be publicly made by anyone because an oral or written notice of objection conveyed to one's party leader is sufficient to stall action.

The minority party or individual members gain power not from affirmative grants of authority within the Standing Rules but rather from the relative absence of restrictive provisions. For example, the rules do not contain provisions authorizing unlimited debate. Instead, the right to unlimited debate exists because it is not circumscribed, except for fairly modest restraints imposed by the cloture process or rule-making statutes, as discussed in this chapter.

Creating additional restrictions requires unanimous consent, to which any senator can object. Under such conditions, the power of any senator is vast.

THE SECOND PILLAR: RULE-MAKING STATUTES

A rule-making statute is a law that specifies procedures to be followed during the consideration of subsequent legislation arising under its provisions. For example, the Congressional Budget and Impoundment Control Act of 1974 (the "Budget Act") established the congressional budget process and provided in part that debate on concurrent budget resolutions would be limited to fifty hours.[6] In the three decades since enactment of the budget process, annual budget resolutions have been debated under this formula. Such a debate limitation would normally come in a consent order, but the debate restriction is imposed as a matter of law and not by unanimous consent.

Rule-making statutes customarily state that the special, expedited provisions they contain have been adopted pursuant to Congress' article 1 rule-making authority. A provision in the Congressional Review Act is typical:

(g) This section is enacted by Congress

(1) as an exercise of the rulemaking power of the Senate and House of Representatives, respectively, and as such it is deemed a part of the rules of each House, respectively, but applicable only with respect to the procedure to be followed in that House in the case of a joint resolution described in subsection (a), and it supersedes other rules only to the extent that it is inconsistent with such rules; and

(2) with full recognition of the constitutional right of either House to change the rules (so far as relating to the procedure of that House) at any time, in the same manner, and to the same extent as in the case of any other rule of that House.[7]

Provisions enacted pursuant to the rule-making power can be changed by subsequent statute but need not be. House or Senate resolutions,[8] concurrent resolutions,[9] and even unanimous consent orders would be sufficient to adjust the procedures. If a statute is used, the change is not effective until the legislation is signed. If a concurrent resolution is used, the change is effective on bicameral agreement. If a Senate resolution or a unanimous consent order is the mechanism, it is effective on Senate action alone.

Stanley Bach, former senior specialist at the Library of Congress, has described the major purposes for expedited procedure statutes:

> Congress typically has enacted sets of expedited procedures into law when (1) the same law imposes a deadline for congressional action on a measure in one or both houses, and (2) Congress wants to ensure, or at least increase the likelihood, that the full membership of the House and Senate have an opportunity to vote on the measure before the deadline is reached.[10]

Twenty-five such rule-making statutes exist, the first being the 1939 Reorganization Act and the most significant of which has been the 1974 Budget Act. The use of expedited procedures in lieu of normal rules has significant ramifications for the Senate. Such procedures tend to diminish the autonomy of committees,[11] neutralize the right to filibuster by limiting debate, and restrict the right to amend, all of which convert the Senate into a miniaturized version of the House. As Bach has stated,

> Because effective fast-track procedures limit floor debate and preclude amendments, whether germane or not, these procedures probably have greater consequences for the Senate than for the House, given the historic importance to the Senate and the strategic importance to senators of the right to filibuster and to offer non-germane amendments.[12]

The following case study illustrates the profound impact on the Senate of an expedited procedures statute.

CASE STUDY: THE YUCCA MOUNTAIN RESOLUTION

In the lame-duck session of 1982, Congress enacted the Nuclear Waste Policy Act.[13] Among the act's provisions is a process by which a decision could be made on designating a permanent repository for nuclear waste.[14] The authors of the legislation understood that such a decision would be politically charged, so they established an unusual procedure to address the controversy it would generate.

The statute provides that once the president designates a repository site, the governor or legislature of the affected jurisdiction would have thirty days to certify unwillingness to accept the waste. If such a certification were made, Congress would have sixty days to override the state's decision. If both houses of Congress acted affirmatively within sixty days, the president's decision would be affirmed. Otherwise, the state would prevail.

To govern proceedings in the Senate, the act sets forth expedited procedures:

- The chairman of the jurisdictional committee is required to introduce an override resolution.
- The jurisdictional committee has thirty days to consider the resolution and report its recommendations to the Senate; if the committee fails to report, the resolution is automatically discharged.
- Any senator can move to proceed to the consideration of the override resolution. This factor would prove to be critically important. The act's provision is similar to ones found in six of the twenty-five rule-making statutes.[15]
- By inference, the motion to proceed to the consideration of the resolution is nondebatable. Although the act is silent on this point, the Senate operates under a parliamentary construction that says if underlying proceedings are time controlled, the motion to proceed is nondebatable. The same construction serves to eliminate debate on the motion to proceed to the budget resolution or budget reconciliation bills.
- Ten hours of debate are permitted on the resolution itself, with no motion to recommit or any motion to proceed to alternative business being in order.
- By inference, no amendments are in order. The statute is silent on this point, but amendments are deemed out of order because to permit them would frustrate the expedited procedures envisioned in the law. This is the same theory that rendered the motion to proceed nondebatable.
- If the House acts on its resolution first and if the House resolution is identical in form to that of the Senate, the House resolution is automatically substituted for the Senate resolution when the time comes for a vote on final passage. If the Senate acts first, the process would be reversed. This provision obviated any dilatory tactics that might be used in establishing bicameral agreement.

Consider the alteration these statutory provisions made to normal Senate procedure:

- Customarily, neither the committee chairman nor any other senator would be required to introduce an override resolution.

- Normally, there is no deadline for committees to report, and the mechanism to discharge reports is so awkward and difficult to implement that it is never used. As a practical matter, without a statute imposing automatic discharge, such arrangements require unanimous consent.
- While it is within the rights of any senator to move to proceed to any measure or matter, under modern practice the motion is made by the majority leader. If another senator makes a motion to proceed that the majority leader opposes, majority party senators will oppose it as well. Because of the statute's specific reference to the motion to proceed, certain majority party senators felt empowered to vote for a motion made by a minority party senator and opposed by the majority leader.
- The motion to proceed is usually debatable without limitation, subject only to cloture.
- There is normally no restriction on offering amendments, be they germane or not.
- The resolution customarily would be debatable without limitation, subject only to cloture.
- Substitution of the House text for that of the Senate would not occur automatically, and delays could occur in the process of getting both houses to act on the same legislative vehicle.

In February 2002, President George W. Bush designated Yucca Mountain, Nevada, as the site for the nation's first permanent nuclear waste repository. Within his allotted time, Nevada Governor Kenny Guinn certified that his state did not wish to accept the waste.

On April 9, 2002, pursuant to statutory mandate, Senator Jeff Bingaman (D-NM), chairman of the Senate Committee on Energy and Natural Resources, introduced S.J. Res. 34 to override the governor's veto. The committee held a hearing, and on the twenty-eighth day of its thirty-day window of consideration, it reported the resolution affirmatively on June 5 by a vote of 13–10.

On May 8, 2002, the House passed and messaged to the Senate H.J. Res. 87, the companion resolution, which would be available for automatic substitution at the end of floor deliberations on S.J. Res. 34.

In both public and private comments, Majority Leader Tom Daschle (D-SD) stated that he had no intention of moving to proceed to S.J. Res. 34. Even though a number of majority party senators supported the substance of S.J. Res. 34, none of them would challenge Daschle and offer the motion to proceed in his place. Unless someone stepped forward to offer the motion, Governor Guinn's veto would stand.

Finally, Senator Frank Murkowski (R-AK), ranking minority member of the Committee on Natural Resources, announced his willingness to make the motion, as was his right under both Senate rules and the statute. The overarching question was whether Democrats who otherwise backed S.J. Res. 34 would vote for a motion to proceed that the majority leader opposed, especially one propounded by a senator from the minority.

Knowing they would not prevail on an up-or-down vote, opponents of S.J. Res. 34 decided to focus attention on that key procedural issue. Accordingly, they negotiated a unanimous consent order that would make the motion to proceed debatable for four and one-half hours and, if the motion were agreed to, permit a vote to occur on the resolution without further debate. This consent order is an example of how a rule-making provision grounded in statute law can be overridden by unanimous consent.

On July 9, 2002, by a vote of 60–39, Senator Murkowski moved to the consideration of S.J. Res. 34. When he did so, it was one of the rare moments since the office of the majority leader evolved eight decades ago that a hostile motion to proceed succeeded.[16] At the conclusion of the roll call vote and pursuant to the consent order, the House resolution, H.J. Res. 87, was substituted for S.J. Res. 34, and the Senate passed it by voice vote.[17]

The tight, expedited procedures set forth in the act profoundly altered Senate deliberation of the Yucca Mountain waste repository issue. Potential filibusters on the motion to proceed and on the substance of S.J. Res. 34 were impossible. Amendments that could have introduced further controversy and prevented bicameral consensus were avoided. Most important, the fundamental leadership prerogative of floor scheduling was weakened, at least in that instance.

It is difficult to say whether the Yucca Mountain precedent will erode leadership scheduling prerogatives when similar circumstances arise, although such a case nearly occurred in the 108th Congress. On July 15, 2003, Senator Byron Dorgan (D-ND) introduced S.J. Res. 17, a resolution to disapprove Federal Communications Commission media ownership rules. Procedures set forth in the Congressional Review Act[18] governed consideration of the resolution and provided, among other things, for its automatic discharge on a petition of thirty senators and expedited treatment on the floor.[19] Dorgan produced his thirty petitioners and made clear he would press for a vote. The law did not require proceeding to the consideration of Dorgan's resolution.

Although Majority Leader William Frist (R-TN) was a Bush administration supporter, he understood that the resolution enjoyed substantial backing and did not attempt to keep the measure off the floor. Engineering a consent order to call the resolution up, he avoided a direct challenge under the Yucca Mountain precedent, barely more than one year old. Frist voted against the resolution, which passed 55–40, leaving questions about the strength of the precedent open for another day.

THE THIRD PILLAR: SENATE PRECEDENTS

The third pillar of Senate procedure is the precedents. A precedent is established when the presiding officer rules on a point of order. The ruling may be appealed. Senate disposition of an appeal would create a precedent of highest standing. Former Senate Parliamentarian Floyd M. Riddick explained how precedents are created:

> Anytime that a point of order is made, and the Chair rules, if no appeal is taken from the decision of the Chair, that becomes the order of the day for the Senate, and remains just as binding on the Senate in future procedure as the rules themselves where they are specific. If an appeal is taken, and the decision of the Chair is sustained, that too becomes binding on the Senate. But if an appeal is taken, and the decision of the Chair is reversed, the decision of the Senate becomes binding on the Senate. This is how precedents are established.[20]

The presiding officer sometimes issues an advisory opinion in response to a parliamentary inquiry from the floor. Usually, these advisory opinions will reflect prior precedents, but occasionally new ground is broken. Because no appeal can be taken from an advisory opinion, the parliamentarian uses such responses for guidance only, but they do not serve as precedents of the Senate.[21] On this point, Riddick notes,

> Parliamentary inquiries are not binding on the Senate like a ruling of the chair, because a ruling of the chair pursuant to a point of order can be appealed. A response to a parliamentary inquiry is not subject to appeal and therefore is not necessarily the will of the Senate, because whatever the chair says is in effect only a guidance as to how he would rule if a point of order should be made, but it is not binding on the Senate.[22]

For a measure or matter to be open to a point of order, it must be pending on the floor.[23] No anticipatory point of order can be asserted. Once the proposition has been disposed of, any point of order would be moot.

No one can make a point of order until he or she is recognized, so a point of order cannot be raised while another senator is in control of the floor.[24] An additional timing consideration is whether the proposition being debated is subject to a time agreement imposed by unanimous consent.[25] If so, a senator may not offer a point of order until all time has been used or yielded back.[26]

Further, no point of order may be made during a quorum call or after a vote has commenced.[27]

A point of order is not debatable, except at the sufferance of the presiding officer,[28] unless the Senate is operating under a consent order or statutory provision that bars debate on points of order, in which case the point of order may not be debated at all. After cloture has been invoked, a point of order is not debatable.[29]

Under Senate Rule XX, the presiding officer may decline to rule on any point of order and may elect to submit the question to the Senate for determination.[30] If the point of order regards an issue of constitutional interpretation, it must be submitted to the Senate.[31] Once submitted, the point of order is fully debatable, unless cloture has been invoked on the underlying proposition.[32] A submitted point of order is subject to being tabled.[33] A successful tabling motion would end debate and kill the point of order.

Senate Rule XVI mandates that all questions of germaneness on appropriations bills be submitted to the Senate without debate. As discussed in the material on the appropriations process, precedent has eroded the blanket application of this rule. For example, issues of germaneness on appropriations bills will not be submitted when the amendment involves language that is not legally binding, such as Sense of the Senate provisions.[34] Further, if germaneness is raised as a defense to a point of order that an amendment constitutes legislation on an appropriations bill, the question will not be submitted if the presiding officer first determines that the defense is a sham.[35] Additional discussion on this point may be found in chapter 9.

A ruling of the presiding officer on a point of order may be appealed as long as other business has not intervened.[36] No appeal is possible from a response of the presiding officer to a parliamentary inquiry, such being nothing more than an advisory opinion. If a senator wishes to reverse that opinion, he would have to assert a point of order and then appeal the ruling of the presiding officer.

Appeals are debatable, except after cloture or when related to an underlying question that is nondebatable.[37] If a question of order is raised while an appeal is pending, the presiding officer without debate shall decide it, and any appeals from his ruling shall also be resolved by the Senate without debate.[38]

Points of order if submitted, or appeals if taken, are decided by a simple majority of senators present and voting. The Budget Act establishes a set of exceptional points of order, under which sixty votes are required to overturn the presiding officer or to waive application of the act.[39] Such waivers must be propounded before a ruling is made on a Budget Act point of order.[40] Motions to waive may even be made before the point of order is asserted. The waiver process set out in the Budget Act is unique. In no other case may points of order be waived.

Except under cloture and in a few other circumstances, the presiding officer does not take the initiative to enforce Senate rules. Failure to assert a point of order acts as an informal waiver. In many cases, a point of order would lie but is never raised. Forgoing the point of order results in the absence of a parliamentary judgment, but such circumstances do not create a precedent for later proceedings.

THE SENATE PARLIAMENTARIAN

Among his many important tasks, the parliamentarian is procedural counselor to the presiding officer.[41] Because it has become the practice to rotate the chair hourly among majority party senators, the parliamentarian's influence becomes central. Few senators have the knowledge or experience presiding to manage Senate procedure by themselves, so they often will rely heavily on the advice of the parliamentarian.

It is often misstated that the parliamentarian makes rulings. The presiding officer rules after having received the parliamentarian's counsel. Although the presiding officer has the power to ignore the parliamentarian's advice and simply rule on his own, it would be extraordinary for him to do so.

If the Senate wishes to break new ground, contrary to the parliamentarian's views, it will vote on or in relation to an appeal to overturn the presiding officer's ruling.[42] The presiding officer is not frequently overturned.[43]

The Senate created the position of parliamentarian in 1937.[44] Since then, a total of five persons have served as parliamentarian: Charles Watkins (1937–1964), Floyd Riddick (1964–1974), Murray Zweben (1974–1981), Robert Dove (1981–1987 and 1995–2001), and Alan Frumin (1987–1995 and 2001 to the present). The Secretary of the Senate supervises the parliamentarian's office. The parliamentarian serves for an indefinite term at the pleasure of the secretary, who is elected by the full Senate at the recommendation of the majority leader.

The parliamentarian is an essential resource on questions of Senate procedure and can be relied on for confidential and unbiased advice. Because rulings of the presiding officer frequently involve issues of judgment or interpretation, consultation with the parliamentarian is fundamental to understanding procedural context, options, and exposure. In conducting such consultations, it is important to provide the parliamentarian with as much context as possible so that the procedural advice given will be sound and not based on misunderstandings.

RIDDICK'S SENATE PROCEDURE:
A SEMINAL REFERENCE WORK

Senate precedents as well as material on rules and rule-making statutes and procedural formats are compiled in *Riddick's Senate Procedure*, most recently edited by Senate Parliamentarian Alan S. Frumin. Floyd M. Riddick, former parliamentarian of the Senate, published the first compilation of precedents in 1954.[45] Later editions were produced in 1974 and 1981. The last edition was published in 1992. Precedents and other parliamentary changes developed since 1992 are maintained in the parliamentarian's office.

In *Riddick's Senate Procedure*, each precedent is annotated to the Standing Rules of the Senate, the *Senate Journal*, or the *Congressional Record*. Reference to the *Record* will set out a complete description of the procedural situation described in *Riddick's Senate Procedure*. The compilation also includes some advisory opinions in response to parliamentary inquiries. Such references can be distinguished from binding precedents by the word "see" in the footnotes in that book.

Riddick's Senate Procedure is not written as a narrative. Instead, it is an alphabetical reference work that is an indispensable starting point to research specific parliamentary questions. Consultation with the parliamentarian's office is also advisable, especially because of developments that may have occurred since *Riddick's Senate Procedure* was last revised.

ROBERT C. BYRD'S SENATE HISTORY:
A COMPREHENSIVE RESEARCH TOOL

On March 21, 1980, then–Majority Leader Robert Byrd (D-WV) initiated a series of speeches on Senate history. Seated in the gallery that day was his granddaughter's school class on a visit to the Capitol. Senator Byrd believed that the students ought to learn something about Senate history during their tour, so he prepared a floor statement.[46]

Senator Byrd's speeches would continue for a decade, mostly given during lulls in the Senate's schedule. All were personally delivered in full and not inserted in the *Record*. By the time the Senate's Bicentennial arrived, in 1989, a set of these speeches was the foundational material for volume 1 of *The Senate 1789–1989 Addresses on the History of the United States Senate*. Eventually, four volumes would be produced.

Senator Byrd's history is a work of unparalleled importance and scholarship for students of the Senate. It provides critical context for understanding how the Senate has evolved, what about it has changed, and what great characteristics have remained constant over time.

Chapter Two

Legislative Business

PRESIDING OVER THE SENATE

Under a Standing Order, entered at the beginning of each new Congress, the Senate has a formal daily convening hour at noon. It is customary to adjust the convening hour by unanimous consent at the close of the previous session day to fit the needs of the next day.

The vice president is the Senate's constitutional presiding officer and the only presiding officer empowered to break ties.[1] Over the past sixty years, it has become rare for the vice president to sit in the chair, except to cast tie-breaking votes. Prior to that time, vice presidents would preside much more frequently. The last vice president who spent substantial time presiding was Alben Barkley, formerly a senator from Kentucky and Senate majority leader. Vice president during President Truman's full term (1949–1953), Barkley presided more than 50 percent of the time the Senate was in session.[2]

The Constitution provides that in the absence of the vice president or when the vice president is performing the duties of president, the Senate shall choose a president pro tempore.[3] With the vice president usually absent, the president pro tempore or his designee calls the Senate to order. By custom, the president pro tempore is the senior member of the majority party, although any senator could be elected to the post.

The president pro tempore holds office continuously until his senatorial term expires or the Senate elects his successor.[4] He stands in the line of presidential succession after the vice president and the Speaker of the House.

The presiding officer has no right to participate in Senate debate. He can speak, but only in response to parliamentary inquiries or points of order. When a senator presides, however, he retains the right to suggest the absence

of a quorum, acting in his individual capacity. As to the decorum expected of
the presiding officer, Senator Byrd observes,

> Senators, when called on to preside, should not speak from the chair. If the chair
> is complimented by a Senator from the floor, the chair should not respond. . . .
> All too often, members who should know better will unburden themselves of
> some pearly words of wisdom from the chair. This does not leave a very good
> impression. The chair is supposed to say as little as possible, beyond making rul-
> ings on points of order, responding to parliamentary inquiries, making certain
> announcements, and securing order in the chamber and the galleries. A Senator
> is not supposed to speak from the chair, even to answer criticism from the floor.
> The vice president—who is not a member of the Senate—may not address the
> Senate, except by unanimous consent.[5]

A DAY OF SESSION

The Senate convenes at an hour recommended by the majority leader and set
in a consent order entered on the previous session day. The president pro tempore or his designee gavels the session open and calls on the chaplain to lead
the Senate in prayer.[6] Following the prayer, the president pro tempore will
lead the Pledge of Allegiance. Under a Standing Order entered at the beginning of the Congress, the two leaders are next recognized, for up to ten minutes each. It is customary for a portion of the leader time to be consumed then
and the remainder to be reserved for use later in the day.

Following leader time, there will usually be a period for the transaction of
routine morning business that permits administrative matters, such as the introduction and referral of bills and the filing of committee reports, to be
processed. It also gives an opportunity for Senators to make speeches on subjects of their own choosing. Sometimes, Senators will want to speak on a subject other than pending business and to do so outside of morning business. In
that case, they will ask consent to speak "as in morning business."

It has become standard practice to divide morning business time equally
between the two parties, alternating each day which party takes the first half
of the time and which one concludes. If morning business does not occur at
this point in the day, it will be scheduled to happen later.

If a morning business period is not ordered by unanimous consent, it will
occur automatically as part of the Morning Hour starting a new legislative
day,[7] provided that a consent order does not state that the Morning Hour is
deemed expired.[8] Discussion of Morning Hour procedure follows in the next
section.

Following the Morning Hour, the Senate will turn to the consideration of
the pending or unfinished business, which will occur either by a consent or-

der or by operation of the rules. Floor managers[9] will assume the leaders' desks at opposite sides of the aisle in the front of the chamber.[10]

After consideration of any such business has ended, the leaders or their designees will replace the managers and begin the ritual of daily "wrap-up." This means working through noncontroversial legislative or executive items that do not require roll call votes or debate and that seldom need amendment.[11] Both party cloakrooms have cleared these items with the jurisdictional committees and any senators who have expressed special interest in them.[12] The leaders will also enter consent orders for the following session day. Subsequently, the majority leader will move that the Senate adjourn or recess, in accordance with the orders just entered.

The wrap-up for Wednesday, October 15, 2003, illustrates this daily routine. Senator Conrad Burns (R-MT) was the majority leadership designee. His minority counterpart was the assistant Democratic leader, Harry Reid (D-NV). On the conclusion of proceedings that day on S. 1689, an Iraq-Afghanistan supplemental appropriations bill, Senator Burns began the wrap-up by asking unanimous consent to proceed to S. Res. 243, designating National Childhood Lead Poisoning Prevention Week, which had been introduced the same day by Senator Jack Reed (D-RI).[13] No objection was made. With the resolution pending, Burns asked consent that the preamble[14] be agreed to, that the motion to reconsider be laid on the table, that there be no other intervening action or debate, and that related statements be printed in the *Record*. There was no objection, and the resolution was passed.

Burns then sought consent that the Senate consider H.R. 3229, a bill held at the desk, which transferred to the public printer the authority over individuals responsible for preparing *Record* digests. There was no objection. Once the bill was pending, Burns asked consent to go to the third reading,[15] to pass the bill, to lay on the table a motion to reconsider, and to print related statements. There was no objection.

Burns followed by asking for the immediate consideration of a conference report on H.R. 1474, the Check Clearing for the 21st Century Act. The conference report was placed before the Senate without objection. Burns sought consent that the conference report be adopted and that related statements be printed. There was no objection.

Following disposition of the conference report, Burns set forth proposed orders of procedure for the next session day. These included an hour for convening, that the Morning Hour be deemed expired, that the *Journal* be approved, that leader time be reserved, that there be a sixty-minute equally divided morning business period, that the Senate thereafter resume consideration of the Iraq-Afghanistan supplemental appropriations bill, and that an amendment by Senator Robert C. Byrd be designated as the pending business. No objection was made.

Burns concluded with an announcement of the next day's program, advising senators of the likelihood of roll call votes and a late evening session, and then secured consent that the Senate stand in adjournment pursuant to the order just entered.

The majority and minority secretaries and their staffs conduct preparation for wrap-up, including development of negotiated consent orders, such as those put forth by Senator Burns. Among the tools available to the secretaries are annotated calendars reflecting communications sent to party leaders by members of their own caucuses. Such communications can vary widely. For instance, a senator may ask to be alerted to negotiations for a time agreement so that certain amendments may be included. Another may address scheduling. A third may voice objection to proceeding to a measure and promise extended debate on the motion to proceed as well as the substantive legislation. The secretaries take note of these communications and develop annotated calendars.

The annotated calendars give the party leaders a sense of the relative complexity of moving legislation, nominations, or treaties. Calendar items that are noncontroversial can be cleared for disposition by voice vote. As in the wrap-up example just given, when there is no further business to be transacted, the leader or his designee will move that the Senate stand in recess or adjournment.

CASE STUDY: A DAY IN THE LIFE OF THE SENATE: HARD TIMES AND EASY TIMES

For most of Thursday, September 25, 2003, the Senate was debating H.R. 2765, the fiscal year 2004 District of Columbia appropriations bill. A pending Senate substitute for the measure already contained controversial language concerning a pilot school-choice educational-scholarship program for the District of Columbia. The provision was about to be strengthened by Senator Dianne Feinstein (D-CA). Democratic leaders opposed the amendment and wished to avoid a roll call. When Senator Feinstein and the majority bill manager, Senator Mike DeWine (R-OH), insisted on a roll call and secured the yeas and nays, Democrats would not permit the amendment to come to a vote.[16]

Ordering the yeas and nays means only that whenever a vote occurs, it will be by roll call. However, the presiding officer cannot put the question on the amendment if any senator is speaking or seeks recognition.[17] Thus, Democrats had it within their power to prolong consideration of the amendment by not permitting debate to conclude.[18] Debate continued thereafter, clouding prospects that the Senate could complete work on the substitute amendment to H.R. 2765 and then on the bill itself.[19]

This brief story about the pilot school-choice educational-scholarship program illustrates the axiom that moving things through the Senate almost always requires minority cooperation, without which the workload can easily become unmanageable and conclusive action can be impossible.

The same day, the Senate gave consent to interrupt consideration of H.R. 2765 to address H.R. 3161, a bill to ratify the authority of the Federal Trade Commission to establish a "Do Not Call" registry. The legislation was intended to relieve consumers from unsolicited telephone contact by telemarketers. Introduced in the House on September 23, 2003, it was referred to committee for one day and then was passed by the House on September 25 by 412–8. The same day, it was sent to the Senate, where it was held at the desk in lieu of referral to committee, then read three times by consent and passed 95–0. Speeches supporting the legislation were pointed, brief, numerous, and bipartisan.

The treatment of H.R. 3161 shows how fast the Senate can move if it wishes to act expeditiously. Doing so requires unanimous consent. If one senator had objected, the three readings of the bill would have been required to occur on separate legislative days. If that senator wished to extend debate, he could have prevented passage until the Senate worked through cloture on a motion to proceed and again on the bill. Put otherwise, if there were only one dissenting senator who insisted on the full exercise of his rights, passage of a bill that took less than two hours could have been delayed well in excess of a week.

Following passage of H.R. 3161, the Senate returned to the consideration of H.R. 2765, which remained stalled over the controversy on educational scholarships. H.R. 2765 finally passed the Senate on November 19, 2003, after the provision on educational scholarships had been dropped. When the bill was brought back to the floor minus that provision, only minimal debate time was required.[20]

PROCEEDINGS IN THE MORNING HOUR ON
A NEW LEGISLATIVE DAY

The President having taken the Chair and a quorum being present, the journal of the preceding day shall be read, to the end that any mistakes may be corrected that shall have been made in the entries.

—Senate Rule I, 1789

When the Senate reconvenes following an adjournment of whatever duration, a new legislative day is created. The first two hours of a new legislative day are called the Morning Hour. Senate Rule VII sets out a sequence of Morning Hour activity that is customarily waived by unanimous consent.[21] Almost invariably, a consent order entered on the previous session day will provide that when the Senate reconvenes on the forthcoming legislative day, the Morning Hour shall be deemed expired.

The Morning Hour litany of business set out in Rule VII is as follows:

1. The Senate *Journal*[22] is read and may be amended, although a nondebatable motion is in order to approve the *Journal*.[23] When the Senate is operating under cloture, the *Journal* is automatically considered as having been read and approved.[24] Otherwise, the reading and correction of the *Journal* is a matter of highest privilege. These proceedings cannot be interrupted and take priority over any motion, including a motion to adjourn. On a point of order, a vote to approve the *Journal* cannot be delayed by dilatory tactics.[25]
2. On demand of any senator, presidential and other executive messages and House messages, as well as matters on the presiding officer's desk that carry over from the previous legislative day, are laid before the Senate.[26]
3. Petitions and memorials are presented.[27]
4. Committee reports are received.
5. Bills and joint resolutions are submitted.
6. Simple and concurrent resolutions are submitted.[28]

Steps 2 through 6 constitute what is known as morning business. Although morning business can occur by operation of Rule VII, it almost never does. Morning business is ordered daily by unanimous consent.

If objection were heard to such a consent order, it would be necessary to adjourn the Senate so that morning business could be created as part of the Morning Hour. In a morning business period ordered by consent, it is customary for the order to provide time for senators to speak. Under this authority, senators usually address matters of current policy or political interest that may be unrelated to the business on the Senate's immediate agenda. Absent consent, senators may not speak in morning business.[29]

At the conclusion of morning business or at the end of the first hour of the Morning Hour, whichever occurs first, it is in order to move by nondebatable motion to any item on the legislative calendar, but this right does not cover motions, resolutions, or proposals to change the Standing Rules.[30] Except in relation to privileged measures, such as a conference report or a budget reconciliation bill, a "motion to proceed" is debatable and subject to filibuster. Making this motion during the Morning Hour renders it nondebatable.

The nondebatable motion to proceed is not available when the Morning Hour falls on a Monday. This is due to the requirement for a calendar call set out in Rule VIII. After morning business has concluded, the call is mandatory, and it is not in order to proceed to another measure unless the call has been exhausted or the Senate has granted consent.[31]

When the Morning Hour ends, a measure brought up on a nondebatable motion is displaced by the unfinished business and is returned to the calendar. Unfinished business is defined as any legislative business that was pending at the moment of adjournment. Even if there were unfinished business, a measure brought up during the Morning Hour could be continued on motion. If there were no unfinished business, the consideration of a bill motioned up during the Morning Hour would continue as the pending business after the Morning Hour expired.

Even should a measure be displaced by the unfinished business, making it pending during the Morning Hour could still be useful. For example, while the measure was pending, a cloture motion could be filed against it. Two session days later, the cloture motion would ripen under the terms of Rule XXII. The measure would automatically be brought back to the Senate for disposition of the cloture vote and the certainty of continued floor consideration if cloture were invoked.

A CALL OF THE CALENDAR UNDER RULE VIII

When a new legislative day occurs on a Monday, Rule VII mandates that after morning business has ended, the calendar be called until the Morning Hour expires. The call, as set forth in Rule VIII, requires proceeding through the calendar in order to consider all measures to which there is no objection. As each such measure is reached, senators may speak once for a period not to exceed five minutes.[32] If objection is heard when a measure is reached, the legislation is passed over. On motion, consideration of that measure can be continued, without debate restrictions.[33]

In practice, formalities of the Rule VIII calendar call are no longer observed. They have been replaced by unanimous consent orders that allow the Senate to "cherry pick" the calendar for measures that are noncontroversial or at least on which there is no controversy on the motion to proceed. The rule remains in force, however, but its only lasting effect is to render impossible using a nondebatable motion to proceed during a Morning Hour that occurs on Mondays.

ADJOURNING RATHER THAN RECESSING

The consequences of adjourning rather than recessing are summarized as follows:

- If the Senate adjourns, morning business occurs automatically as part of the Morning Hour. If the Senate recesses, morning business happens only by consent, and there could be an objection. If morning business does not take place, the Senate cannot receive presidential and other executive communications, nor can it receive House messages that include House-passed bills. Bills and resolutions cannot be introduced, committee reports cannot be filed, and petitions and memorials cannot be received and referred.
- Measures reported from committee must lie over one legislative day before they are eligible for floor consideration. If a legislative day has not elapsed, a point of order could be lodged against a motion to proceed to the measure.
- Senate rules require disposition of particular legislative steps on separate legislative days. For instance, a committee report cannot be considered on the same legislative day it is filed.[34] A motion to proceed to the consideration of a bill is not in order on the same legislative day it is filed.[35] No senator may speak more than twice on the same question on the same legislative day,[36] so the change in legislative days provides fresh opportunities for speeches. If the Senate has not adjourned to create a new legislative day, points of order may arise under each of these rules.
- Other than on Mondays,[37] a nondebatable motion to proceed is available within the Morning Hour. If the Senate has not adjourned, no Morning Hour is created.
- Any measure pending at the time of adjournment becomes the unfinished business of the Senate.[38] Unless set aside by unanimous consent or temporarily suspended by a motion to proceed to a privileged measure, the unfinished business recurs before the Senate until its disposition or its displacement.[39] Moving to proceed to a nonprivileged measure would displace the unfinished business and return it to the calendar.[40]
- Any motions to proceed that are pending at the time of adjournment die.[41]

The following case study will illustrate the operation of some of these rules.

CASE STUDY: EXTENSION OF THE
EQUAL RIGHTS AMENDMENT IN 1978

In 1971, Congress passed and sent to the states the Equal Rights Amendment to the United States Constitution, accompanied by a seven-year deadline for ratification. By September 28, 1978, an insufficient number of states have ratified the amendment, and the time for ratification is about to expire.

Pending before the Senate is H.J. Res. 638, a resolution to extend the ratification deadline. Senate Majority Leader Robert Byrd (D-WV) seeks to pass H.J. Res. 638 before the deadline expires. On the Republican side, Senator Lowell Weicker (R-CT) wishes to demonstrate Republican advocacy of the extension and looks for a way to put his party in the forefront of the issue.

On the afternoon of September 28, Weicker moves that the Senate proceed to the consideration of H.J. Res. 638. He secures the yeas and nays. Senate Democrats are surprised. To permit them to regroup, Senator Harrison Williams (D-NJ) suggests the absence of a quorum.

During the quorum call, Majority Leader Byrd comes to the floor. He secures consent to rescind the quorum call, determines from the presiding officer that the pending business is Weicker's motion to proceed, and initiates a new quorum call.

Following strategic discussions, Byrd obtains consent to rescind the quorum call. He then makes a nondebatable motion that the Senate stand in adjournment for ten seconds. The motion is adopted 54–35 on a party-line vote, killing Weiker's motion.

The Senate reconvenes ten seconds later. Byrd is recognized and asks consent that the reading of the *Journal* be waived. Weicker objects, and the reading of the *Journal* proceeds.[42]

After some conversation between interested parties, Weicker asks consent to dispense with further reading of the *Journal*. On a new legislative day, as has existed from the moment the Senate reconvened, the next order of procedure would be the morning business litany under Rule VII. Byrd preempts the operation of the rule through a unanimous consent agreement that there be a period for morning business not to extend beyond one minute in length.

The one-minute morning business period having concluded, Morning Hour time remains available. Within the Morning Hour, Byrd offers a nondebatable motion to proceed to H.J. Res. 638. The motion carries by voice vote.

Once H.J. Res. 638 is pending, Byrd files a cloture motion. Ultimately, the cloture motion is vitiated, and the Senate proceeds to consider and pass H.J. Res. 638 before the deadline for ratification expires.

This case study is noteworthy for the following elements:

- In theory, a motion to proceed may be made by any senator, and Senator
  Weicker so moved. In practice, the majority leader makes the motion, as
  Senator Byrd did after the Senate reconvened.
- Rather than having Democrats table Senator Weicker's motion, which
  could have created a politically confusing or damaging vote for them, Sena-
  tor Byrd moved to adjourn. By voting for adjournment, Democrats killed
  Senator Weicker's motion to proceed without political complications.[43]
- Senator Byrd made effective use of Morning Hour procedure to obviate debate on the motion to proceed to consider H.J. Res. 638.
- By filing a cloture motion once H.J. Res. 638 was pending, Senator Byrd
  demonstrated his intent to secure timely passage of the resolution. At the
  end of the Morning Hour, H.J. Res. 638 would have returned to the calendar, and the legislation pending at the time of adjournment would have re-
  curred as the unfinished business of the Senate. Nevertheless, by operation
  of Rule XXII, the cloture motion would have matured two days later, caus-
  ing H.J. Res. 638 to be brought back before the Senate automatically. Faced
  with these facts, senators concluded a consent order that streamlined further
  proceedings.[44]

TWO OBJECT LESSONS IN MINORITY POWER

The minority party can exercise enormous power in the Senate, impairing the
ability of any majority leader to control the Senate's schedule too tightly. Two
examples drawn from the first session of the 108th Congress will illustrate
this point:

On Monday, March 17, 2003, the Senate proceeded to the consideration of
S.Con. Res. 23, the fiscal year 2004 concurrent resolution on the budget. The
majority leader announced that he intended for the Senate to complete its
work on the budget resolution no later than close of business Thursday,
March 20. Such pronouncements have value as an expression of hope and a
signal of determination, but in the absence of controlled procedures, they are
nothing more than a guideline.

The budget resolution was subject to a fifty-hour overall debate limitation,
so finishing by the leader's deadline was theoretically possible. For important

strategic reasons, the minority did not want to complete work according to that timetable, so it engaged in a slowdown, chiefly through offering dozens of amendments for roll call votes after all debate time had expired. The budget resolution was adopted only on Wednesday, March 26, and only after the minority had scored important political and policy victories by extending floor consideration and was ready to let the measure pass.

Later in the year, the majority leader stated his objective to consider and pass S. 1689, the Iraq-Afghanistan supplemental appropriations bill, during the week of September 29, 2003. The leader expressed his desire that the Senate complete work on the bill before a forthcoming recess, scheduled to start on Friday, October 3.

The minority claimed that the announced schedule was too compressed and made clear that it would not assent to the bill's expedited movement through committee and through the full Senate. In light of the minority's capacity to slow matters down, a bipartisan understanding was reached that extended committee proceedings and delayed commencement of floor action until Wednesday, October 1. These arrangements carried consideration of the bill past the recess. The Senate resumed action on the bill on Tuesday, October 14, and finally passed it on Friday, October 17, in accordance with a timetable pretty much dictated by the minority.

The key lesson in these examples is that if a minority is sizable and disciplined and can hold forty-one votes against cloture, most of the time it can have a decided effect on the pace at which the Senate can conduct its business. The majority party can decide when the Senate begins considering legislation. The minority can greatly influence when the Senate concludes it or whether it concludes it at all.

UNANIMOUS CONSENT ORDERS

Much of Senate business is transacted by unanimous consent, absent which the Senate would have great difficulty operating. Among the principal objectives served by consent orders are sequencing floor activity, expediting business, controlling and allocating time, and imposing a germaneness or relevance requirement for amendments. Consent orders represent a temporary waiver of the rules. Needing to obtain unanimous consent to work through a significant portion of its agenda tends to dampen partisan differences in the Senate. Many times daily, the words "I ask unanimous consent" are spoken on the Senate floor.

Reliance on unanimous consent orders is indispensable for Senate operations. At earlier points in Senate history, they were used to an even greater degree than they are now. Under Majority Leaders Lyndon Johnson (D-TX)[45] and Robert Byrd (D-WV) and to a somewhat lesser extent under Majority Leader Howard Baker (R-TN), it was common to secure comprehensive consent orders before bringing legislation to the floor. In *Master of the Senate*, Robert Caro describes Johnson's frequent use of unanimous consent agreements to change dramatically the operation of the Senate:

> Lyndon Johnson's use of the unanimous consent agreement to drastically limit debate ran contrary to the principles on which the Senate had been founded, and to the customs which had, during the previous century and a half of its existence, been most fundamental in its functioning. Unlimited debate had been sacred Senate custom, the device by which, more than any other, it fulfilled the Founding Fathers' vision of it as the bulwark against the "fickleness" and "transient impressions" of the majority, as the guarantor of the sovereignty of the individual states. And it was debate—in its highest sense: unhurried thoughtful discussion to educate first the Senate and then the people, to raise issues and examine them in depth and at length—that had made the Senate a great deliberative body. Johnson's agreements limited debate so drastically that with their increased use the very nature of the Senate was altered.[46]

That practice has changed substantially. Legislation is now more often considered without securing a comprehensive agreement in advance, and consent orders are secured to add structure and restrictions later, if orders are possible at all. Quite often, a bipartisan understanding between the party leaders operates in lieu of a consent order. It is as if the Senate has somewhat returned to an earlier era. Caro describes the Senate before Johnson:

> Prior to World War II, most unanimous consent agreements had come near the end of a session, when the bill in question had already been debated for days, if not weeks; the Senate would then agree that after a certain number of additional days of debate, a vote would be taken. The mounting impatience after the war with the Senate's inefficiency had led to the increased use of these agreements, but they still had generally been employed only after substantial time on a measure had already occurred, and they still generally allowed additional time for debate.[47]

A unanimous consent proposal can be blocked by a single objection. Although debate is not in order on a consent request, senators will sometimes reserve the right to object so that the terms of the request can be clarified or adjusted. Debating the consent request is not in order, however. If the reservation of objection appears to extend into a speech, the exercise will soon terminate. Either on his own or on demand for the regular order, the presiding officer will ask, "Is there objection?" which will require senators to accede to the consent request or object to it.[48] If time is controlled, then time consumed by a senator who reserves the right to object will be charged to the senator who had propounded the consent request.

If a unanimous consent order restricts time, it usually provides that the time be evenly divided between two opposing sides and be under the control of specified senators. On a bill, the majority and minority managers of the legislation generally control the time. On the amendment, the mover of the amendment and the majority manager usually control the time. If the majority manager favors the amendment, then the minority manager or his designee controls time in opposition.

Each senator who controls time may yield some of it to a senator who wishes to speak on his side of the proposition. If no one yields time, the senator cannot be recognized. If no one wishes to speak and time remains, the senators in control of time may yield it back to the presiding officer, at which point all time is exhausted.

The terms of each unanimous consent order differ and are designed to meet specific circumstances. For this reason, each such order stands on its own foundation.

In addition to suspending the terms of the rules by unanimous consent, a rarely used alternative method is available under Rule V. This involves moving to suspend the rules after one calendar day's notice has been given. The motion must be specific as to the provision(s) of the rules to be suspended and is debatable. In lieu of unanimous consent, Rule V provides a mechanism to suspend the rules on an affirmative vote of two-thirds of all senators present. The Rule V suspension motion is debatable.

There is a fundamental and noteworthy distinction between the operation of a unanimous consent order and the suspension procedure under Rule V. A unanimous consent agreement imposes new conditions on considering a proposition. By contrast, Rule V suspends the usual operation of the rules but contains no positive authority to impose other conditions in its place. For example, in the case of an appropriations bill, Rule XVI, paragraph 4, requires that amendments be germane. This prohibition could be waived by unanimous consent or, alternatively, by suspension of the rules. In either case, a nongermane amendment could be offered to the bill. However, if the Senate wished to impose a time limitation on debate of the amendment, a unanimous consent order would be necessary.

Motions to suspend the rules are not common. An example of such an effort occurred on October 27–28, 2003. Senator Richard Lugar (R-IN) wished to offer a legislative amendment to the fiscal year 2004 foreign operations appropriations bill. As a legislative amendment to an appropriations bill, the amendment was subject to a point of order under Rule XVI. On October 27,

Lugar gave the requisite one day's notice of his intention to suspend Rule XVI so that the amendment would be in order:

> Mr. LUGAR: Mr. President, I hereby provide notice that I intend to move to suspend rule XVI of the Standing Rules of the Senate during the Senate's consideration of H.R. 2800 in order to offer the amendment No. 1974 to that bill.[49]

The following day, Senator Harry Reid (D-NV) made the point of order. Lugar responded as follows:

> Mr. LUGAR: I move to suspend rule XVI of the Standing Rules of the Senate during the Senate's consideration of H.R. 2800 in order to offer amendment 1974 to that bill.[50]

After brief debate, the motion to suspend came to a vote and was defeated by 40–57. The presiding officer then announced the following:

> The PRESIDING OFFICER: On this vote, the yeas are 40, the nays are 57. Two-thirds of the Senators not voting in the affirmative, the motion to suspend rule XVI pursuant to notice previously given in writing is rejected. The point of order is sustained and the amendment falls.[51]

Rather than moving to suspend the rules, Lugar could have appealed the ruling of the chair. If he had done so, he would have needed a simple majority vote rather than two-thirds. The effect of winning, however, would have gone beyond avoiding the point of order. A successful appeal would have seriously damaged enforcement of Rule XVI in future cases. In 1995, just such a case arose when Senator Kay Bailey Hutchison (R-TX) appealed the ruling of the chair, who had sustained a point of order against her legislative amendment to a supplemental appropriations bill. Senator Hutchison prevailed, but the impact extended beyond the amendment itself. Under the parliamentarian's interpretation that the Senate had voted to make legislative amendments in order to appropriations bills, the rule was not enforced for some four years until its restoration via Senate resolution in 1999. By proceeding with a Rule V suspension motion, Lugar increased his burden to win, but he did not follow a process that threatened enforcement of the rule.

Unanimous consent orders are printed in the daily calendar of business, except for orders that are entered and executed on the same calendar day. For instance, the calendar for Monday, October 20, 2003, set forth five consent orders of varying complexity. One of those orders was comprehensive, addressing S. 139, a greenhouse gas emissions bill. The terms of that order, entered on July 31, 2003, are set out here, followed by commentary to illustrate the effect of the order on normal Senate procedures:

Ordered, That at a time determined by the Majority Leader, following consultation with the Democratic Leader, the Environment and Public Works Committee be discharged of S.139 . . . that the Senate then proceed to its consideration; that the measure be considered under the following limitations: that there be a total of 6 hours of debate on the bill and substitute amendment, with the time equally divided and controlled between the proponents and opponents; provided further, that the only amendment in order be a substitute amendment to be offered by the Senator from Arizona (Mr. McCain) and the Senator from Connecticut (Mr. Lieberman); that upon the use or yielding back of all time, the Senate vote on the amendment; that upon the disposition of the amendment, the bill as amended, if amended, be read a third time and without any further intervening action or debate, the Senate proceed to vote on passage of the bill.

Comment on the committee discharge provision. Except in rare circumstances, committees are not discharged, except by unanimous consent. Normally, such a consent-driven discharge would be triggered by an event such as the expiration of a set number of days for a sequential referral. Here, a somewhat unusual event caused the discharge, that being the essentially unilateral act of the majority leader. Although he must consult with the minority leader, the minority leader cannot veto the discharge.

Comment on the motion to proceed provision. A motion to proceed is debatable, except for privileged measures. S. 139 was not a privileged measure, and debate on the motion to proceed was waived by this order. Without the order, the only other way to waive debate would be for senators to forbear from debating the motion.

Comment on the limitation of debate provision. Debate on the bill would normally be unlimited unless cloture was imposed or senators chose not to debate. The order limits debate to a maximum of six hours and provides for an equal division of time. A specific limitation of this kind could be achieved only by unanimous consent.

Comment on the limitation of amendments provision. Absent an order, S. 139 would be fully amendable, and, without cloture, such amendments would not even have to be germane. This agreement makes only the McCain-Lieberman amendment in order, and provides that no amendments may be proposed to it, a result that could be achieved only by unanimous consent. If the order had limited only the time for debate, additional amendments could have been proposed when time expired, but this order ties down the amendments to just the one specified.

Comment on tabling motions and points of order. The agreement states that a vote shall occur on the amendment. That wording precludes a tabling motion. If the agreement had said that the vote would occur "on or in relation to" the amendment, a tabling motion would be in order. The agreement does not preclude points of order against the amendment, to be asserted while the amendment is pending.

Comment on the final passage provision. After third reading, the amendment process is closed, but additional debate can occur and motions can be made, such as a motion to recommit. Points of order can also be made. This consent order eliminates such possibilities by providing that a vote on final passage follows immediately after third reading without intervening action.

Another unanimous consent agreement, entered while the fiscal year 2004 foreign operations appropriations bill was pending, also shows the use of consent orders to structure and expedite business:

> Mr. McCONNELL: I ask unanimous consent that the only first-degree amendments remaining in order to the Foreign Operations bill be the following, and that they be subject to second-degrees which are relevant to the first: DeWine No. 1966; Feinstein No. 1977; McConnell No. 1970; one McConnell technical, and two McConnell relevants; a Frist relevant; Allard-Feingold-Leahy, Indonesia; Durbin on AIDS; Bingaman on AIDS; two Leahy relevants; Daschle relevant; McConnell-Leahy cleared managers' amendment.
>
> I further ask unanimous consent that following the disposition of the above listed amendments, the bill be read a third time and the Senate proceed to a vote on passage of the bill with no intervening action or debate. Further, I ask unanimous consent that following passage of the bill, the Senate insist on its amendments, request a conference with the House, and the Chair be authorized to appoint conferees on the part of the Senate, which will consist of the subcommittee plus Senator Stevens and Senator Byrd.[52]

Comment on the limitation of first-degree amendments. Because the underlying measure was an appropriations bill, amendment possibilities were not unlimited. Under Rule XVI, a point of order would lie against any legislative or nongermane amendments.[53] The agreement qualifies certain amendments notwithstanding this rule but also states that these will be the only amendments in order.

Comment on limitation of second-degree amendments. The order also limits second-degree amendments, which are amendments proposed to the first-degree amendments. Under the order, they must be relevant to the underlying amendment. Without the order, Rule XVI would control, and second-degree amendments would have to be germane either to the underlying amendment or to the underlying bill text.

Comment on procedures after disposition of the amendments. Third reading follows the last amendment. While no further amendments are in order after third readings, motions are possible, as are points of order and additional debate. The order bars any such motions, points of order, or debate.

Comment on conference arrangements. Motions to insist on the Senate amendments and to request a conference with the House and that the chair appoint conferees are all separate, debatable motions. The order collapses and expedites this process.

RULE XXII MOTIONS

Rule XXII, paragraph 1, sets forth and prioritizes a list of motions. In descending order of priority, these are motions to do the following:

- Adjourn (nondebatable)
- Adjourn to a time certain (nondebatable)
- Recess (nondebatable)
- Proceed to the consideration of executive business (nondebatable)[54]
- Table (nondebatable)
- Postpone indefinitely (debatable)
- Postpone to a time certain (debatable)
- Commit (debatable)
- Amend (debatable)

Although any senator has a right to make these motions, all but the motions to amend, to commit, to postpone, and to table are considered prerogatives of the majority leader. In addition, by norm it is the leader's prerogative to make motions to proceed to the consideration of a measure or matter. If another senator wishes to bring legislation to the floor, he may resort to offering amendments, including amendments that are nongermane.[55]

Further discussion follows on each of these Rule XXII motions.

To Adjourn

A motion to adjourn is the motion of highest priority. It can be neither debated nor amended.[56] It is in order at any time except when the *Journal* is being read,[57] the Senate is conducting a roll call vote,[58] or the Senate is in a quorum call.[59] If a quorum call discloses that no quorum is present, motions to adjourn and motions to produce a quorum are the only motions in order, with the motion to adjourn taking priority between them.[60] Successive motions to adjourn may not be made unless intervening business has occurred.

Adoption of this motion creates a new legislative day.[61] The Senate will reconvene at noon, under a Standing Order agreed to at the beginning of the Congress, or else will reconvene at a time set by a consent order, if such has already been entered. When the Senate adjourns, any pending motion to proceed is killed.[62]

Under article 1, section 5, clause 4, of the Constitution, neither house can adjourn for more than three calendar days without the consent of the other body. Such accords on adjournments are embraced in adjournment resolutions, which are privileged. In the absence of an adjournment resolution, the Senate and/or the House may meet in pro forma sessions in order to have convened frequently enough to meet constitutional requirements.[63]

To Adjourn to a Time Certain

With permission of the House, the Senate has adjourned for more than three days to a time certain. For example, when the Senate adjourns for the August recess, it adjourns to reconvene on a particular date. The Senate has also adjourned and reconvened within the same calendar day in order to create a new legislative day. A motion to adjourn to a time certain is amendable in two degrees to provide for alternative times, but the amendments cannot be debated.[64]

To Recess

When the Senate adopts a motion to recess, the legislative day does not change and will remain constant until the Senate next adjourns.[65] Whatever was the unfinished or pending business at the time of the recess remains such when the Senate reconvenes.[66] If the Senate has recessed rather than adjourned, a Morning Hour is not created, so morning business activity such as the presentation of bills and committee reports occurs by unanimous consent.

A motion to recess, like motions to adjourn or to adjourn to a time certain, cannot be made during the reading of the *Journal*,[67] while the Senate is in a quorum call,[68] or during a roll call vote.[69] The motion to recess cannot be made in the absence of a quorum unless the Senate has previously adopted a consent order that at the close of that day's business it shall stand in recess.[70]

Motions to recess can be amended in two degrees to change the time for reconvening, but the amendments are not debatable.[71] They cannot specify the business to be considered when the Senate reconvenes.[72] Motions to recess can be renewed if business has intervened between them.[73]

To Proceed to Executive Business

Although it is normal to proceed from legislative session to executive session by unanimous consent, a nondebatable motion is available if there is objection. Similarly, a motion to return to legislative session would be nondebatable.

Adoption of a motion to proceed to executive session, or accomplishing the same result by unanimous consent, freezes the legislative business in place.[74] When the Senate returns to legislative session, it picks up legislative business where it left off. The same result happens in the opposite direction when the Senate returns to legislative session. Whatever business was pending in executive session is suspended in place, to be renewed when the Senate returns to executive session. For example, the leadership could schedule consideration of a particular bill, interrupt it with debate on a treaty, and then set aside the treaty to return to the bill. It is possible for the leadership to do this because legislative business is suspended, not displaced, when the Senate goes into executive session. Similarly, proceedings on the treaty would be suspended, not displaced, when the Senate returns to legislative session.[75] Legislative business cannot be conducted in executive session, and executive business cannot be addressed in legislative session, except by unanimous consent.[76]

Even though Rule XXII does not say so, a motion to proceed to executive session may specify the business to be considered, as in "I move that the Senate proceed to executive session to consider the nomination of John Doe."[77] Conversely, a motion to proceed to legislative session cannot specify the proposal to be considered.

The reason for this disparity is a pair of 1980 precedents set at the urging of then–Majority Leader Robert C. Byrd (D-WV). Prior to that time, Senate practice had been to reach the first nomination on the executive calendar without debate once the Senate had proceeded to executive session. Any other calendar items could be reached only through a debatable motion to proceed. For instance, in 1968 there was contentious debate on a motion to proceed to the nomination of Abe Fortas to be chief justice of the United States Supreme Court. A cloture motion was filed, but cloture was not invoked, and the Fortas nomination was withdrawn. Through these 1980 precedents, these procedures were altered. Thereafter, any executive calendar item could be reached on a nondebatable basis by coupling nomination or treaty with the motion to proceed to executive session.

A motion to proceed to executive business is not amendable. The Pastore Rule governs debate in executive session,[78] meaning that debate must be germane for the first three hours after the pending or unfinished business has been laid before the Senate. The two-speech rule[79] also applies, but in the executive session the word "day" means calendar day, so each turn of the calendar is a fresh opportunity for speeches under the rule.[80]

To Table

The motion to table may be used to terminate debate and dispose of any pending debatable proposition because it takes priority over any nondebatable motion.[81] A tabling motion may be offered at any time, provided that the underlying proposition is not subject to a time limitation imposed by unanimous consent or by statute. If time is controlled, the motion to table may not be offered until all time has expired or been yielded back.[82]

A tabling motion will end debate on the underlying proposition because it is itself nondebatable and the Senate must consider it as a priority motion when offered. A successful tabling motion is a final disposition of the question against which it is aimed.[83] For instance, if an amendment has been tabled, it cannot be offered again in identical form. A second-degree amendment would also fall with a first-degree amendment that had been tabled, but its disposition would have been incidental to the tabling motion, and it could be proposed again in the same form.[84] If an amendment to an underlying measure is tabled, the measure itself is not prejudiced.[85]

If a tabling motion fails, then the proposition against which it is aimed remains before the Senate for further disposition.[86]

To Postpone Indefinitely

Adopting the motion to postpone indefinitely kills the underlying proposition. Such a motion is sometimes used to clear the calendar of business of Senate bills when companion House measures have been amended by the Senate and are enacted into law. An illustration of the motion to postpone indefinitely follows:

> Mr. REID: Mr. President, I ask unanimous consent that Calendar No. 88, S. 1178, be indefinitely postponed.
> The PRESIDENT pro tempore: Without objection, it is so ordered.
> Mr. REID: Mr. President, for the information of the Senate, this item is an appropriations bill. The conference report on the House numbered bill is now public law.[87]

Along the path to bicameral agreement, it is more common to return Senate bills to the calendar after their text has been incorporated as an amendment to a House bill rather than indefinitely postponing them, at least until the legislative process has been concluded. For instance, in the 108th Congress, the Senate passed S. 1050, the fiscal year 2004 defense authorization bill. Shortly thereafter, it considered the House companion measure, H.R. 1588. The Senate amended H.R. 1588 with the text of S. 1050. Following passage of H.R. 1588, as amended, the Senate by consent vitiated passage of S. 1050 and returned that bill to the calendar.

To Postpone to a Time Certain

Adoption of a motion to postpone to a time certain will bring a proposition back before the Senate when the specified time arrives. Extraneous provisions cannot accompany the motion, such as establishing the conditions for debate or voting when the measure returns. Imposing such conditions would require unanimous consent.[88]

To Commit

This motion could also be phrased as a motion to refer or as a motion to recommit. The motion can be offered against any measure pending before the Senate[89] but not against an amendment to that measure.[90] If the measure were considered under a consent order providing for a time certain to vote on final passage, then a motion to recommit would contravene the intent of the consent agreement and would not be in order.[91] Similarly, a motion to recommit cannot be made against a measure on which cloture has been invoked because Rule XXII requires that the Senate remain on the "clotured" proposition until it is completed.[92] Otherwise, the motion is in order at any time prior to passage of the bill.[93] If a motion to recommit fails, another may be offered after a reasonable time or after an amendment has been adopted to the bill.[94]

A motion to recommit may be accompanied by instructions, such as directions to a committee to report on a date certain or perhaps to report a particular amendment. Such instructions are amendable in two degrees.[95] It is not in order to amend the motion to commit in order to refer the measure to a different place.[96] Once the measure has been marked up and reported back from committee, it does not automatically return to the Senate floor as the pending business.

An important variation on this theme involves a motion to recommit with instructions to report back forthwith. In such a case, the concept of a committee markup is nothing more than a fiction. In fact, the bill never leaves the floor, and the committee never actually meets.[97] Adopting a motion to recommit has the effect of stripping a bill of all pending amendments and any amendments that have been adopted prior to that time.[98] The instruction could be accompanied by proposed amendment language that might include provisions to keep intact some or all of the amendments that had already been agreed to in the Senate while stripping pending amendments.

An example of how this motion is used arose during consideration of S. 14, a comprehensive energy bill extensively debated on the Senate floor during the summer of 2003. Faced with an indeterminately long list of amendments and trying to conclude action on the bill before the impending August recess, Majority Leader Bill Frist (R-TN) filed a motion to recommit to the Committee on Energy and Natural Resources with instructions to report forthwith a complete substitute. Senator Frist then offered germane first- and second-degree amendments to the substitute. Once the amendment tree was filled, Frist filed a cloture motion on the pending motion to recommit.[99]

Instructions to recommit cannot require a committee to do something that would otherwise be outside its authority.[100] When the measure has been reported back forthwith, the bill is open to further amendment on the floor. The instructions to a committee cannot structure or obligate the Senate's consideration of the measure once the legislation is back on the floor. To structure such floor consideration would require a consent order.[101]

Because the motion to recommit takes priority over amendments, offering this motion can add layers and complexity to the amendment process. Its use enables senators to override an amendment tree full of pending amendments and can result in undoing floor proceedings on amendments previously adopted. Accordingly, unanimous consent orders intended to limit amendments sometimes contain a provision restricting the use of this motion.

To Amend

The motion to amend is detailed in substantial depth during a review of the amendment process that follows. Note that it is of lowest priority among Rule XXII motions. For example, while an amendment is pending, any of the other motions can be offered and must be addressed before the Senate returns to deliberations on the amendment.

Although it stands least in priority, the motion to amend is the most significant of the Rule XXII motions. Freedom of amendment is a great distinguishing characteristic of the Senate. The following example contrasting Senate amendment procedure with that of the House is instructive.

On February 5, 2003, Representative Jim Greenwood (R-PA) introduced the HEALTH Act. Among other things, Greenwood's legislation provided for caps on medical malpractice claims. The Speaker referred the bill to the House Committee on the Judiciary and also to the House Committee on Energy and Commerce. By March 11, both committees had reported amended versions of the bill. On March 12, the House Rules Committee reported H. Res. 139, a rule setting forth procedures to govern the consideration of H.R. 5. In testimony before the Rules Committee, proposals were heard for thirty-four amendments, thirty-two of which were to be offered by Democrats. As reported from committee, the rule provided for no amendments at all.[102]

On March 13, the House agreed to the rule and then passed the medical malpractice bill after several hours of debate on a near–party-line vote. No amendment was offered on the floor because none was possible under the rule.

Senate procedure on amendments could not be more different. The Senate lacks a forum like the House Rules Committee to impose amendment restrictions that can be adopted by majority vote.[103] To secure amendment limitations, the Senate would have to enter a consent order, which could be blocked by a single objection, or impose cloture, which requires sixty votes. Even under cloture, amendments could be proposed so long as they were germane. Absent these circumstances, companion legislation before the Senate would be wide open to amendments of all kinds.

Chapter Three

Floor Debates

QUORUMS

Article 1, section 5, of the Constitution states that a quorum of the Senate consists of a majority of all senators duly chosen and sworn.[1] In daily practice, the Senate operates on the principle of a presumptive quorum, which means that the presence of a quorum is assumed unless its absence is suggested. The typical way to raise a point of no quorum is to obtain recognition and state, "Mr. President, I suggest the absence of a quorum."

For a senator to initiate a quorum call, he must have the floor,[2] although the presiding officer may act from the chair to suggest the absence of a quorum.[3] If the Senate is operating under a time agreement, time consumed in the quorum call will be charged against the senator who raised the point of no quorum.[4] Under these circumstances, a senator must be in control of time to initiate a quorum call and must have at least ten minutes of time remaining.[5] A quorum call is always in order before a vote and can be ordered once all time has expired.[6]

Once the absence of a quorum is suggested, the presiding officer will then direct that the roll be called, and two bells will sound. The quorum call commences when the first senator's name is called.[7]

Except during postcloture proceedings, the presiding officer has no authority to count a quorum, and its presence or absence can be ascertained only through calling the roll.[8] Once a quorum call has commenced, no business can be transacted, and no debate is in order.[9] Senators who have withheld their votes through the announcement of pairs[10] are considered present for purposes of a quorum, as are senators who are physically present in the Senate chamber but do not answer to their names.[11] Other than in post-cloture

37

proceedings the presiding officer is not permitted to determine whether a call of the roll is needed even if he can see that a quorum is present. Once the roll call has commenced, however, he can take notice of a Senator who is there and count him as present, even if that Senator refuses to respond to the call.[12]

Most quorum calls are intended to fill time rather than to produce an actual quorum of senators. For example, quorum calls are typically used to await the arrival of a senator on the floor or to delay floor proceedings while a procedural path or legislative compromise can be negotiated. When the reason for the hiatus has expired, a senator will seek recognition and ask consent that the quorum call be vitiated.

Without objection, the call of the roll will cease, and the Senate will go on with its business. If objection is heard, the clerk must continue with the call. When all senators' names have been read out and a quorum has not been produced, the call of the absentees is in order, and three bells will ring. This is what is known as a live quorum, and attendance of senators is necessary. Once the roll call discloses the absence of a quorum, the quorum call can no longer be suspended by unanimous consent.[13]

It can take substantial time to produce a quorum as senators trickle in, so a common means of speeding matters along is to move that the sergeant at arms be directed to request the attendance of the absentees.[14] A roll call is customarily requested on this motion, and as senators respond to the vote, they make a quorum. Further proceedings relative to the sergeant at arms are then moot.

The Senate's power to compel a quorum is set forth in the Constitution. Article 1, section 5, says of each house of Congress that "a majority of each shall constitute a Quorum to do Business; but a smaller Number may adjourn from day to day, and may be authorized to compel the Attendance of absent Members, in such Manner, and under such Penalties as each House may provide."[15]

Quorum-producing motions are decided with debate.[16] Due to the constitutional provisions just cited, an affirmative vote of less than a quorum is sufficient to agree to the motion. If a motion to request attendance fails to produce a quorum, a motion can be offered to instruct the sergeant at arms to compel the attendance of absent senators or even to compel such attendance by arrest.[17] Motions to arrest senators have been rare. An arrest motion was last used on the evening of February 23–24, 1988, as part of an extended Senate session that lasted more than fifty-three hours.

That night, the Senate was considering campaign finance reform legislation. Minority Whip Alan Simpson (R-WY) suggested the absence of a quorum. Senator Byrd asked consent to rescind the quorum call, but Simpson objected, and the call was completed. Thirteen senators answered to their names, all but one of whom was from the majority Democrats. Byrd then moved that the sergeant at arms be instructed to request the attendance of absent senators and secured the yeas and nays. The vote on the roll call was 47–1, with fifty-two senators not voting. No Republican voted.

The presiding officer announced the result and said that the clerk would continue to call the roll for absent senators. Byrd then offered the following motion: "Madam President, I move that the Sergeant at Arms be instructed to arrest the absent Senators and bring them to the Chamber, and I ask for the yeas and nays on the motion."[18] By a vote of 45–3, with no Republican voting, the Senate agreed to the motion. The presiding officer announced that the clerk would continue to call the names of the absentees and that the sergeant at arms would execute the order of the Senate. A quorum was finally made when officers of the sergeant at arms carried Senator Bob Packwood (R-OR) into the Senate chamber.[19]

In volume 2 of his Senate history, Senator Byrd describes several additional instances when failure to produce a quorum led to the issuing of arrest warrants.[20] His account of the 1942 arrest of Senator Kenneth McKellar (D-TN) at Washington's Mayflower Hotel demonstrates that the arrest authority of the sergeant at arms can be exercised away from Capitol Hill.

In the absence of a quorum, no business or debate can be transacted, and the only motions in order are motions to produce a quorum or motions to adjourn or to recess pursuant to a previous order.[21]

One quorum call cannot follow another unless some business intervenes. For this purpose, business generally includes offering or adopting a motion, including a motion to amend, a ruling on a point of order, proposing and acting on a unanimous consent request, the ordering or refusal of the yeas and nays, and presentation and reference of House or presidential messages.[22] When a quorum call is suspended by unanimous consent, then a request for another quorum call can be made even if no business has intervened.[23] Intervening debate is not business for purposes of a renewed quorum call, nor is receipt of House or presidential messages on which no action is taken, nor is making a parliamentary inquiry or posing a unanimous consent request on which no action is taken.[24]

Under Rule XII, a quorum call is required before the Senate may enter into a unanimous consent order fixing a time certain to vote on final passage of a bill or joint resolution.[25]

SENATE DEBATE: RECOGNITION OF SENATORS

Every member, when he speaks, shall address the chair, standing in his place, and when he has finished, shall sit down.

—Senate Rule III, 1789

No member shall speak more than twice in any one debate on the same day, without leave of the Senate.

—Senate Rule IV, 1789

When two members shall rise at the same time, the President shall name the person to speak; but in all cases the person first rising shall speak first.

—Senate Rule V, 1789

A Senator is granted the opportunity to speak after he rises and addresses the presiding officer.[26] While holding the floor, a senator must remain standing. All recognition comes through the presiding officer, and a senator cannot obtain the floor in his own right by having it yielded to him by a colleague.[27] Conventions of Senate debate require that senators address each other in the third person and speak to each other through the presiding officer.[28]

Rule XIX, paragraph 1(a), states that "the Presiding Officer shall recognize the Senator who shall first address him." Application of this rule is conditioned by precedent, first established by Vice President John Nance Garner in 1937, which accords preferential recognition to four senators. As expressed in *Riddick's Senate Procedure* at page 1098: "The Presiding Officer is required to recognize the Senator who in his discretion first sought recognition. However, in the event that several Senators seek recognition simultaneously, priority of recognition shall be accorded to the Majority and Minority Leader, the majority manager and the minority manager, in that order."

Senator Mike Mansfield's biographer, Don Oberdorfer, captures the importance of the right to preferential recognition:

> Stripped to its essence, the power of the Majority Leader is based on senatorial courtesy and custom and especially on the right to be recognized first by the presiding officer ahead of all others to speak on the Senate floor. This power of first recognition is more potent than it sounds, for it permits the Majority Leader to outflank any other Senator in offering motions or amendments, and to have the most important voice, rarely overruled, in shaping the nature and timing of Senate business.[29]

Preferential recognition is granted to each leader personally and not to another senator, such as the assistant majority leader who may be acting as majority leader. Thus, a majority whip temporarily standing in for his leader would have no greater right to recognition than any other senator and a lesser right than the minority leader. Greater flexibility is granted for substitute managers, and a senator who acts as manager will accrue preferential recognition rights as if he were the original manager.

The right to preferential recognition does not mean that a senator who is speaking can be taken off his feet so that the floor may be given to a "preferred" senator. For example, if a freshman member of the minority party is speaking and the majority leader wants the floor, he must ask if the speaker will yield to him. If the senator refuses to yield, the majority leader must wait until that senator sits down. What preferential recognition really means is that when the floor is open, a preferred senator will be recognized over another senator who may have sought recognition first.

When time is controlled under a unanimous consent order, a senator may speak only if yielded time by someone who controls it, as specified by the order. Customarily, this will be either the majority or the minority bill manager or the proponent of an amendment. As noted in *Riddick's Senate Procedure* at page 1103, "Under a unanimous consent agreement giving certain stipulated Senators the control of time for debate for a stipulated period of time, the Chair is restrained from recognizing anyone not yielded to by the Senators in control of that time."

A senator must have the floor to offer an amendment or other motion, proffer a consent request, ask for the yeas and nays, or request the absence of a quorum. Once he takes such an action, he loses the floor and does not automatically regain it.[30] A senator is entitled to yield for a question but will lose the floor if he yields for a speech.[31] Further, he may lose the floor for circumstantial reasons, such as the expiration of time under a consent agreement or the arrival of a cloture vote pursuant to Rule XXII.

DECORUM IN DEBATE: NORMS

No member shall speak to another, or otherwise interrupt the business of the Senate, or read any printed paper while the journals or public papers are reading, or when any member is speaking in any debate.

—Senate Rule II, 1789

No member shall speak more than twice in any one debate on the same day, without leave of the Senate.

—Senate Rule IV, 1789

When a member shall be called to order, he shall sit down until the President shall have determined whether he is in order or not; and every question of order shall be decided by the President, without debate; but, if there be a doubt in his mind, he may call for a sense of the Senate.

—Senate Rule XVI, 1789

If a member be called to order for words spoken, the objectionable words shall be immediately taken down in writing, that the President may be better enabled to judge the matter.

— Senate Rule XVII, 1789

The presiding officer is responsible for maintaining decorum on the Senate floor. It is common to see him gavel for order when a senator makes the point that the Senate is not in order. Nevertheless, he is empowered to bring the Senate to order on his own without need for a demand from the floor.

The norms for Senate debate are set out in Rule XIX. In debate, a senator may not impute to a colleague conduct or motives unbecoming to a senator or refer offensively to any state of the union.[32] On a demand for the regular order,[33] a senator could theoretically lose the floor for violating these rules, subject to his seeking permission of the Senate to continue. A remonstration from the presiding officer would precede a sanction, and disciplinary action would be avoided if at all possible. If the presiding officer requires a senator to take his seat, that decision may be appealed without debate.[34]

Another debate norm is the Pastore Rule,[35] which stipulates that debate must be germane for the first three hours of actual session after the pending or unfinished business has been laid down. "Germane" in this instance means related to the subject matter of the underlying business.[36] The Pastore Rule is seldom enforced, but, more frequently, the prospect of enforcement has been raised in order to press adherence to the rule. For instance, on November 7, 2003, the Senate was considering Internet tax legislation. During the hours when the Pastore Rule was still in effect, Senators Harry Reid (D-NV) and Byron Dorgan (D-ND) entered on a colloquy concerning judicial nominations. Senator John McCain (R-AZ) made a parliamentary inquiry as follows:

Mr. McCAIN: Parliamentary inquiry, Mr. President.

Mr. REID:—Senators from California or what the reason might be.

The PRESIDENT pro tempore: Does the Senator yield for a parliamentary inquiry?

Mr. REID: For a parliamentary inquiry? I will be happy to do that, without losing my right to the floor. Yes.

The PRESIDENT pro tempore: The Senator from Arizona.

Mr. McCAIN: Mr. President, I have a parliamentary inquiry: Wouldn't rule XIX 1(b) begin to apply concerning proceedings while legislation is before the Senate?

The PRESIDENT pro tempore: That is correct. Under the procedures of the Senate, there would be a warning issued to Senators speaking on matters other than the business before the Senate in the first 3 hours.

Mr. REID: Mr. President, I appreciate that very much. I appreciate my friend from Arizona bringing that to my attention. What I am going to talk about for a while is the Internet tax problem.[37]

Another debate norm is the two-speech rule, a provision, with origins in the Senate rules of 1789, that provides that no senator may speak more than twice on the same subject on the same legislative day.[38] Dr. Stanley Bach explains the application of the rule:

A Senator does not have to speak for very long at all before that statement will be counted under the two speech rule. According to the Senate's precedents, the Senate has rejected the position "that recognition for any purpose constituted a speech," and that "certain procedural motions and requests were examples of actions that did not constitute speeches for purposes of the two speech rule." These matters include such things as making a parliamentary inquiry and suggesting the absence of a quorum. On the other hand, a substantive comment, however brief, on the pending question may count as a speech.[39]

The precedent to which Dr. Bach refers was set on September 25, 1986. The presiding officer had ruled that securing recognition for any purpose constituted a speech. After considerable and contentious debate, the Senate voted to overturn the ruling. *Riddick's Senate Procedure* explains where matters stand in light of that vote:

[I]t was determined that standing alone, the following procedural motions and requests were examples of actions that did not constitute speeches for purposes of the two speech rule: parliamentary inquiries, appeals from rulings of the Chair, points of order, suggesting the absence of a quorum, withdrawal of appeals, requests for the yeas and nays, requests for a division vote, requests for reading of amendments, and requests for division of amendments. Therefore, the two speech rule requires not a mechanical test, but the application of the rule of reason.[40]

If a senator loses the floor for whatever reason, such as yielding for a colleague's speech or for a consent request, putting in a quorum call, or permitting an intervening motion, it will terminate his speech, unless he secures consent that, on being recognized again, it not count as a second speech.[41]

The two-speech rule is not particularly effective as a filibuster constraint, especially when the filibuster has support from a significant number of senators. Every debatable proposition is a fresh opportunity for two speeches under the rule.[42] Thus, if a measure is pending, a senator could speak twice on the bill, twice on every amendment, and twice on every debatable motion. Moreover, although speeches may be brief and yet counted, they also can be extremely lengthy. The rule limits the number of speeches but not their duration. Although it has been part of the Senate's rules for more that two centuries, the two-speech rule has never been utilized as a cloture-type device, even during times when filibusters proved vexatious and a cloture rule did not yet exist. Under existing precedents and interpretations, enforcement of the two-speech rule for cloture purposes would be highly cumbersome and time consuming.

FREEDOM TO DEBATE AND ITS RESTRICTIONS

In general, the Senate operates on the foundation of unlimited debate. This principle is fundamental to the right to filibuster. Senate rules do not specifically authorize filibusters; rather, extended debate is possible in the absence of debate restrictions.

In the Senate, debate can be limited only by the following methods:

- Tabling motions: Rule XXII, paragraph 1, authorizes the motion to table. It is nondebatable and may be asserted against any motion of lesser priority. These include motions to amend, to commit, to postpone to a date certain, and to postpone indefinitely. Absent a consent order to the contrary, a tabling motion may be offered against any other debatable proposition.

  Bill managers commonly propose tabling motions as an efficient means of disposing of floor amendments that the committee opposes. A tabling motion takes priority over amendments or other debates or propositions. Once the tabling motion is made, the Senate suspends consideration of the underlying amendment and addresses the tabling motion itself.

  If the motion to table fails, debate resumes on the pending amendment.[43] If the motion to table succeeds, the net effect will have been to halt debate immediately on the amendment and then to dispose of that amendment with prejudice.[44]

  While tabling motions are effective to dispose of hostile amendments, they are ineffective to control debate on a proposal that a senator wishes to pass. For example, a majority party bill manager would be unlikely to use a tabling motion to curtail debate on a committee substitute because the effect of prevailing would be to kill the substitute itself.
- Unanimous consent agreements
- Restrictions in rule-making statutes
- Cloture: Cloture procedure is set forth in Rule XXII, paragraph 2. Although the cloture procedure has evolved over more than eight decades, its fundamental purpose has not changed. Cloture is the fulcrum on which is bal-

anced the right of senators to engage in extended debate and the right of the Senate to work its will. Cloture provides a means by which the Senate can bring consideration of a question to a gradual close. Invoking cloture has always required more than a simple majority vote, meaning that a filibuster can be halted only by a significant consensus of the Senate. Discussions of the cloture process and the evolution of the cloture rule follow.

CLOTURE: THE PROCESS

To initiate the cloture process, a cloture motion signed by sixteen senators is presented at the desk.[46] A senator may be interrupted for presentation of a cloture motion without losing his right to the floor.[47] A quorum call, roll call, approval of the *Journal*, or reading of an amendment cannot be interrupted to present a cloture motion. An example of a cloture motion, as read by the Clerk, follows:

> We the undersigned Senators, in accordance with the provisions of Rule XXII of the Standing Rules of the Senate, do hereby move to bring to a close debate on the motion to proceed to S. 1751, a bill to amend the procedures that apply to consideration of interstate class actions to assure fairer outcomes for class members and defendants, and for other purposes. Bill Frist, Orrin G. Hatch, Charles Grassley, George Allen, Kay Bailey Hutchison, Rick Santorum, Susan M. Collins, Elizabeth Dole, Lindsey Graham of South Carolina, Wayne Allard, Pat Roberts, John Ensign, Thad Cochran, John Warner, Jon Kyl, John E. Sununu, Saxby Chambliss.[48]

Once the cloture motion is proffered and before there is a vote, a day of session must intervene. On the next day of session (two session days after the cloture motion was initiated), a quorum call will occur one hour after the Senate has convened. Once a quorum is established, the cloture vote occurs. Frequently, the quorum call is waived by unanimous consent.

If the Senate has been in continuous session and so does not "reconvene," then the cloture vote will occur one hour after the Senate's normal convening hour, unless another time has been established by unanimous consent. At the beginning of each Congress, the Senate by resolution establishes that the normal convening hour will be noon. Absent a consent order to the contrary, the process of quorum call and cloture vote would therefore commence at 1:00 P.M.[49]

The following hypothetical will illustrate operation of the rule:

- On Monday, a Senator presents a cloture motion, signed by a minimum of sixteen Senators.

- On Tuesday, there is an intervening day of session. No action is taken on the cloture motion, but the rule imposes a special 1:00 P.M. filing requirement on amendments in the first degree, that is, amendments to the text against which the cloture motion has been presented.[50] If cloture is subsequently invoked and an amendment has not been timely filed, that amendment cannot be considered. If cloture is not imposed, the filing requirement is meaningless.
- On Wednesday, the Senate convenes at 10:00 A.M. Amendments in the second degree (amendments to the first-degree amendments) need to have been filed by the time the session begins. One hour later, Senate proceedings are interrupted for the quorum call required by the rule. If the quorum call has been waived, then the Senate will proceed straight to the cloture vote.

The affirmative votes of three-fifths of all senators duly chosen and sworn (sixty senators) are necessary to invoke cloture, unless the proposal involves an amendment to the Standing Rules, in which case an affirmative vote of two-thirds of those present and voting is required.[51] If cloture fails, additional cloture votes may be taken.

There is no restriction on the number of cloture motions that may be presented, and a senator need not await the outcome of one cloture vote before filing a second cloture motion. For instance, while awaiting a cloture motion to ripen on Wednesday, a senator could file a second motion on Tuesday. If the Wednesday cloture vote fails, the second motion will ripen on Thursday. If the first cloture vote succeeds, further proceedings on the second cloture motion would be moot.

If cloture is invoked, it triggers imposition of a new set of rules and precedents. Rule XXII provides:

- There is a thirty-hour cap on overall consideration of the proposition on which cloture has been imposed. This is not simply a limitation on debate but includes all time consumed. The thirty-hour cap may be expanded by nondebatable motion if agreed to by sixty senators.
- At the conclusion of the thirty hours, the Senate votes on amendments that are then actually pending, followed by a vote on the proposition against which the cloture motion was originally filed. If an amendment was timely filed but was not made pending by the end of the thirty hours, it cannot be considered.
- A one-hour-per-senator time limitation is placed on debate, with tight restrictions on yielding time between colleagues. Up to two hours may be yielded to each of the two leaders and each of the two managers, and they, in turn, may yield time to other senators. For example, a senator could "lay

claim" to his hour of debate time and then yield it to the majority leader as part of the overall two hours the leader could accumulate. The leader could use the additional time himself or serve as a conduit to other senators up to the two-hour limitation. As to debate, the thirty-hour limitation is somewhat elastic. When the thirty hours have expired, if a senator wishing to speak has not used or yielded ten minutes of time, he may debate for any part of ten minutes he has not consumed.

- All amendments must be germane.[52]
- Amendments that have been printed and available to senators for at least twenty-four hours need not be read. Normally, the reading of amendments is waived only by unanimous consent.
- No senator may call up more than two amendments if other senators who have yet to call up their second amendment seek recognition to offer an amendment.
- Amendments that have been filed may be withdrawn by their sponsor and thus be unavailable to other senators to call up. Otherwise, there is no restriction on a senator calling up an amendment that another senator has filed.[53]
- Dilatory motions and amendments are out of order.
- The presiding officer will enforce the rules without need for a point of order from the floor.[54] In general, Senate rules are not self-enforcing, and, if a rules violation is not noted through a point of order, the presiding officer will ignore it. In postcloture practice, the presiding officer is empowered to act without awaiting a point of order. His ruling is subject to appeal, provided that the appeal is made before the Senate has moved on to the next amendment. A simple majority of senators present and voting is required to overturn the ruling.
- Points of order and appeals after cloture are nondebatable.
- The presiding officer is empowered to tally a quorum without resorting to a quorum call, merely by counting senators present on the floor. Normally, when the absence of a quorum is suggested, the presiding officer asks the clerk to call the roll.[55]

A cloture motion may be filed against any pending debatable proposition, such as bills, all debatable motions, appeals, nominations, and treaties. Once cloture is imposed, Rule XXII requires that the Senate remain on the "clotured" proposition until it is completed.

Cloture is an effective but cumbersome remedy to use against a filibuster. Under the hypothetical previously outlined in this discussion, cloture was imposed on a Monday. An intervening day of session occurred on Tuesday. Cloture was successful on the first attempt, the vote coming on Wednesday.

Thirty hours of postcloture consideration followed and did not conclude until Friday.

Compare this scenario with a tabling motion, which can end debate instantly (as well as kill the underlying proposition) on a simple majority vote. If one is trying to pass something, the tabling motion is impractical. If unanimous consent to limit debate cannot be achieved and if no statutory restrictions apply, then only cloture is available. Particularly late in the session, when floor time becomes increasingly precious, resort to cloture may be difficult. Given the tortuous and lengthy nature of the cloture process, it is little wonder that for every real or threatened filibuster that is confronted, many others are not.

SPECIAL NOTE: FILIBUSTER BY AMENDMENT AND ITS RELATIONSHIP TO THE CLOTURE RULE

Unanimous consent agreements and rule-making statutes often control time for debate, but unless they restrict amendments after all debate time has expired, nondebatable amendments can continue to be offered.[56] Cloture imposes a limitation on consideration, not only on debate, and creates finality when all time has elapsed. A consent order or statutory provision that does not provide finality contains a loophole that will permit filibuster by roll call or quorum call, notwithstanding the presence of time-controlled procedures.[57] There is discussion in the section of this book that concerns the Budget Act about how the loophole has been exploited to create an unlimited possibility for amendments after debate has concluded. This procedure is known without affection as a "vote-a-rama."

CLOTURE AND RELATED DEBATE RESTRICTIONS: A BRIEF HISTORY

When the Senate first sat in 1789, its rules authorized a motion for the previous question. Codified at Rule IX, the motion read, "The previous question being moved and seconded, the question for the chair shall be: 'Shall the main question now be put?' and if the nays prevail, the main question shall not then be put."

As the previous question motion evolved in the House of Representatives and many other legislative bodies, it became a cloturelike mechanism. It shuts off debate with the suddenness of a tabling motion, but its adoption does not kill the underlying proposition. Origins of the previous question motion date back to the seventeenth-century British Parliament.

Students of the Senate's previous question rule have disputed its purpose. Some have argued that in its original usage it could serve as a cloture device. Others contend that it was used only as a motion to postpone. In the context of the civil rights issue, a lengthy and repeated debate took place during the 1950s, led principally by Senators Paul Douglas (D-IL) and Richard Russell (D-GA). Through floor debate and *Record* inserts and via committee prints and correspondence, the two senators advocated opposite conclusions. Douglas attempted to show that the previous question motion had been used to halt debate. Russell argued that it was only a mechanism to postpone consideration of delicate questions.

Beyond disagreement is that the motion was rarely attempted, and even less often did it prevail. In fact, over seventeen years, the motion had been agreed to only four times.

When the Senate first recodified its rules in 1806, it took the suggestion of Vice President Aaron Burr and eliminated the previous question motion altogether. As explained in the diary of then-Senator John Quincy Adams, Burr

> mentioned one or two rules which appeared to him to need a revisal, and recommended the abolition of that respecting the previous question, which he said had in the four years been only once taken, and that upon an amendment. This was proof that it could not be necessary, and that all its purposes were certainly much better answered by the question of indefinite postponement.[58]

Once the previous question motion was eliminated, no substitute mechanism to close debate was imposed. In dropping the motion, the Senate opened itself to the possibility of filibusters without recourse. It cannot be said, however, that the Senate consciously opted to tolerate unlimited debate. The Senate of 1806 had no tradition of filibustering, a practice that would not emerge for some three decades. As noted in a Brookings Institution study, "Although the lack of a previous question motion after 1806 meant that any minority could theoretically obstruct passage of pending legislation, no real filibusters took place until the late 1830s."[59]

For 111 years after the 1806 rules change, there was no means to close Senate debate. Filibusters became a graver problem in the 1840s, beginning with legislation in 1841 to charter the Second Bank of the United States. Extended debate led to a call by Senator Henry Clay (W-KY) to revive the previous question motion and to use it as a cloture device.[60] Franklin Burdette, a scholar of nineteenth-century Senate debate, has said of Clay's effort:

> The Kentucky leader asserted he would act to allow a majority to control the business of the Senate, that he would offer a measure to that end, and that he believed a limitation of debate would be approved. Senator King of Alabama retorted that the majority had consumed most of the time, and he demanded to

know whether the Senator actually intended to introduce a gag measure. Said Mr. Clay: "I will, sir; I will." Mr. King, defiantly, "I tell the Senator, then, that he may make his arrangements at his boarding house for the winter." Never before had the Senate listened to so plain an avowal of the intention to filibuster.[61]

Opponents of Clay's plan to close debate included Democrats John C. Calhoun of South Carolina and King but also Whig senators concerned about the negative political atmosphere a gag proposal would create. Clay stood down, understanding he had no way to proceed successfully.[62]

In 1850, another prominent Senator, Stephen Douglas (D-IL), sought to impose a previous question motion but was stymied. The practice of filibustering grew in the second half of the nineteenth century, as did calls for reform, but senators empowered by availing themselves of lenient debate rules continually deflected proposed restrictions. Additional efforts to create a previous question motion occurred in 1873 and 1883, each time with substantial but insufficient support.[63]

A further effort occurred in 1890, when the Senate was addressing legislation to authorize federal troops to supervise elections in southern states. Its principal sponsor, Senator Nelson Aldrich (R-RI), was perhaps the most powerful and prominent majority party senator of his era. Frustrated by a filibuster on the bill, he promoted a procedural maneuver that would have allowed a simple majority of senators to curtail debate on demand that such debate be closed. Aldrich's resolution provided:

> When any bill, resolution, or other question shall have been under consideration for a considerable time, it shall be in order for any Senator to demand that debate thereon be closed. On such demand, no debate shall be in order, and pending such demand no other motion except one motion to adjourn shall be made. If such demand be seconded by a majority of the Senators present, the question shall forthwith be taken thereon without debate.[64]

Aldrich's proposal had no foundation in the Senate rules. Nevertheless, he was confident he could secure a majority in favor of his cloture mechanism, provided that the issue could be brought to a vote. Burdette describes the Senator's strategy:

> The plan of Senator Aldrich was to allow debate to proceed for a time on the cloture resolution, then to make a point of order that debate had gone far enough and that an immediate vote should be had. It was admitted that the Vice President would overrule such a point. No Senate parliamentarian could respectably do otherwise. But, when the point had been overruled, an appeal would be taken; and Aldrich hoped that the Vice President would cooperate to the extent of ruling (though against precedent) that the appeal itself could not be debated.

Aldrich evidently believed that if a vote could be taken on the appeal, the Republicans would reverse the decision of the chair, on the basis of a distinction between dilatory and legitimate debate, and thus make possible an immediate vote on cloture.[65]

Vice President Levi P. Morton, who served under President Benjamin Harrison, was reluctant to assist Aldrich in any way, but the matter was soon rendered moot when the Senate proceeded to the consideration of other legislation.[66]

The reform debate raged into the twentieth century inside the Senate, among the press, within academic institutions, and in the political parties. It took the threat of war and the Senate's initial response to that threat to bring about the first cloture rule.

On January 19, 1917, Americans were angered to learn of the Zimmerman Note (hereafter the "Note"), a communication from the German Foreign Ministry to the German ambassador to Mexico. The ministry advised that Germany was about to launch unrestricted submarine warfare in the North Atlantic and that such might provoke a change in American neutrality toward the war belligerents. If America took the side of the Allied powers, the Note said, the German ambassador should explore with the Mexican government the possibility of an alliance against the United States.

Unrestricted submarine warfare commenced. On March 1, 1917, the Senate began consideration of President Wilson's proposal to arm American merchant ships. Although the bill had passed the House with overwhelming support and enjoyed parallel support within the Senate, a group of eleven isolationists led by Senator Robert La Follette (R-WI) filibustered. Prior to adoption of the Twentieth Amendment in 1937, Congresses ended at noon on March 4 of odd-numbered years. LaFollette and his allies would not permit the bill to come to a vote, and the 64th Congress expired.

Public reaction was negative and immediate. Wilson made a famous declaration against the "little group of willful men" who represented no interest other than their own and called for filibuster reform. The rules of the Senate, said Wilson, must be changed so the Senate might act.

A special session of the 65th Congress was to begin on the following day. Special sessions were commonplace every four years in the March following a presidential election. The new Congress, which otherwise would not meet for thirteen months after the elections, would convene for several days to confirm presidential nominations and sometimes for longer periods to address legislation.[67] Pursuant to his constitutional power to convene Congress, President Wilson had issued a February 23, 1917, call for a special session to commence on March 5.

When the special session opened, there was brief debate over what kind of business the Senate would be able to consider. Senators such as Henry Cabot

Lodge (R-MA) and Thomas Walsh (D-MT) successfully argued that although acting in special session, the Senate's power would not be limited to considering nominations and could embrace adoption of rules changes.

Although the Senate might consider rules reform, no rule existed that would permit a majority to shut down a rules-change filibuster. Senator Walsh offered a solution. Walsh theorized that the Senate had a constitutional right to make new rules at any time, notwithstanding the fact that customarily existing rules carried over from Congress to Congress by acquiescence. Accordingly, he proposed that all Senate rules be formally readopted, save Rule XXII, and that a special committee recommend a procedure for cloture. While these reforms were being debated, Walsh said, the Senate could operate under general parliamentary law. Doing so would permit someone to move the previous question to shut down a rules-change filibuster, he argued.

Walsh's opponents contended that the Senate is a continuing body whose rules and procedures carry over from one Congress to the next and bind the deliberations of future Congresses until changed. Were that view to prevail, Walsh's proposal would have no standing. In response, Walsh said,

> The idea of a 'continuing Senate' is at war with the theory of parliamentary government the world over. It is an essential conception in such a system that at intervals representatives assemble in one or more houses, transact such business as demands their attention, and then as a legislative body pass out of existence, a new assembly coming into being in conformity with organic law, or at the call of the sovereign authority.[68]

Walsh went on to observe, "When the Senate is spoken of as a 'continuing body,' nothing more is meant or can be meant than that two-thirds of its Members remain in office at the expiration of each two-year period. . . . There is a vast difference between the Members of the Senate and the Senate."[69]

With Walsh's proposal looming, the two parties each appointed five senators to negotiate a cloture rule. The two party caucuses endorsed their compromise. Introduced by Majority Leader Thomas Martin (D-VA), the cloture resolution was debated for six hours and then passed by 76–3 on March 8, 1917. The rule permitted cloture to close debate on "any pending measure." To obtain cloture, two-thirds of all senators present and voting would be necessary. Whether the reform process would have gone so smoothly or would have happened at all without the threat of Walsh's procedure is impossible to say, but later filibuster reformers argued that his proposal was central to the result.

Although cloture was first invoked in 1919 on the Treaty of Versailles, the procedure was seldom attempted and more rarely successful in the first four decades following its adoption. Unlike modern practice, to propose invoking cloture was an extraordinary thing. Between 1917 and 1962, cloture was imposed only five times.

The cloture rule was again amended in 1949. The previous year, President Pro Tempore Arthur Vandenberg (R-MI) ruled that Rule XXII did not apply to motions to proceed to the consideration of a measure. Under Vandenberg's ruling, although cloture could be invoked on a measure once pending, no mechanism existed to stop debate on the motion to bring that measure to the floor. The Senate had no effective cloture rule at all, said Vandenberg.

Presiding over a new Democratic majority in 1949, Vice President Alben Barkley attempted to reverse the Vandenberg precedent, but the Senate overturned his ruling.[70] Only a formal rules change would remedy the obvious anomaly in the rules.

The 1949 amendment broadened the reach of cloture to embrace any debatable proposition except for a motion to proceed to a rules-change resolution. Nominations, which were not the reason for the amendment, were brought under Rule XXII for the first time. As a compromise with senators who did not want to expand use of Rule XXII, cloture was made more difficult. Instead of needing the affirmative vote of two-thirds of those present and voting, cloture would now require two-thirds of all senators. Imposition of a higher cloture threshold and the lack of any mechanism to obviate a filibuster on motions to consider rules amendments foretold a long and bitter struggle to modify the rules through extraordinary devices.

In 1953 and 1957, advocates of filibuster reform proposed Walsh-like methods to bring about rules changes. Senator Clinton Anderson (D-NM) and bipartisan allies claimed constitutional authority to propose new Senate rules. So when the 83rd Congress convened in 1953, Anderson offered the following motion: "In accordance with Article I, Section 5 of the Constitution which declares that 'Each House may determine the rules of its proceedings,' I now move that this body take up for immediate consideration the adoption of rules for the Senate of the Eighty-third Congress."[71]

While those rules were under consideration, Anderson argued, the Senate could be governed by general parliamentary law. The new Majority Leader, Robert Taft (R-OH), tabled Anderson's proposal 70–21, with the support of the new minority leader, Lyndon Johnson (D-TX). Taft contended that the Senate is a continuing body whose rules carry over from one Congress to the next and that although the rules could be amended at any time, any effort to do so would have to abide by procedures set out in the rules themselves.[72]

In 1957, using similar reasoning, Majority Leader Johnson tabled a nearly identical Anderson resolution by 55–38. Once again, both party leaders cooperated to oppose Anderson. Johnson enjoyed full support from Minority Leader William Knowland (R-CA).

Also in 1957, Vice President Richard Nixon issued an advisory opinion in response to a parliamentary inquiry from Senator Hubert H. Humphrey (D-MN). Nixon stated that the Senate has a constitutional right to adopt rules at the beginning of a new Congress without resort to the procedures set out in rules carrying over from the old. Nixon posited the following theory:

> It is the opinion of the Chair that while the rules of the Senate have been continued from one Congress to another, the right of a current majority of the Senate at the beginning of a Congress to adopt its own rules, stemming as it does from the Constitution itself, cannot be restricted or limited by rules adopted by a majority of the Senate in a previous Congress.
>
> Any provision of the Senate rules adopted in a previous Congress that has the expressed or practical effect of denying a majority of the Senate in a new Congress the right to adopt the rules under which it desires to proceed is, in the opinion of the Chair, unconstitutional.[73]

Nixon added, however, that a rules-change procedure must be undertaken when the new Congress commences and before it begins to operate under carryover procedures. Once the Senate has acquiesced in the carryover rules by operating under them, said Nixon, rules changes could be made only under the old procedures. In any event, Nixon continued, the matter at issue was a constitutional question, one that only the Senate and not its presiding officer had the power to decide.

Nixon's advisory opinion was without consequence for that Congress when Johnson successfully tabled Anderson's resolution. Nevertheless, his opinion was a landmark in the history of efforts to change the cloture rule by constitutional methods. Nixon's words set the stage for 1967 and 1969 rulings from Vice President Hubert Humphrey and a 1975 ruling from Vice President Nelson Rockefeller.

The election of 1958 added thirteen new Democrats to the Senate and supplied substantial momentum to filibuster reform efforts. These initiatives would be renewed in the Congress convening the following January.

Early in the 1959 session, Anderson would again attempt a constitutional rules change, hoping to lower the cloture requirement from two-thirds of all senators to three-fifths of senators present and voting. In another advisory opinion, Vice President Nixon repeated the essence of his 1957 statement:

> It is the opinion of the Chair, as he has expressed it both yesterday and at the beginning of the first session of the last Congress, the rules of the Senate continue from session to session until the Senate, at the beginning of a session indicates its will to the contrary.
>
> In the opinion of the Chair, also, however, any rule of the Senate adopted in a prior Congress, which has the express or implied effect of restricting the con-

stitutional power of the Senate to make its own rules, is inapplicable when rules are before the Senate for consideration at the beginning of a new Congress.[74]

In response to an inquiry from Majority Leader Johnson, Nixon later added this caveat: "During the course of the Congress, after the original decision as to adoption of rules has been made, the Senate would be bound by whatever rules it adopted, whether by acquiescence or by action."[75]

Majority Leader Johnson, with the support of Minority Leader Everett Dirksen (R-IL), preempted Anderson with a rules change of his own, proposing to apply cloture to motions to proceed to rules-change resolutions and to lower the cloture threshold back to the pre-1949 level of two-thirds present and voting. Johnson also attempted to end or at least to quiet the debate about whether the Senate is a continuing body. As a bow in the direction of Senator Russell, Johnson proposed language that the Senate is a continuing body whose rules can be changed only pursuant to the provisions of the rules themselves.[76] Efforts by Senators Jacob Javits (R-NY) and Clifford Case (R-NJ) to eliminate that provision failed, although Javits would argue that the language was a constitutional nullity. Constitutional rights, Javits claimed, would always supersede the Standing Rules.

Johnson had convinced filibuster reform opponents led by Senator Russell to support the leadership proposal as the only alternative that could preempt Anderson's reforms. Johnson tabled Anderson's constitutional motion by 60–36, and the leadership reform was adopted by 72–22.

In January 1961, Anderson proposed S. Res. 4, amending Rule XXII to provide for three-fifths present and voting cloture. After extended debate, the new Senate majority leader, Mike Mansfield (D-MT), successfully moved by 50–46 to refer Anderson's resolution to the Rules Committee.[77] In September of that year, Mansfield brought S. Res. 4 back for an unsuccessful cloture vote (37–43).

In January 1963, Anderson attempted again to move a resolution providing for cloture by three-fifths of senators present and voting. That month, Anderson sought a ruling from Vice President Lyndon Johnson that, under constitutional authority, only a simple majority would be required to cut off debate. Johnson did not rule but referred the issue to the Senate as a debatable constitutional question. As Johnson framed it, the question was, "Does the majority of the Senate have a right under the Constitution to terminate debate at the beginning of a session and proceed to an immediate vote on a rule change notwithstanding the provisions of the existing Senate rules?"[78]

By consent order, the Senate set a time several days later to vote on a motion to table the question that Johnson had submitted. The tabling motion carried by 53–42, meaning that Anderson was required to proceed under existing Senate rules rather than being able to cut off debate with a simple majority. A cloture motion filed under Rule XXII procedures was rejected by 54–42.

At the beginning of the 90th Congress, in January 1967, Senators George McGovern (D-SD) and Thruston Morton (R-KY) introduced S. Res. 6 to amend Rule XXII, hoping to reduce the cloture requirement to three-fifths present and voting.

On January 18, 1967, and under claim of constitutional authority, McGovern offered a motion to limit debate on the motion to proceed to S. Res. 6. McGovern's motion would create a new cloture-type procedure in lieu of the Rule XXII cloture process. The motion had multiple parts:

- That without intervening debate, the presiding officer immediately put to a vote McGovern's motion to adopt a substitute cloture procedure.[79]
- On adoption of that motion by a simple majority of senators present, debate on the motion to proceed to S. Res. 6 would be limited to only two hours.
- After the two hours of debate had concluded, the presiding officer should immediately put the question on the motion to proceed.

Arguing that McGovern's motion was nothing other than an attempt to circumvent Rule XXII, Minority Leader Senator Everett Dirksen (R-IL) made a point of order against it. Vice President Humphrey submitted the point of order to the Senate as a constitutional question. He indicated that if the point of order were tabled, he would construe that the Senate had approved the terms of McGovern's motion, and he would therefore be bound by those terms.

Notwithstanding Humphrey's announcement about how he would interpret a vote on tabling, reform proponents still lacked sufficient support. McGovern moved to table Dirksen's point of order, but his motion failed by 37–61. The point of order thereafter carried by 59–37. Later a cloture vote on S. Res. 6, undertaken under the supermajority cloture requirements of Rule XXII, failed by 53–46, and the resolution was returned to the calendar.

In early January 1969, Senator Frank Church (D-ID) introduced S. Res. 11 to provide for cloture by three-fifths present and voting. Vigorous debate followed. On January 14, Church filed for cloture on the motion to proceed to S. Res. 11, then made a parliamentary inquiry, grounded in the constitutional authority to make new rules at the beginning of a Congress. Church asked, "If a majority of the Senators present and voting, but less than two-thirds, vote in favor of this motion for cloture, will the motion have been agreed to?" Vice President Humphrey responded in the affirmative, setting the stage for a major procedural confrontation when the cloture vote occurred.

On January 16, the cloture motion ripened. The vote to invoke cloture was 51–47. Humphrey announced that, consistent with his previous response to the parliamentary inquiry, cloture had been invoked and that debate would proceed under the limitations of Rule XXII. Humphrey's ruling allowed Church to take advantage of the Rule XXII process to curtail debate without requiring that he secure the two-thirds then required under the rule to invoke cloture.

Senator Spessard Holland (D-FL) appealed Humphrey's ruling. With the support of Leaders Mansfield and Dirksen, Holland prevailed. On the question "Shall the judgment of the Chair stand as the judgment of the Senate?" the vote was 45–53.[80] Humphrey was overturned.[81] Yet again, reform advocates lacked the votes to implement a favorable ruling from the vice president.

In 1971, the question of whether constitutional methods could be used to change the cloture rule arose again when Senator James Pearson (R-KS) attempted to proceed to the consideration of S. Res. 9, a resolution to provide for cloture by three-fifths of senators present. Pearson and his allies hoped that Vice President Spiro T. Agnew would assist their constitutional approach by taking an interventionist approach as Humphrey had done in 1967 and 1969. However, Agnew, like Vice President Johnson in 1963, refused to play an activist role. Agnew was unwilling even to issue an advisory opinion, saying,

Advisory opinions or responses to parliamentary inquires of the Chair are not subject to appeal by the Senate. Hence, the Senate would have no opportunity to work its will thereon. Under the circumstances stated, such opinions could serve no useful purpose other than to give a particular conclusion of the Chair.[82]

Agnew stated that if a constitutional point of order were raised, he would submit it to the Senate for decision. The point of order would, of course, be debatable, and Pearson would be unlikely to gain a two-thirds vote for cloture.

Having to confront the requirements of Rule XXII instead of being able to proceed on a constitutional theory, Pearson did not make the point of order. Instead, Pearson tried four cloture votes on the motion to proceed, each securing substantially more than a simple majority but never a two-thirds vote.[83]

In 1975, the issue was joined once more. On January 14, Senators Walter Mondale (D-MN) and James Pearson (R-KS) introduced a resolution to permit cloture by three-fifths present. Although they did not move to its immediate consideration, they announced that they were asserting their constitutional rule-making rights and put the Senate on notice that they would later press for consideration of their reform. January efforts to secure floor action on S. Res. 4 led to several days of desultory debate but no resolution of the issue.

On February 20, under claim of constitutional authority, filibuster reformers made an extraordinary motion to bring debate to an immediate close by simple majority vote. This act resulted in lengthy parliamentary maneuvering that frustrated their efforts but ultimately concluded on March 7 with passage of a compromise for cloture by three-fifths of all senators duly chosen and sworn. The Senate operates under provisions of that rule today. A detailed discussion of the procedural maneuvering is set out in a case study titled "1975: Critical Procedural Moments." The case study appears following this discussion of cloture history.

In 1976, the Senate adopted a proposal by Senator Edward Kennedy (D-MA) that permitted any germane amendment to be considered after cloture as long as the amendment had been filed with the journal clerk before the cloture vote was announced. Prior to that time, for an amendment to be considered after cloture, it had to have been presented and read before the cloture vote.

Notwithstanding that situation, the leadership could qualify amendments for consideration by a consent order containing a list of amendments that could be called up although they had not been read. This provided the leadership with some control in negotiating limits on the number of eligible amendments. The Kennedy reform vastly expanded the number of amendments that could be considered after cloture.[84]

During the 1970s, cloture motions became much more frequent, and after 1975, cloture had become easier to secure. In response, Senator James Allen (D-AL) exposed serious loopholes in Rule XXII as he perfected the "postcloture filibuster." At that time, the rule limited senators' speaking time to one hour after cloture was invoked, but it did not limit the number of amendments that could be offered, the reading of amendments, how much time could be spent in quorum calls and roll call votes, and how much time could be consumed overall. Under these conditions, the postcloture period was open to a filibuster by amendment and by quorum calls.

In 1977, the postcloture filibuster reached its zenith. Opposed to a natural gas price deregulation bill, Senators Howard Metzenbaum (D-OH) and James Abourezk (D-SD) filibustered for thirteen days after cloture was invoked. Empowered by the 1976 Kennedy reform, they filed at the desk hundreds of amendments and put the Senate through a great many quorum calls and roll call votes. Except when they took a moment to debate, none of the time consumed was charged to either senator's hour-long debate rights.

Senator Robert Byrd (D-WV), in his first year as majority leader, engaged in extraordinary tactics to break the filibuster. Byrd secured a ruling from Vice President Walter F. Mondale that, after cloture, defective amendments could be ruled out of order on their face without need for a point of order from the floor.[85] Thereafter, Byrd began calling up certain Abourezk amendments. Mondale would rule each amendment out of order, and before an appeal could be lodged, Byrd would secure priority of recognition to call up the next amendment.[86] In all, Byrd disposed of thirty-three amendments in this fashion. Vigorous complaints were lodged from both sides of the aisle about the denial of appeals, but the filibuster was broken.

In 1979, Leader Byrd successfully proposed amending Rule XXII to control the postcloture filibuster. Byrd's resolution placed a one-hundred-hour cap on postcloture consideration, an overall time limit that captured not only debate but also all time consumed of any nature. The rule imposed a filing requirement on first- and second-degree amendments.[87]

One senator could not fill debate time to the disadvantage of other senators. The rule carried over a limitation that no senator could debate longer than one hour after cloture was invoked. A limited amount of yielding time was permitted. Both leaders and both managers could obtain up to two hours of time claimed by other senators and could act as conduits of such time to those who wished to debate. If the one hundred hours expired and a senator still had not had a chance to speak, the rule offered limited elasticity. A senator who had not used or yielded ten minutes of debate time could speak for up to ten minutes.

Nor could a senator offer amendment after amendment to the exclusion of amendments by his colleagues. The new rule provided that a senator could not offer more than two amendments unless every other senator had the chance to do likewise.

Perhaps the most important reform of all was to bring finality to the cloture process. At the end of one hundred hours, the Senate would proceed to vote on all amendments actually pending and then on adoption of the clotured proposition.

After 1979, it would not be possible to conduct a postcloture filibuster by amendment. Members could not cause the Senate to spend hours in roll calls and quorum calls with no end in sight. The combination of subsuming all time into the one-hundred-hour limitation and voting only on pending amendments at the conclusion of the time closed the loopholes that had permitted the postcloture filibuster to flourish. If the purpose of invoking cloture was to allow the Senate to work its will, individual senators lost the capacity to deny the Senate that opportunity.

In 1986, the Senate adopted a resolution to televise its proceedings. In connection with that resolution and under the leadership of Senator Byrd and Majority Leader Bob Dole (R-KS), the Senate further amended its cloture rule. Pursuant to the 1986 amendment, the one-hundred-hour postcloture cap was reduced to thirty hours. One hundred hours of postcloture consideration could consume eight twelve-hour days or even four around-the-clock days. Although the 1979 amendment had created finality for postcloture consideration, the expansiveness of the one-hundred-hour cap had still led some senators to deter the use of cloture by filing hundreds of amendments before the cloture deadlines.

Facing the risk that the whole of the one hundred hours might be used, a Senate leader might consider carefully whether to initiate the cloture process. By capping postcloture consideration at thirty hours, the potential burden of invoking cloture was substantially reduced.

CASE STUDY: 1975 CRITICAL PROCEDURAL MOMENTS

The 1975 cloture reform effort was a procedural maze far more intricate than the Senate usually encounters. The complexity was due mainly to the skills of one senator, James Allen (D-AL), who strongly and deftly resisted constitutional rules change procedures. The following discussion tracks through the maze. Procedural details that would further explain the various twists and turns taken can be located at different passages in this book.

FEBRUARY 20

On the calendar is S. Res. 4, the Mondale-Pearson resolution that will reduce the cloture requirement from two-thirds present and voting to three-fifths present and voting. Senator Pearson understands that if he makes an ordinary motion to proceed to S. Res. 4, he will confront a filibuster on that motion. Immediately, he tries to circumvent the filibuster by offering an extraordinary, self-executing procedure to avoid debate. He relies on the same constitutional rule-making theory advanced by Senators Walsh, Anderson, McGovern, and others before him. Modeling his approach on McGovern's 1967 effort, Pearson proposes a form of majority cloture. His motion contains three parts:

1. That the Senate proceed to the consideration of S. Res. 4
2. That under the rulemaking powers found in article 1, section 5, of the Constitution, debate on this motion to proceed be brought to an immediate conclusion[88]
3. That on the adoption of this motion, the presiding officer put the question on the motion to proceed without further debate

Majority Leader Mike Mansfield (D-MT) counters that the Senate is a continuing body and that it amended the Standing Rules in 1959 to affirm this fact.[89] He contends that he favors the end of three-fifths cloture but not the use of the constitutional approach to achieve it. He raises a point of order against Pearson's motion. Vice President Nelson Rockefeller notes that a constitutional question has been raised and, accordingly, submits the point of order to the Senate.[90] Senator Jacob Javits (R-NY) makes a parliamentary inquiry: if the point of order is tabled, will Rockefeller interpret the vote to affirm the procedural validity of Pearson's motion?

Rockefeller responds affirmatively, saying that tabling the point of order would constitute a judgment by the Senate that Pearson's motion is proper in all respects. Thus, he will adhere to special procedures set out in the motion and call for a vote without debate. If the motion prevails, S. Res. 4 will be pending before the Senate, Rockefeller announces.

Senator James B. Allen (D-AL) poses a central question. He asks Rockefeller whether tabling the point of order still leaves Pearson's motion before the Senate, subject to debate under existing Senate rules. If so, Allen inquires, are not the terms of the motion inoperative until the Senate has agreed to the motion? In other words, how can the Senate be bound by the terms of a motion it refused to table but has not yet adopted?

Rockefeller responds that by tabling the point of order, the Senate will have judged the motion to be proper and he will follow the procedure the motion sets out. In essence, Pearson has offered a previous question motion.[91] Although Pearson's motion runs contrary to the Senate rules, Rockefeller will abide by it because, when it tabled Mansfield's point of order, the Senate expressed its will that he do so.

Senator Robert C. Byrd (D-WV) decries the ramifications of such a self-executing procedure and draws a road map as to how this process can lead to majority cloture at any time it is executed, not only at the beginning of a Congress. Whenever a majority departs from the regular order and insists on imposing its will, it can do so, Byrd contends. Just because reliance on constitutional rule-making authority has traditionally been claimed at the start of a Congress, future Senates will not necessarily follow that course. The majority of a given moment might not consent to be bound by the old rules even though they had begun a Congress by operating under them.[92] That same majority, observes Byrd, might insist that constitutional rule-making authority trumps entrenched procedures any time it is asserted.

Senator Walter F. Mondale (D-MN), the principal sponsor of S. Res. 4, rebuts. He claims that he, Pearson, and their allies do not favor majority cloture but cloture by three-fifths. Nevertheless, Mondale notes, they have no possibility to reach that substantive end unless they use constitutional methods to bring the rules change resolution before the Senate and override provisions in the Standing Rules requiring a two-thirds vote to shut off debate.

Allen condemns Rockefeller's ruling to permit the self-executing motion. He argues that the vote on the tabling motion is dispositive of that question only and cannot result in implementing the terms of Pearson's motion.

Senator Edward Kennedy (D-MA) defends the use of constitutional powers to bring about the rules change. He interprets the Senate's overturning of Vice President Humphrey's 1969 ruling not as a defeat for majority cloture but rather as a snapshot of majority will in that instance. Kennedy concludes that a different majority could as legitimately reach an opposite conclusion now.

Mondale moves to table Mansfield's point of order. He is successful by a vote of 51–42. It is the first of three times in 1975 that the Senate will go on record supporting constitutionally based procedures to make rules changes.

Interpreting the vote on tabling as validating Pearson's method, the vice president is now prepared without debate to put the question on the motion to proceed to S. Res. 4. Before Rockefeller can do so, Allen calls for a division. Allen claims that the first part of Pearson's motion (moving to proceed to S. Res. 4) is divisible from the second part (that no debate shall be in order). He further claims that the first part is not grounded in any constitutional theory and is clearly debatable. Rockefeller rules that Pearson's motion is in fact divisible and that debate can ensue on the first part.

Allen gains the floor and holds it throughout the remainder of the day, being interrupted and sustained by questions from allies. During debate, Allen disputes the notion that the Senate can rely on inherent rule-making powers to effect rules changes at the start of a Congress. Echoing a point Senator Byrd made earlier in the day, Allen claims that the Senate's constitutional power is no different at the beginning of a Congress than at any point before adjournment.

At the close of business on February 20, the Senate adjourns. An effect of doing so is to kill Pearson's motion to proceed to S. Res. 4.[93]

FEBRUARY 24

Mondale renews the battle. He offers a new self-executing cloture-type motion based on constitutional authority. He moves for the following:

- To close debate on the motion to proceed to S. Res. 4 immediately without intervening debate, motions, or amendments
- That on closure of debate, the chair immediately put the question on the motion to proceed to S. Res. 4 without intervening debate, motions, or amendments

Majority Leader Mansfield makes a point of order against Mondale's motion, and Mondale moves to table the point of order. Although Rockefeller tries to put the question on Mondale's tabling motion, Allen begins a series of delaying tactics. These include quorum calls, roll calls on motions to recess, appeals of points of order, and motions to reconsider.

Eventually, Rockefeller is able to put the question on Mondale's tabling motion, which carries 48–40. This is the second time that the Senate endorses constitutional procedures to effect a rules change.

Now that the point of order has been tabled, the question recurs on Mondale's motion to proceed. Because Rockefeller has again construed that tabling the point of order validates the underlying procedure, he is prepared to put the question to the Senate with no further debate or intervening motions.

Before Rockefeller can do so, Allen moves to recess until 7 P.M. Javits makes a point of order that because the Senate tabled Mansfield's point of order, Allen's motion is out of order. Because this point of order is grounded in an interpretation of inherent constitutional powers and not the Standing Rules, Rockefeller submits the question to the Senate, and debate ensues. Allen holds the floor throughout the afternoon, debating the point of order. Bipartisan allies, consisting mostly of southern Democrats and conservative Republicans, help Allen rest periodically by spelling him with questions.

Much as the Senate adjourned on February 20 and killed Pearson's motion to proceed, Allen would like the Senate to adjourn on February 24 to dispose of Mondale's motion. However, at 7:10 P.M., the Senate recesses for the day, leaving the motion alive.

FEBRUARY 25

The presiding officer begins with an announcement on the status of Javits's constitutional point of order made the previous day. Javits had asserted the point of order against an Allen motion to recess until 7:00 P.M. of that day. Because the Senate was in session past the time specified in Allen's motion, observes the presiding officer, the entire question has become moot. Thus pending is Mondale's motion to proceed to S. Res.

4. After roll calls on several other delaying motions, Allen moves to postpone consideration of the motion to proceed for one month. Rockefeller states, "The motion is not debatable,[94] but if the Senator wants to make a few remarks he may."[95] Allen's few remarks are actually quite lengthy. He holds the floor for a substantial time, interspersed with questions from allies, and they continue to filibuster through instituting live quorums and roll calls on motions to recess, motions to postpone, points of order, and appeals. As the Senate recesses for the day, an Allen motion to postpone consideration of S. Res. 4 for one month is pending.

FEBRUARY 26

When the Senate reconvenes on February 26, Senator Charles Mathias (R-MD) successfully moves to table Allen's motion to postpone. Mansfield makes his third point of order, this one against the Mondale self-executing motion in that it precludes debate, intervening motions, and amendments.

Senator Edward Brooke (R-MA) successfully moves to table Mansfield's point of order, this time by a vote of 46–43, the third occasion on which constitutional methods have been upheld. As the clerk is ordered to call the roll on Brooke's tabling motion, Allen tries several times to gain recognition for a parliamentary inquiry. Rockefeller ignores him, instructing the clerk to proceed with the roll call. Thereafter, Allen's allies, led by Senator Russell Long (D-LA), chastise Rockefeller for allegedly breaching Senate decorum.[96]

Having lost three times in efforts to table Pearson's and Mondale's constitutional motions, Mansfield suggests that he will be open to a compromise.[97] The Democratic leadership will propose amending the cloture requirement to three-fifths of all senators in lieu of the then-current requirement for two-thirds present and sworn or the Pearson-Mondale proposal for three-fifths present and sworn. From this moment on, the leadership assumes command of cloture reform. Senator Byrd, the Democratic whip, will become the point man. Pearson and Mondale, the chief initiators of reform, will recede from dominance.

FEBRUARY 28

Democratic Whip Robert Byrd (D-WV) introduces S. Res. 93 embracing the proposed sixty-vote compromise. Allen objects to its immediate consideration, and the resolution goes over, under Rule XIV, paragraph 6, for possible consideration on the next legislative day.

Related to his endorsement of the leadership compromise, Senator Roman Hruska (R-NE) enters a motion to reconsider the vote by which the last Mansfield point of order was tabled. Hruska acts for a number of conservative Republicans in tying the two questions together. His purpose is to undo, as far as possible, the constitutional precedents that have been established. Mondale announces that he will personally oppose the motion to reconsider but will support the compromise for an absolute sixty-vote cloture requirement. He acknowledges that certain of his backers will support Hruska's efforts to reconsider the precedents.

The leadership compromise, as set forth in S. Res. 93, reduces the vote necessary to impose cloture and comes close to Pearson and Mondale's desired outcome. The two senators have sought to amend Rule XXII to require cloture by three-fifths of senators present. Under their formula, absentees would have been a factor in the vote. If all senators voted, there would be no difference between their cloture number and the leadership's.

The leadership proposal somewhat resembles the cloture rule in effect between 1949 and 1959. The rule then required cloture by two-thirds of all senators. Now it would be cloture by three-fifths. Then, as now, absentees did not matter, and the burden for the vote would fall solely on those who wished to impose cloture.

MARCH 3

The Senate takes up Hruska's motion to reconsider the vote by which the last Mansfield point of order was tabled. Hruska's motion is agreed to by a vote of 53–38. Mondale's motion to table Mansfield's third point of order (against a portion of Mondale's self-executing motion) is again before the Senate. This time, the tabling motion fails 40–51.

Now pending is the point of order itself, which is debatable. Before the point of order is further addressed, the Senate adjourns for five minutes. Byrd will later explain that he moved to adjourn as a tactic to expedite consideration of S. Res. 93, the sixty-vote compromise resolution.[98] Meanwhile, the five-minute adjournment results in killing Mansfield's newly pending point of order and the underlying Mondale motion to proceed to S. Res. 4.

Following the five-minute adjournment, the Senate reconvenes. Byrd moves on an alternative track to proceed to S. Res. 4 and files cloture on that motion to proceed. By moving himself to S. Res. 4 as well as through his maneuvering on S. Res. 93, Byrd has reclaimed the motion to proceed as a leadership initiative.

MARCH 4

Debate on filibuster reform continues. Allen makes a lengthy floor statement concerning why Byrd's five-minute adjournment killed the Mansfield point or order and left constitutional precedents undisturbed. If senators think they reversed those precedents when they reconsidered the vote to table Mansfield's point of order, Allen says, they are mistaken, because the point of order was never adjudicated before the Senate adjourned.

An adjournment of the Senate kills a pending motion to proceed. It does not generally kill a point of order. The Mansfield point of order, however, was directed at procedures tied to a motion to proceed, which is why the point of order died when the motion to proceed died.

Byrd will later defend his motion to adjourn. He did not attempt to secure a vote to affirm the point of order, Byrd explains, because the point of order was debatable, and the question could not have been brought to a conclusion. Byrd argues that when the Senate reconsidered the tabling motion, that was sufficient to undo the constitutional precedent and, in any case, was as far as the Senate could reasonably go. He urges support for the sixty-vote compromise and contends that if the Senate does not take this path, a majority exists to use extraordinary means to effect cloture reform.

At the close of business on March 4, the Senate adjourns. Adjournment kills Byrd's motion to proceed to S. Res. 4, but that consequence is not problematic. Once the cloture motion he filed on March 3 matures on March 5, the motion to proceed to S. Res. 4 will automatically be brought back before the Senate by operation of Rule XXII.

MARCH 5

The Senate reconvenes in a new legislative day. In the Morning Hour, Byrd hopes to reach S. Res. 93, his cloture reform vehicle, which has carried over under the rule.[99] If he can do so, he can move to proceed to S. Res. 93 by nondebatable motion and lay down a cloture motion once S. Res. 93 is pending. Allen filibusters during the entire two hours of the Morning Hour, and Byrd is unable to execute this strategy.

In light of Allen's remarks from the previous day that the constitutional precedents are still viable, Senator Carl Curtis (R-NE) secures unanimous consent that the Senate be able to vote on affirming the third Mansfield point of order. Consent is necessary because the Senate definitively killed the point of order when it adjourned on March 3.

Now resurrected by consent, Mansfield's point of order is sustained by 53–43. Through parliamentary inquiries to the presiding officer, Allen establishes that the vote to affirm Mansfield's third point of order addressed only a portion of the constitutional precedents:

> Mr. ALLEN: Would the Chair, for the information of the Senator, state what the Mansfield point of order is and as to what it is directed?
>
> The PRESIDING OFFICER: The Mansfield point of order was directed against that part of the motion by the Senator from Minnesota that provided that the motion would not be debatable, subject to intervening motions, or amendment.
>
> Mr. ALLEN: It was not directed against that part of the Mondale debate choke-off motion that said that a majority could cut off debate?
>
> The PRESIDING OFFICER: It was directed against what the Chair just stated.
>
> Mr. ALLEN: And not what the Senator from Alabama has just stated?
>
> The PRESIDING OFFICER: And nothing else.[100]

Further on March 5, cloture ripens on Byrd's motion to proceed to S. Res. 4. The vote to invoke cloture is 73–21. The motion to proceed to S. Res. 4 is thereafter adopted. With S. Res. 4 now pending, Byrd moves to amend the resolution with a substitute that reflects the sixty-vote compromise, mooting the need to act further on S. Res. 93. By consent, the substitute is made original text for purposes of further amendment. Byrd files cloture on the resolution as amended by the substitute.

MARCH 6

Debate continues on S. Res. 4, as amended.

MARCH 7

Cloture is invoked on S. Res. 4 as amended by 73–21. Allen complains that the sixty-vote compromise was coerced under threat of extraordinary procedures imposed by those he labels the "gag rule senators." For that reason, Allen says, he condemns the compromise and will continue

to offer postcloture resistance. In the course of that resistance, Allen proposes some thirty-five amendments, all of which are rejected, some by
roll call.

Following recapitulations by Allen, Javits, and Mondale on the path
the Senate has just taken that led to the compromise, the Senate agrees
to S. Res. 4 by a vote of 56–27. Senator Byrd moves to postpone indefinitely S. Res. 93, the original leadership compromise resolution.

MAJOR QUESTIONS THAT ARE NOT DEBATABLE

Although Senate debate is generally unlimited, subject to certain controls
such as the cloture process, there are major questions that cannot be debated.
The list follows:

- Certain motions under Rule XXII, paragraph 1: The rule sets out five motions, in descending order of priority, on which debate cannot be had. They
  are motions to adjourn, to adjourn to a time certain, to recess, to proceed to
  the consideration of executive business,[101] and to table.
- Motions to proceed to House messages, a process otherwise known as
  amendments between Houses:[102] When a House message is received in the
  form of a House amendment to Senate-passed language, a motion to proceed to the consideration of that House message is not debatable. Once before the Senate, the House message can be debated.
- Motions to proceed to conference reports: The motion to proceed is not
  debatable, but the conference report can be debated once it is before the
  Senate.[103]
- Motions to proceed to measures time restricted by statute: Rule-making
  statutes expedite the consideration of measures that are later to be considered under their terms. Even in cases where these laws do not contain explicit restrictions on debating the motion to proceed, so long as time on the
  underlying measure is controlled, the motion to proceed is construed to be
  nondebatable. An example of this construction is the 1974 Congressional
  Budget and Impoundment Control Act, which controls time on budget resolutions and budget reconciliation bills but is silent on the motion to proceed
  to either vehicle. These motions to proceed are always treated as privileged
  and nondebatable.
- Motion to proceed during the Morning Hour: During the Morning Hour,
  which occurs during the first two hours after the Senate convenes on a new
  legislative day, a motion to proceed to any measure on the calendar of business is nondebatable, except for "motions to proceed to the consideration

of any motion, resolution, or proposal to change any of the Standing Rules of the Senate."[104] Under Rule VIII, which provides for a calendar call procedure on Mondays, the nondebatable Morning Hour motion is not available when the new legislative day falls on that day.[105]

- Any activity during morning business:[106] Morning business is a component of the Morning Hour and includes a litany of business set forth in Rule VII, such as submission of bills and committee reports and the receipt of petitions and memorials. No debate is in order during morning business, but it is customary to obtain unanimous consent for a morning business period and to order that debate be permitted during that time.
- Unanimous consent requests: Unanimous consent requests are not debatable. At times, senators will reserve the right to object, and the presiding officer will tolerate a limited amount of discussion for purposes of clarifying the request or the possible response to it. Nevertheless, he can close the discussion at any time by asking if there is objection. A call from the floor for the regular order will also prompt the presiding officer to press the same question, after which either consent will be granted or objection will be heard.[107]
- Points of order generally, except when submitted to the Senate: The presiding officer resolves points of order without debate, unless he submits a point of order to the Senate for decision, in which case it is debatable.[108]
- Points of order after cloture: Rule XXII provides that all points of order are not debatable postcloture.[109]
- Certain appeals: Although appeals are generally debatable, certain appeals are not. If an appeal is taken from the presiding officer's ruling and a question of order arises before that appeal is decided, then any appeal of a ruling before the main appeal is decided will be nondebatable.[110] Appeals following the imposition of cloture are nondebatable.[111]

  If the underlying question is nondebatable, an appeal in connection with that question is also nondebatable. If an appeal is taken relative to a proposition that is subject to a time agreement, the appeal will be nondebatable, unless time has been provided for it. All appeals are subject to being tabled.[112]
- Questions of germaneness on appropriations bills: Rule XVI states that all questions of germaneness on appropriations bills "shall be submitted to the Senate and decided without debate."[113]
- Motions to consider a presidential message: A motion to proceed to a veto message or other presidential message is nondebatable. Debate can be had on the message itself.[114]
- Motions to produce a quorum: In the absence of a quorum, motions may be offered to instruct the sergeant at arms to request or to compel the attendance

of absent senators or even to arrest absentees. As no debate is in order in the absence of a quorum, these motions are nondebatable.[115]

- Motions to permit a senator to speak: If a senator has spoken twice on the same question on the same legislative day, a motion to allow him to speak again or a motion to allow a senator to regain the floor after having been called to order is nondebatable.[116]

Chapter Four

Legislation and Committee Procedures

DRAFTING LEGISLATION:
OFFICE OF THE LEGISLATIVE COUNSEL

Although senators are free to draft legislation without professional assistance, almost universally they rely on the Office of the Legislative Counsel of the Senate. Doing so helps ensure that legislative proposals have proper statutory context and will be less subject to ambiguities or misinterpretations that could arise from inexpert drafting. Securing assistance from legislative counsel is a vital part of developing legislation.

Located on the sixth floor of the Dirksen Senate Office Building, the office provides nonpartisan drafting services. The president pro tempore appoints the legislative counsel, who works subject to oversight and guidance from the Committee on Rules and Administration.

SPONSORS AND COSPONSORS

A principal sponsor, who may be joined by cosponsors, introduces legislative measures. In general, cosponsorship is less common in the Senate than in the House. Senators joining on the day of introduction are called original cosponsors. Senators may later ask unanimous consent that they be added to or deleted from the cosponsor list.

Numerous cosponsors can indicate substantial support for a measure, but the list has no direct bearing on whether the legislation will move forward. As a matter of committee practice, some committees require certain levels of cosponsorship before agreeing to act on certain measures.[1]

SENATE COMMITTEES

All committees shall be elected by ballot, and a plurality of votes shall make a choice.

—Senate Rule XV, 1789

There are sixteen standing committees and four special or select committees. In addition, there are four Senate-House joint committees. The jurisdiction, size, and membership restrictions for these committees are set out in Rule XXV.[2]

The Senate has operated with standing committees since 1816, and over the years the number of such committees has grown and shrunk in response to periodic reforms. The current rule reflects the last major systemic reorganization of Senate committees, which was the 1977 reform effort spearheaded by Senator Adlai Stevenson III (D-IL).[3]

Exceptions to the rule are made at the beginning of each Congress, when resolutions are adopted to establish committee memberships that reflect leadership agreements on committee sizes and ratios. The resolutions also designate who shall serve as chairmen and who shall be the ranking minority members.[4] Committee sizes, as well as party and funding ratios, are negotiated between the two leaders, assisted principally by leadership staff and the two party secretaries. When the resolutions are submitted, they begin, "Notwithstanding the provisions of Rule XXV"[5]

Rule XXIV, paragraph 1, provides that committee chairmen shall be elected by resolution, which shall be amendable. If the designation of chairmen is included in the resolution appointing overall committee memberships, a separate vote on one or more chairmen may be ordered on demand of any senator.

Separate resolutions are submitted for the majority and minority parties. The resolutions are privileged. They may be debated and amended to substitute alternative names but not to expand committee sizes.[6] The committees thus elected serve until their successors are appointed.

In addition to Senate rules, there are Republican and Democratic conference rules that also govern eligibility to serve on committees. For example, Republican conference rules will not permit a Republican senator to serve on more than one of the following committees: Appropriations, Armed Services, Finance, and Foreign Relations.

Separate resolutions are adopted for committee budgets,[7] customarily on report of the Committee on Rules and Administration. The fiscal year for Senate committees runs from March 1 until the last day of February of the following year.[8]

Rule XXVI governs committee procedure[9] and empowers Senate committees to hold hearings, to subpoena witnesses and documents, and to conduct investigations into matters within its jurisdiction.[10] Committees are required to publish by March 1 of the first session of each Congress committee rules that are "not inconsistent" with the Standing Rules of the Senate.[11]

Notwithstanding this provision, there will be features of the Senate rules that simply cannot be mimicked at the committee level. For instance, there is never a cloture procedure in committee, and unlike the Senate's presiding officer, the chairman has the power to gavel debate to a close.

Standing committees are also required to fix regular meeting days, which may be supplemented by additional meetings called by the chairman.[12]

Public notice of committee hearings shall be given at least one week in advance, although committees have the discretion to expedite the hearings.[13] Written witness testimony must be submitted at least one day before a hearing,[14] although many committees require testimony to be provided somewhat earlier than that deadline.

A committee's majority staff primarily assembles witness lists, but the minority is entitled to call witnesses during at least one day of hearings.[15] Implementing these rights requires action by a majority of the minority party members. This rule is not construed to mean that the minority gets its own day of hearings. Instead, the provision results in a negotiation between the chairman and the ranking minority member as to how minority-selected witnesses will fit into the overall hearing.

Committees cannot meet on a day the Senate is in session beyond two hours after the Senate convenes and in no event after 2:00 in the afternoon, unless consent has been obtained from the two leaders.[16] In practice, this means that during daily wrap-up, the majority leader or his designee will seek unanimous consent for committees to meet during the meeting of the Senate on the following session day. An example of such a request follows:

> Mr. STEVENS: Mr. President, I ask unanimous consent that the Committee on Finance be authorized to meet during the session of the Senate on Wednesday, October 15, 2003, at 10 A.M., to hear testimony on "Company Owned Life Insurance."
>
> The PRESIDING OFFICER: Without objection, it is so ordered.[17]

If there is objection, as sometimes occurs, committee meetings will be limited to the time permitted under the rule. It is also possible to move permission for a committee to meet, but the motion would be debatable and, therefore, could be readily frustrated. If a committee reports a measure or matter while meeting without leave of the Senate, a point of order will lie, and the item will be recommitted.

Committees and their subcommittees have a right to determine what will constitute a quorum, but the quorum must be at least one-third of their members for the conduct of committee business. A lesser number can take sworn testimony.[18] Proxies may not be used to make a quorum, although committees may permit proxy voting to record a senator's position, provided that the senator has been informed of the matter on which he has been recorded and affirmatively asked that his proxy be noted.[19]

A majority of the committee must be physically present contemporaneously in order to report a measure, matter, or recommendation.[20] This means that an item cannot be "polled" out of committee without exposing the measure or matter to a point of order. Furthermore, proxies cannot be used to establish the quorum to order something reported.[21] On a point of order, a measure not reported by a contemporaneous quorum will be sent back to committee as having been improperly reported.

The vote by a majority of a quorum to report a measure or matter ratifies all prior committee action taken with respect to that item, and no point of order shall lie on the basis that activity during the markup did not comply with Senate rules.[22]

A committee can order a measure reported favorably, unfavorably, or without recommendation. In general, only if a committee were willing to make a favorable recommendation would it let a measure or matter be reported out. As noted by Thomas Carr of the Congressional Research Service:

> Reporting unfavorably or without recommendation is unusual, but may occur when the committee is required to report by a statutory rule or an instruction from the full Senate. A favorable report signifies that a committee wishes to see further action on a measure. An unfavorable report signifies the opposite—that the Senate take no further action—and committees usually accomplish the same aim by not reporting at all.[23]

Once a committee orders a bill reported, the chairman is obliged to cause it to be reported promptly to the Senate.[24] If it is accompanied by a committee report, then on a demand of a majority of committee members, the report must be filed within seven session days after the request for reporting has been made.[25] These provisions of Rule XXVI limit to some degree the ability of a committee chairman to frustrate the wishes of a majority of committee members.

The committee staff, appointed by the chairman, is responsible for drafting the committee report, which describes the rationale and justification for the committee's action in addition to reflecting certain content requirements established in Rule XXVI.

Pursuant to the rule, a report must recapitulate roll call votes taken during the markup.[26] In addition, the report must contain government cost impact analyses;[27] regulatory, economic, and paperwork impact evaluations;[28] and a comparison of the current legislation with any statutory provision it amends or repeals.[29] Any bill or joint resolution whose report does not set forth this information is subject to a point of order, which can be lodged when a motion is made to proceed to the measure or matter.[30]

A member of the committee who gives notice of intent to file minority, supplemental, or additional views is entitled to not less than three calendar days to file his views with the committee clerk for inclusion in the report.[31]

Although written reports are not required, they are customary. A committee report is an important part of the legislative history of a bill or the history of a nomination or treaty. Committees are the great filters of the legislative process. Their expertise is greatly respected and influential during floor debate. Thus, it is no surprise that agencies, courts, and the affected public will rely on a committee report to add explanation and nuance to statutory language.

If the legislative history the report creates is problematic, there are opportunities to offset or contradict it, but the report cannot be undone via floor amendment to its text. Countervailing history could be established through floor debate and the amendment process, the committee and floor process in the House, and the content of a conference report as well as its floor debate and its accompanying Explanatory Statement of Managers.

A COMMITTEE REPORTS AN ORIGINAL BILL

Rule XV bars consideration of any committee amendment that contains significant subject matter falling within the jurisdiction of another committee.[32] A point of order against such an amendment would cause it to fall. No point of order would lie against the vehicle to which the amendment was proposed. The amendment could be reoffered as a floor amendment.

In addition to reporting legislation that has been referred to it, a committee may also generate an original bill. If the committee reports an original bill, Rule XV would not apply, as the rule affects only amendments and not original legislation. Rule XV bars amendments that contain "any significant matter not within the jurisdiction of the committee proposing such amendment."[33]

Although Rule XV does not pertain to original bills, committees must remain within their jurisdictional boundaries. If a committee reports an original bill whose predominant subject matter falls in the jurisdiction of another committee, then on a point of order the bill will be taken off the floor and referred to the other committee.

A BILL OR RESOLUTION IS REPORTED FROM COMMITTEE:
THE ONE- AND TWO-DAY RULES

Before a bill or resolution reported from committee is considered on the floor, it is generally subject to a one-day rule[34] and a two-day rule.[35]

The one-day rule states that when a measure is reported from committee, it must lie over for one legislative day. The two-day rule provides that a committee report must be available to members in printed form for two calendar days before the measure to which it relates can be considered. The two-day period is construed to mean forty-eight hours, which commences when the Government Printing Office delivers copies of the committee report to the Republican and Democratic cloakrooms. Sundays and holidays never count against the two-day rule, even when the Senate is in session on such days. If the committee does not file a report and there is no requirement that it do so, the two-day rule is inapplicable.

Rule XVII permits the waiver of the two-day rule by joint agreement of the majority and minority leaders and on measures for the declaration of war or the declaration of a national emergency. It is also inapplicable to any measure related to an executive decision or an action that would be effective unless invalidated by one or both houses of Congress.[36] In practice, the leader's waiver is manifested through a unanimous consent agreement or the absence of a point of order.

DISCHARGING A COMMITTEE OF LEGISLATIVE BUSINESS

To discharge a committee, a unanimous consent order must be entered, or the Senate must adopt a Senate resolution. To consider a resolution on the day of its introduction requires unanimous consent. Absent consent, the resolution goes to a special section of the calendar entitled "Resolutions over Under the Rule." Bringing resolutions forward that are in that category is impossible as a practical matter. This process is explained more fully in the portion of this book entitled "Introduction and Treatment of Resolutions." In the alternative, the resolution could simply be introduced without seeking its immediate consideration. In that case, it will be referred to the very committee its proponents hope to discharge. Although a discharge petition process exists in the House, no such procedure exists in the Senate.

If such a unanimous consent agreement is elusive on a bill or joint resolution, a possible remedy is to introduce a fresh legislative vehicle and to place it on the calendar using Rule XIV. An additional method to generate floor consideration of business bottled up in committee is through the use of nongermane amendments.

At the beginning of the 107th Congress, an equally divided Senate adopted a procedure to discharge committees that failed to report legislation or nominations because of a tie vote. Under this procedure, the committee posted a notice of its deadlock in the *Congressional Record*. Thereafter, either the majority or the minority leader could move a resolution to discharge the committee. The resolution could be debated for four hours and could not be amended. A simple majority vote was required to adopt the discharge resolution.

This special procedure was contained in S. Res. 8, which made arrangements for power sharing. The special discharge procedure was never used, and, along with the remainder of S. Res. 8, it died after Senator James Jeffords (I-VT) left the Republican conference and ended the 50–50 partisan split.

DISCHARGING A COMMITTEE OF EXECUTIVE BUSINESS

Nominations and treaties are considered in executive session, which is separate from legislative session. Accordingly, the Senate must be in executive session before a motion can be considered to discharge a nomination or a treaty. During executive session, a senator may offer a motion to discharge a committee and ask unanimous consent for its immediate consideration. Without objection, the motion will be brought before the Senate. The discharge motion is debatable and subject to a sixty-vote cloture requirement. Adoption of the motion requires a simple majority of senators present.

If there is objection to the immediate consideration of the discharge motion, the motion goes to the executive calendar, where it must lie over for one calendar day before it is eligible for floor consideration. The following example illustrates this process:

On July 7, 2003, Majority Leader Bill Frist (R-TN) sought immediate consideration for a resolution to discharge the Senate Judiciary Committee of four judicial nominations, beginning with that of David W. McKeague:

> Mr. FRIST: I now send a resolution to the desk to discharge from the Judiciary Committee the nomination of David W. McKeague, of Michigan, to be a United States Circuit Judge for the Sixth Circuit. I ask for its immediate consideration.
>
> The PRESIDING OFFICER: Is there objection?
>
> Mr. DURBIN: Mr. President, reserving the right to object, this nomination for the Sixth Circuit, and the others that will be made by the majority leader, have not had the benefit of any hearing before the Senate Judiciary Committee. I believe that hearing should take place before a lifetime appointment is given to any person to the Circuit Court. So, on behalf of Senators CARL LEVIN and DEBBIE STABENOW of Michigan, I object.
>
> The PRESIDING OFFICER: Objection is heard.[37]

Following Senator Durbin's objection to the McKeague resolution, he objected to three additional resolutions on other nominations. All four resolutions went to the executive calendar.

Executive calendar items may be brought before the Senate on nondebatable motion to consider if the Senate is in legislative session. The leader or his designee moves to proceed to executive business for the purpose of considering the discharge motion. While any senator is entitled to offer this motion, doing so is considered a leadership prerogative. Once the discharge motion has been brought before the Senate, the motion is fully debatable.

Chapter Five

Bills and Joint Resolutions

One day's notice at least shall be given of an intended motion for leave to bring in a bill.

—Senate Rule XII, 1789

Every bill shall receive three readings previous to its being passed; and the President shall give notice at each, whether it be the first, second, or third; which readings shall be on three different days, unless the Senate unanimously direct otherwise.

—Senate Rule XII, 1789

No bill shall be committed or amended until after it shall have been twice read, after which it may be referred to a committee.

—Senate Rule XIV, 1789

Bills and joint resolutions can be brought to the desk for introduction at any time on a day when the Senate has a morning business period.[1] This is permitted under a Standing Order entered by unanimous consent on the first day of each Congress, so senators may introduce legislation at their convenience rather than just during morning business.[2] Simple or concurrent resolutions can also be introduced in this way, but their disposition under the rules and precedents differs from that of bills and joint resolutions.

Senate Rule XIV provides that each bill or joint resolution must be read three times by title only on separate legislative days, twice before referral to committee and once again at the conclusion of the amendment process. Normally, when such a measure is brought to the desk, this process is collapsed. The measure is deemed to have been read twice, is reviewed by the parliamentarian for

79

jurisdictional determination, and is referred to committee by the presiding officer, all on the same calendar and legislative day.

Bills are referred to the committee of predominant jurisdiction.[3] Unlike the Speaker of the House of Representatives, who has broad authority to refer measures to multiple committees, the Senate's presiding officer can refer bills to only one committee. If there is a dispute over reference, the presiding officer decides the question without debate, but his decision may be appealed immediately thereafter.[4] The appeal is debatable, subject to being tabled.

Joint or sequential referrals occur by unanimous consent. Such consent agreements for joint or sequential referrals arise when a second committee has a lesser claim to a measure, however important its interest in the legislation may be.

In the alternative, the majority and minority leaders may offer a joint referral motion. Authority for that motion is contained in Rule XVII, paragraph 3. The rule requires a one-day notice printed in the *Record* and is not amendable, except for an amendment to any instructions it may contain. Under Rule XVII, paragraph 3, the instructions may contain provisions limiting the time of referral and providing for automatic discharge. Debate of the motion is limited to two hours. Although part of the Standing Rules since 1977, this motion has never been used. Leaders have chosen to honor objections from within their own party conferences and have not attempted to override them via the joint motion.

Frequently, joint or sequential referrals are limited in time and scope for the secondary committee and sometimes provide for automatic discharge if that committee has not acted within a specified period.

In addition, referral may also be accomplished through a motion to commit, which may be proposed once a measure is actually pending on the floor and after second reading.[5] The motion to commit cannot be amended to refer the measure to a different committee or provide for a sequential referral to a second committee.[6] Such a sequential referral would require unanimous consent. The sole amendments in order would be those to add instructions.[7]

When a measure arrives from the House of Representatives, it is read twice, and the presiding officer refers it to the predominant jurisdictional Senate committee.[8] An important exception to this procedure arises when a companion Senate measure is also on the calendar. In that case, the House measure likewise goes to the calendar and is not referred.[9]

House measures may be held at the desk by unanimous consent, especially when Senate committee action on companion legislation is imminent but not yet completed. Further, House measures may be placed directly on the calendar under Senate Rule XIV. The Rule XIV procedure, discussion of which follows, obviates referral of both House or Senate bills and joint resolutions to committee.

ON THE CALENDAR

Bills and joint resolutions reach the calendar by one of four methods:

1. Senate or House vehicles are reported from committee.
2. House vehicles are deemed companion measures to bills or joint resolutions already reported from a Senate committee.
3. Senate or House vehicles are placed there by unanimous consent.
4. Senate or House vehicles are placed there through the exercise of Rule XIV.

THE RULE XIV PROCEDURE TO OBVIATE REFERRAL TO COMMITTEE

Rule XIV presents a method to get measures to the calendar of general orders without the need to have them reported from committee. The following steps are involved.

A measure is presented for introduction. Normally, no objection is made to the introduction of a measure. If objection is heard, then the measure must lie over until the next legislative day.[10] This means that before the measure can be introduced, the Senate must adjourn and reconvene.

After introduction, a measure is customarily deemed to have two readings and then is referred to committee. To avoid referral, the first and second readings of the bill occur openly.[11] Following second reading, a senator says aloud, "I object to further proceedings on this legislation." Without the necessity for unanimous consent, the measure goes directly to the calendar of general orders. Note the following:

- On objection, there cannot be two readings on the same legislative day.[12] Thus, if objection is heard, then, on introduction, the measure will have first reading only. It will remain at the desk, to be laid before the Senate on the next new legislative day.
- If these procedures are followed to the letter and if there are objections throughout, the Senate would have to adjourn three times—once in order to change the legislative day so that the measure could be introduced, a second time to create an opportunity for first reading, and yet again so that second reading can occur.

An example of the operation of Rule XIV procedure is set out next, relative to legislation concerning civil liability for manufacturers and distributors of firearms and ammunition:

Mr. McCONNELL: I understand S. 1805, which was introduced earlier today, is at the desk. I ask for its first reading.

The PRESIDING OFFICER: The clerk will report.

The assistant legislative clerk read as follows:

A bill (S. 1805) to prohibit civil liability actions from being brought or continued against manufacturers, distributors, dealers, or importers of firearms or ammunition for damages resulting from the misuse of their products by others.

Mr. McCONNELL: I now ask for its second reading and object to further proceedings on the matter.

The PRESIDING OFFICER: Objection is heard. The bill will be read the second time on the next legislative day.[13]

On November 3, 2003, the Senate convened a new legislative day, and the bill was read a second time and placed on the calendar, on objection to further proceedings.

To bypass a committee, any senator may unilaterally resort to the Rule XIV procedure. Unanimous consent would be needed only in order to collapse portions of the process, such as securing two readings on the same legislative day. Scheduling the measure, however, remains the majority leader's prerogative. The leader's involvement is needed before measures sent to the calendar under Rule XIV are brought to the floor. Use of Rule XIV can be an exercise in futility if the leader refuses to schedule a measure that has reached the calendar by this means.

The Rule XIV procedure can also be an essential device to move legislation forward. For example, during the 1960s, Senator James Eastland (D-MS) chaired the Judiciary Committee. The committee had jurisdiction over civil rights measures that Senator Eastland was likely to oppose. Wanting to move a civil rights bill, Majority Leader Mike Mansfield (D-MT) used Rule XIV to place the measure on the calendar, avoiding Eastland's roadblock.

In another illustration, in 1980 Senator Birch Bayh (D-IN) proposed a constitutional amendment to abolish the Electoral College. The Judiciary Committee has jurisdiction over constitutional amendments and at the time was chaired by Senator Edward Kennedy (D-MA). A majority of the committee, however, was unfriendly to the proposal. Accordingly, Senator Bayh employed Rule XIV to place his amendment on the calendar, from which Majority Leader Byrd later called it up.

Yet a further example can be found during the the 108th Congress. Bipartisan discussions had become bogged down on class-action-litigation reform. Anxious to try to address the issue before sine die adjournment of the first session and concerned about apparently endless negotiations, Majority Leader William Frist (R-TN) and prime sponsor Senator Charles Grassley

(R-IA) introduced a new class-action bill, S. 1751. The bill received a second reading on October 17, 2003, after which Leader Frist objected to further proceedings, and the bill was placed on the calendar.

INTRODUCTION AND TREATMENT OF RESOLUTIONS

Senate resolutions and Senate or House concurrent resolutions relate to internal housekeeping issues, do not have the force of law, and are subject to procedures distinct from those applicable to bills and joint resolutions.[14] Unlike those vehicles, simple or concurrent resolutions need not be read twice before referral or three times before passage.[15]

Rule XIV, paragraph 6, specifies how such resolutions shall be treated. On introduction, a resolution is referred to committee. It cannot be considered on the legislative day of introduction unless by unanimous consent. If consent is sought and objection heard, a resolution is placed in a separate calendar section titled "Resolutions and Motions Over Under the Rule."

On the next legislative day,[16] a resolution that has gone "over under the rule" is laid before the Senate as the last item in the morning business sequence set out in Rule VII and before the conclusion of the Morning Hour.[17] As each such resolution is disposed of, the next one is put before the chamber. If a resolution remains pending at the end of the Morning Hour, it goes directly to the calendar of general orders, as would a resolution that had been pending for any length of time but was displaced by a motion to proceed to another measure.[18] Any resolution not reached under this procedure remains among the "Resolutions and Motions Over Under the Rule" until the next legislative day.[19]

Morning business is usually created by unanimous consent rather than by operation of Rule VII. In that case, resolutions do not come over under the rule. They remain static, awaiting a morning business period that occurs by operation of the rules rather than by consent.[20]

Given the inherently cumbersome nature of this process, it is extremely rare for resolutions to be brought before the Senate in this manner. As a practical matter, for a resolution to be considered on the floor, it would have to be reported from committee, or consent would have to have been granted for its immediate consideration.

During the daily wrap-up that precedes adjournment, it is customary to secure consent that when the Senate reconvenes on the next legislative day, the Morning Hour is deemed expired. Under the terms of that order, no resolution can come over under the rule.

RESOLUTIONS AND THEIR PREAMBLES

Sometimes preambles accompany simple, concurrent, or joint resolutions, setting out "whereas" clauses in order to justify the resolution to which they relate. The resolution is addressed first, and the preamble is considered only after the resolution has been passed.[21] Amendments to the resolution cannot include amendments to the preamble.

Once the preamble is pending, it may be debated and amended. It may also be tabled without prejudice to the resolution that has already been adopted.[22]

Failure of the resolution means failure of the preamble. By contrast, passage of the resolution does not carry with it the preamble, which requires a separate vote. On noncontroversial resolutions that have a preamble, it is customary to secure consent that the resolution be agreed to and that the preamble be agreed to as well. The following example, drawn from the *Record* of July 29, 2003, illustrates the procedure followed on such resolutions:

> Mr. McCONNELL: Mr. President, I ask unanimous consent that the Senate proceed to the immediate consideration of calendar No. 233, S. Res. 184.
>
> The PRESIDING OFFICER: The clerk will report the resolution by title.
>
> The legislative clerk read as follows:
>
> A resolution (S. Res. 184) calling on the Government of the People's Republic of China immediately and unconditionally to release Dr. Yang Jianli, and for other purposes.
>
> There being no objection, the Senate proceeded to consider the resolution.
>
> Mr. McCONNELL: Mr. President, I ask unanimous consent that the amendments to the resolution be agreed to; that the resolution, as amended, be agreed to; further, that the amendment to the preamble be agreed to, and the preamble, as amended, be agreed to, the motion to reconsider be laid upon the table, and that any statements relating to this matter be printed in the *Record*.
>
> The PRESIDING OFFICER: Without objection, it is so ordered.[23]

HOLDS

Holds are notifications from senators to their respective party leaders that they have an interest in measures or matters that may be considered on the floor. In some instances, holds are initiated simply to ensure that the senator is consulted before something is scheduled. More extreme variations are possible. For instance, a senator can indicate that he will object to the consideration of a bill and will not waive his right to debate the motion to proceed.

A senator's power to impose and enforce a hold is grounded in his right to debate and his unilateral ability to object to unanimous consent requests. Particularly near the end of the session, when floor time is precious, holds can act as a silent filibuster and unilateral veto.

It is up to the majority leader whether to honor a hold. If the leader moves to proceed to the legislation anyway, the objecting senator may need to come to the floor to enforce his rights. It is rare that a senator would be forced to do so. Customarily, his party leadership would stand in on his behalf. Indeed, one of a floor leader's prime responsibilities is to protect the interests of his party members.

Except on "must-pass" bills, majority leaders are normally reluctant to challenge holds. Overcoming holds by invoking cloture to beat a filibuster is sufficiently cumbersome that a leader will move to alternative legislation or nominations, if available. Stanley Bach explains that

> the practice of placing holds on measures has developed informally as a way for Senators to interpose an objection in advance and without having to do so in person on the floor. In turn, the majority leader and the measure's prospective floor manager understand that a Senator who objects to allowing the bill or resolution to be called up by unanimous consent is threatening to filibuster a motion to proceed to its consideration. So, recent majority leaders have tended to honor holds both as a courtesy to their colleagues and in recognition that if they choose not to do so they may well confront filibusters that they prefer to avoid.[24]

Holds are private communications to the leadership. Although there have been proposals to publish holds in the *Congressional Record*, a policy of public disclosure has never been adopted.[25] From time to time, leaders have encouraged internal disclosure of holds as a means of working through them, but even these efforts have not significantly affected Senate practices.

BRINGING A MEASURE OR MATTER OFF THE CALENDAR

A measure or matter may be made the pending business by unanimous consent. Without consent, it is possible to move to proceed to the consideration of any measure on the calendar.[26]

Although any senator may make a motion to proceed, it is customary that only the majority leader or his designee offers the motion. For example, between 1979 and 2000, motions to proceed were made 231 times. On all but seven of these occasions, the motion to proceed was made by either the majority leader or his designee. Those seven times, the motion to proceed was rejected.[27]

Nevertheless, Senate custom does not give the majority leader an absolute veto over what may be brought to the floor. For instance, these pages contain detailed descriptions of extraordinary efforts over a number of Congresses to reform the cloture rule. The leadership of the time opposed each such initiative. To wait for the majority leader to move to proceed to the reformers' rules change resolutions would have doomed their efforts without a fight. Accordingly, the reformers, some of whom were from the majority party, had no choice but to use their rights to offer those motions themselves. Had they not done so, the reforms they attempted to push through would have been impossible from the start.

Thus, it is not correct to say that only the majority leader can offer the motion to proceed. However, when someone other than the leader does so, the motion usually fails.

A motion to proceed[28] to a nonprivileged calendar item is debatable, except when made in the Morning Hour following an adjournment.[29] A motion to proceed to a privileged matter is nondebatable. Conference reports, House messages, presidential messages, statutory fast-track measures,[30] and adjournment resolutions are among the privileged business and can thus be reached by nondebatable motion.[31]

If the motion to consider a nonprivileged measure is agreed to, whatever was previously pending is displaced,[32] whether that underlying measure was privileged or not.[33] The displaced business enjoys no preferential status as to any other measure. For example, if the Senate voted to proceed to H.R. 456 while S. 123 was pending and H.R. 456 were not privileged, S. 123 would go to the calendar. S. 123 would not come back before the Senate except by unanimous consent or on motion.

If the measure brought up is privileged and the underlying business is nonprivileged, then the consideration of the nonprivileged vehicle is merely suspended and not displaced.[34] The latter recurs on the floor automatically on disposition of the privileged measure. For instance, if S. 123 were pending and the Senate interrupted it to consider a conference report on H.R. 789, action on S. 123 would be temporarily suspended, and the Senate would resume considering it as soon as disposition of the conference report was concluded.

A motion to proceed may not be amended.[35] While one motion to proceed is pending, it is not in order to move to proceed to something else. Disposition must first be made of the original motion to proceed.[36]

The situation is different when a proposition is reached by unanimous consent. By precedent, the underlying business is suspended rather than displaced, unless the agreement otherwise specifies. During the consideration of the consent item, a senator may call for the "regular order." If so, the measure is automatically taken down, and the underlying business recurs.[37] Sometimes, consent agreements will make specific provision to preclude this possibility.

Chapter Six

The Amendment Process

A measure is open to amendment at any time after it has become the pending business and before third reading. The amendment process does not proceed title by title. Any unamended portion of the measure is open to amendment.[1]

A committee can propose amendments, as can individual senators on the floor. When a measure is brought up for consideration, committee amendments and any amendments offered to them take priority over floor amendments to other portions of the measure.[2] Sometimes, consent orders are entered to adopt the committee amendments en bloc and to consider them as original text for the purpose of further amendment.[3] These orders customarily provide that no points of order shall be deemed waived.

The orders serve to expedite proceedings on the floor and allow amendments to be drawn to any part of the text. But for the orders, committee amendments would otherwise be considered in the sequence in which they appear in the bill, and floor amendments other than those proposed to the committee amendments would have to await disposition of all committee amendments.

When the committee amendment is in the nature of a substitute for the introduced bill, the committee amendment, although offered first, is voted on last before third reading.

DRAFTING ISSUES: CONTIGUOUS LANGUAGE AND SCOPE OF AMENDMENTS

Amendments may not amend an underlying provision in more than one place and must be drafted contiguously to avoid that result.[4] For example, absent unanimous consent, a senator could not propose an amendment that said, "On page 2, line 5, strike all through page 2, line 10, and insert the following; and on page 5, line 8, strike all through page 5, line 12, and insert the following." A properly drafted amendment would read, "On page 2, line 5, strike all through page 5, line 12, and insert the following."

If a point of order is made against a noncontiguous amendment, the sponsor may demand its division before a ruling. He will then secure separate votes on each of the two parts.

Noncontiguous amendments automatically fall postcloture, and a demand for a division is not in order to rescue them. Such amendments could be considered only by consent.

A second-degree amendment may touch only that part of the underlying bill that is reached by the first-degree amendment. It may not be drafted to change language in any other part of the bill.[5]

On his own initiative and without waiting for a point of order, the presiding officer will rule out of order an amendment that is improperly drafted.[6]

AMENDMENTS TO ORIGINAL BILLS

Although committees customarily amend legislation that has been referred to them, they need not wait to receive a measure before acting. Committees are empowered to report original bills on any subject within their jurisdiction. The text is open to amendment in two degrees.

NOMENCLATURE OF THE AMENDMENT PROCESS

Substitute and Perfecting Amendments

A substitute amendment amends all the language of the underlying legislation that can possibly be reached, leaving no portion unamended. Thus, a substitute amendment for an entire bill would propose to strike all language after the enacting clause and replace it with new language. By contrast, a perfecting amendment goes to only a portion of the underlying legislation and leaves the remainder unamended.

These terms may be clarified by an example. Suppose that Senator A offers an amendment to a bill that strikes language appearing at page 2, line 5, through page 2, line 10, and inserts new language in its place. She leaves the remainder of the bill unamended. Because Senator A amends only a portion of the bill, hers is a perfecting amendment. Further suppose that Senator B offers an amendment to Senator A's amendment that strikes all Senator A's language and inserts new provisions. Because Senator B amended all the language open to him (the underlying amendment) and left no material unamended, his amendment is a substitute.

These issues relate to questions of form, not questions of substance. For instance, Senator A might have proposed to strike all language after the enacting clause and insert new material textually identical to the underlying bill except for the language appearing on page 2, lines 5 through 10. Had she proceeded in this way, her amendment would be a substitute, even though the substantive change in the underlying bill would have been no greater than that achieved by her perfecting amendment.

Types of Amendments

There are three types of amendments: 1) to insert, 2) to strike and insert, or 3) to strike. An amendment to insert seeks to add language to the text of the measure without removing any material. An amendment to strike and insert takes language out of the measure and in the same location inserts new language. An amendment to strike deletes language. A perfecting amendment can take any of these three forms. A substitute is always a strike-and-insert amendment.

Degrees of Amendments

The original text of a measure is amendable in two degrees. An amendment to the text is an amendment in the first degree. An amendment to the amendment is an amendment in the second degree. No third-degree amendment is in order,[7] and were one offered, the presiding officer would disallow it without need for a point of order.

The first complete substitute for a measure is automatically treated as original text for the purpose of further amendment. It is therefore amendable in two degrees. Customarily, the jurisdictional committee will have generated the substitute, although substitutes from floor managers or the leadership are not rare.

The substitute is almost always the language to which floor amendments are directed. In such instances, the text of the bill as introduced, which is also amendable in two degrees, is usually left alone.[8] When the substitute is adopted, the original bill language, inclusive of amendments to it that have been adopted, is stricken.

Printed and Unprinted Amendments

Amendments may be printed or unprinted, depending on whether the proponent sends them to the desk at least a day early for later consideration or simply waits to send up the amendment when he is ready to offer it. It makes no procedural difference whether an amendment is printed or unprinted, except under cloture, when amendments are required to have been filed under Rule XXII deadlines. If an amendment has been filed for printing, any senator, not just its sponsor, may call it up.

Recognition to Offer an Amendment

Under Rule XIX, the presiding officer is required to recognize the senator who may first address him. As previously noted, however, the rule is subject to precedents that have established priority recognition for the majority and minority leaders and then the majority and minority managers, in that order. Such "prioritized" senators may be recognized to offer amendments ahead of other senators seeking the floor at the same time. Moreover, if the Senate is operating under a consent order controlling time, a senator who would propose an amendment will have to be yielded time to do so unless the order specifically allocates time to him.

Recognition is but one factor in determining when a senator can offer an amendment. For example, suppose a senator wishes to amend section 302 of a bill but that section has already been amended in its entirety. A further amendment directed only at section 302 would not be in order. One cannot simply re-open language that has already been amended, and the presiding officer would rule such an amendment out of order without need for a point of order.[9]

Similarly, imagine that Senator A wanted to offer an amendment but that other members have pending amendments in the first and second degree. While the second-degree amendment was pending, no further amendments would be in order. If the second-degree amendment were defeated or tabled, the first-degree amendment would be open to further amendment by Senator A. If the second-degree amendment were perfecting in nature and were agreed to, then Senator A could amend any unamended portion of the first-degree amendment. If the second-degree amendment were a complete substitute for the first degree and were agreed to, then no further amendment to the first-degree amendment could be offered because the entirety of the text would have been previously amended.

AN AMENDMENT IS READ

Once an amendment is sent to the desk, the presiding officer will ask the clerk to report the amendment. As the clerk begins to read the amendment, the sponsor will seek consent that further reading be waived. If objection is heard, the reading must continue and cannot be interrupted for any purpose.[10] Consent is almost always granted to waive the reading of an amendment. The following procedure, involving an amendment proposed by Senator Jeff Bingaman (D-NM), is typical:

> Mr. BINGAMAN: Mr. President, I send an amendment to the desk and ask for its immediate consideration.
> The PRESIDING OFFICER: The clerk will report.
> The assistant legislative clerk read as follows:
> The Senator from New Mexico [Mr. BINGAMAN] proposes an amendment numbered 2035.
> Mr. BINGAMAN: Mr. President, I ask unanimous consent that reading of the amendment be dispensed with.
> The PRESIDING OFFICER: Without objection, it is so ordered.[11]

Immediately thereafter, the presiding officer recognized Senator Bingaman to speak on the amendment.

PRINCIPLES OF PRECEDENCE

Precedence concerns the sequence of offering and voting on amendments. The Principles of Precedence, as illustrated by the four amendment process charts that follow, are these:

Principle I: Second-degree amendments are voted on ahead of first-degree amendments.[12]

Principle II: A perfecting amendment to language proposed to be stricken is voted on ahead of an amendment to strike. Further, a perfecting amendment to language proposed to be stricken is voted on ahead of an amendment to strike and insert new text.[13]

PRINCIPLES OF PRECEDENCE:
A VARIATION OF CONVENIENCE

Until the mid-1990s, it was standard practice for the majority party to offer second-degree amendments to amendments proposed by minority party senators. This would allow the majority to avoid difficult votes. For instance, if the minority proposed a first-degree amendment providing for a new policy, the majority would counter with a second-degree substitute providing for a study. The first vote would come on the substitute. If the amendment were agreed to, the next vote would come on the first degree as amended, which would bring the study into the bill. The minority would never have been able to secure a clean vote on its policy amendment.

To counter this tactic, minority negotiators began to insist on consent orders that separated first- and second-degree amendments into two first-degree amendments. Continuing with the example given previously, the first vote would be on the study, but there would be a separate and unamended vote on the policy. This arrangement would allow majority senators partially to neutralize the policy amendment but not to avoid it completely.

Obviously, both amendments could pass, notwithstanding their potential contradictions. However, no point of order lies against inconsistent amendments. Resolution of the differences would be left to conference, where the majority party would hold a numerical advantage among Senate conferees. While it is unlikely that the minority position would be endorsed in conference, the minority would have accomplished its goal of crystallizing its legislative proposal and creating voting records for its own senators and those in opposition.

If the majority were unwilling to go along with this arrangement and insisted on either tabling or neutralizing minority amendments, the minority would threaten to delay passage of the bill by continuing to offer its amendments until afforded a clean vote. This leveraging sometimes has led to bifurcation periodically, although the traditional use of first- and second-degree amendments also continues.

THE AMENDMENT PROCESS CHARTS

The following charts excerpted from *Riddick's Senate Procedure* illustrate the amendment process. An explanation follows each chart. Chart I applies to an amendment to insert new text. Chart II is used when a senator proposes to strike a portion of the bill. Chart III applies when there is an effort to strike a portion of the bill but also to insert new text. Chart IV occurs when a complete substitute for the bill is proposed. The charts set forth the maximum number of amendments that could be offered in these situations as well as the sequence of voting. The Principles of Precedence can be used to explain and justify the position of amendments on the charts, but one cannot draw upon these principles to add further lines to the charts. The Senate has relied upon these charts for many years. Alongside charts I and III, reference is made to numbered Lott amendments. These references relate to a case study of filling amendment trees. The case study begins on page 100.

An Amendment to Insert: Chart I

Assume that Senator A offers an amendment to insert new material in the bill. Hers is a first-degree amendment and is open to amendment in one further degree. If Senator B offers a second-degree perfecting amendment, no further

AMENDMENT TO INSERT

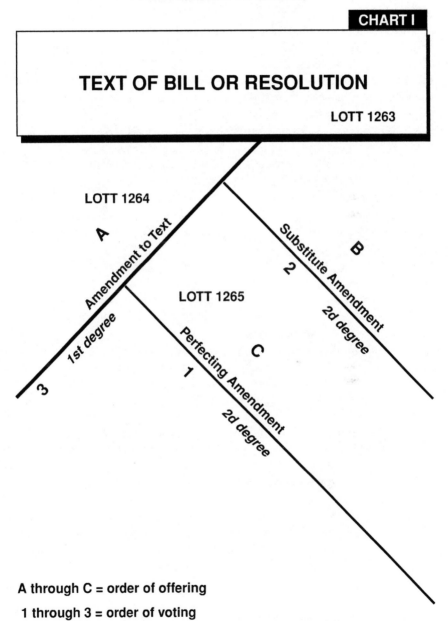

CHART I

TEXT OF BILL OR RESOLUTION

LOTT 1263

LOTT 1264

A

Amendment to Text

1st degree

3

B

Substitute Amendment

2d degree

2

LOTT 1265

C

Perfecting Amendment

2d degree

1

A through C = order of offering

1 through 3 = order of voting

amendment is in order until disposition of Senator B's amendment. After disposition, other senators could offer additional perfecting amendments to material Senator B did not amend. Because it is not in order to reopen previously amended language, these later perfecting amendments cannot be drawn solely to the language that Senator B amended. However, if they are drafted to cut more broadly into the underlying amendment and make a substantive change apart from reopening Senator B's provision, they can traverse the same ground that Senator B previously covered. The governing principle is called the "bigger-bite theory," in which successively larger bites may be taken at the underlying provision as long as there is remaining language to amend. Once a substitute amendment has been agreed to, no further amendments are in order because all the underlying language has been amended.

It is possible to offer a perfecting amendment that strikes all after the first word of the underlying amendment. On its face, such a strategy would appear to undermine the possibility of a bigger bite since it would be difficult to make a substantive change in the unamended language. Nevertheless, once this amendment has been agreed to, a substitute for the first-degree amendment, as amended, will be in order.

Now assume that Senator B offers a complete substitute for Senator A's amendment. As Senator B's amendment is in the second degree, it cannot be further amended. However, under Principle II, an amendment to the text that Senator B's substitute proposes to strike is in order and would be addressed before a vote occurs on the substitute itself.

Accordingly, Senator C offers a second-degree perfecting amendment to Senator A's first-degree amendment. The sequence of voting, as shown by the chart, is Senator C's second-degree perfecting amendment, then Senator B's second-degree substitute, and then Senator A's first-degree amendment, as and if amended. Note that while three amendments are pending, none is an amendment in the third degree. A third-degree amendment would amend Senator B's substitute, a result that is impossible under the rules. Instead, the three pending amendments are one first-degree amendment, proposed by Senator A, and two second-degree amendments, Senator B's substitute and Senator C's perfecting amendment.

Votes on second-degree perfecting amendments will always take priority over a vote on Senator B's substitute. If a series of such perfecting amendments succeeded in amending the entirety of Senator A's text, then Senator B's substitute would fall. There would be no language left for him to amend because all language would previously have been amended.

An Amendment to Strike: Chart II

In this situation, a senator has offered a first-degree amendment to strike a portion of the bill, say, Title III. The question before the Senate at that moment is

AMENDMENT TO STRIKE

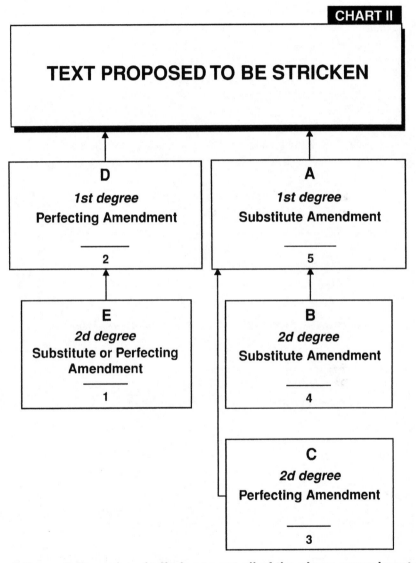

CHART II

TEXT PROPOSED TO BE STRICKEN

D	**A**
1st degree **Perfecting Amendment**	*1st degree* **Substitute Amendment**
2	5

E	**B**
2d degree **Substitute or Perfecting Amendment**	*2d degree* **Substitute Amendment**
1	4

C

2d degree **Perfecting Amendment**

3

A through E = order of offering to get all of the above amendments before the Senate

1 through 5 = order of voting

whether to retain Title III in its original form or to eliminate it. Under Principle II, which permits a senator to amend language proposed to be stricken, Senator A offers a first-degree substitute for Title III. Senator A's amendment is open to amendment in one further degree. Senator B follows with a second-degree substitute for Senator A's amendment.

Senator B's substitute may not be amended, but under Principle II, another senator may offer a second-degree perfecting amendment to Senator A's underlying first-degree amendment, the provisions Senator B has proposed to strike. Senator C offers that amendment.

When Senator A offered a substitute for the original Title III language, her amendment struck Title III but inserted a new title in its place. Using Principle II, the original Title III language that Senator A would strike is open to perfecting amendments in two degrees. These are depicted as Senator D's first-degree

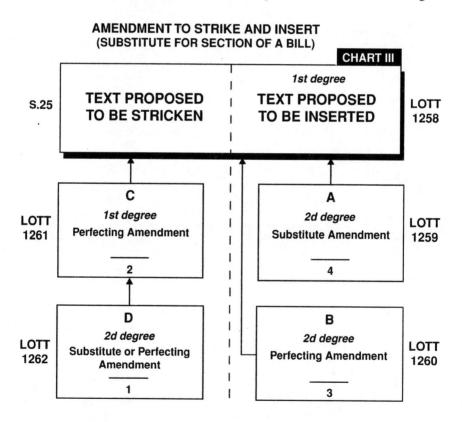

**AMENDMENT TO STRIKE AND INSERT
(SUBSTITUTE FOR SECTION OF A BILL)**

CHART III

	TEXT PROPOSED TO BE STRICKEN	*1st degree* TEXT PROPOSED TO BE INSERTED	
S.25			LOTT 1258

LOTT 1261	**C** *1st degree* Perfecting Amendment —— 2	**A** *2d degree* Substitute Amendment —— 4	LOTT 1259
LOTT 1262	**D** *2d degree* Substitute or Perfecting Amendment —— 1	**B** *2d degree* Perfecting Amendment —— 3	LOTT 1260

**A through D = order of offering to get all of the above amendments
before the Senate**

1 through 4 = order of voting

amendment and Senator E's amendment in the second degree. Note from chart II that it does not matter if Senator E offers a substitute or a perfecting amendment. Even if Senator E proposes a substitute, no senator can avail himself of Principle II to amend the language that Senator E wishes to strike.[14]

The sequence of voting will begin with Senator E's second-degree amendment, then follow with Senator D's first-degree amendment to the underlying Title III language. Next in sequence will come Senator C's second-degree amendment to perfect Senator A's first-degree amendment before the vote on Senator B's substitute for that amendment. Thereafter, there will be a vote on Senator B's second-degree substitute. Finally, a vote will occur on Senator A's amendment to substitute for the language of Title III proposed to be stricken.

A Perfecting Amendment to Strike and Insert: Chart III

Chart III depicts an amendment to strike a portion of a bill and insert other language in its place. Assume that a senator has proposed a first-degree strike-and-insert perfecting amendment to strike Title III and insert new language in its place. The question before the Senate is whether to retain the original Title III or to replace it.

Senator A offers a second-degree substitute for the language proposed to be inserted. Under Principle II, Senator B can go behind the substitute and perfect the text that Senator A wishes to strike.

Also relying on Principle II, Senator C proffers a perfecting amendment to the original Title III language that the original amendment proposed to strike. Senator D amends his provision in the second degree, whether by a substitute or by a perfecting amendment. As per the discussion of a similar circumstance on chart II and the explanatory footnote, it makes no difference whether the amendment is a substitute or a perfecting one.

Voting will begin with Senator D's second-degree amendment, followed by Senator C's first-degree amendment to the original Title III language proposed to be stricken.

Following that vote, the Senate will turn to Senator C's perfecting amendment to the language that Senator B wishes to strike. Senator B's substitute is next, followed by Senator A's perfecting amendment to strike the original Title III and replace it with new provisions.

A Complete Substitute: Chart IV

Chart IV applies when an amendment in the nature of a substitute has been proposed for the entire bill. The question facing the Senate is whether to retain the original text of the bill or to adopt a complete substitute to replace it.

AMENDMENT TO STRIKE AND INSERT
(SUBSTITUTE FOR BILL)

CHART IV

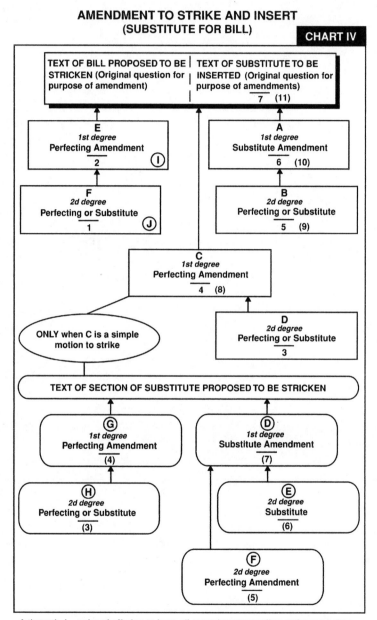

A through J = order of offering to have all amendments pending at the same time
1 through 11 = order of voting
Circled and parenthetical material apply only when C is a motion to strike

As shown in the chart, a maximum of eleven amendments can be pending at once in this situation. For purposes of chart IV, assume that a committee has reported the bill with an amendment in the nature of a substitute. The first substitute offered for an entire measure is always treated as original text for the purpose of further amendment, meaning that it can be amended in two degrees.

Senator A offers a first-degree substitute for the committee amendment. Senator B offers an amendment in the second degree. Whether his amendment is perfecting or a substitute is immaterial. Using Principle II, Senator C offers a first-degree perfecting amendment to the committee language that Senator A proposes to strike. Senator D can amend in the second degree with either a substitute or a perfecting amendment.

If Senator C's amendment to the committee's new language is a simple motion to strike a portion of that text, he triggers five additional amendments. The remaining boxes mirror chart II, which similarly involved a perfecting amendment to strike language (and insert nothing in its place), and the rationales behind the placement of each amendment are identical to the discussion of chart II.

The committee amendment struck the text of the bill as introduced. Senator E uses Principle II to offer a first-degree amendment to the original bill text. Senator F amends in the second degree with either a substitute or a perfecting amendment.

Assuming that Senator C has not offered an amendment to strike, the sequence of voting is Senator F's second-degree amendment and then Senator E's first-degree amendment to the bill text the committee proposes to strike. Following amendments to the bill language, a vote will occur on Senator D's second-degree amendment and then Senator C's first-degree perfecting amendment to the committee substitute. Thereafter, there will be a vote on Senator B's second-degree amendment to Senator A's substitute, then on Senator A's amendment, and finally on the committee substitute, as and if amended.

If Senator C did not offer an amendment to strike, seven amendments could be pending at once. If Senator C proposed a motion to strike, eleven amendments could be pending, and the amendments generated by his motion would be voted on after disposition of amendments to the original text and prior to amendments related to the committee substitute.

Concluding Observations

All the charts depict the maximum number of amendments that can be pending at the same time. In each of these circumstances, the reality of the floor situation is likely to be far simpler. For instance, when a committee reports a substitute, first- and second-degree perfecting amendments are the only amendments likely to be pending.

Nevertheless, there is a useful rationale for why senators would propose amendments to the original bill text, knowing that such language and any amendments added to it will be eliminated when the Senate votes for the committee substitute. The original text is language proposed to be stricken, and votes on amendments to it take priority over votes on amendments to the substitute. Putting senators on record by securing the first vote can have a substantive impact by influencing subsequent voting. These votes will establish a record that can be used to the political advantage or disadvantage of senators.

FILLING THE AMENDMENT TREE AND DUELING MOTIONS: A CASE STUDY IN POLITICAL AND LEGISLATIVE MANEUVERING

Pending before the Senate on October 7, 1997, was S. 25, campaign finance reform legislation sponsored by Senators John McCain (R-AZ) and Russ Feingold (D-WI). Senate Majority Leader Trent Lott (R-MS) opposed the bill.

Using his right of preferential recognition, Lott acted to fill the amendment tree and prevent advocates of the bill from gaining a strategic advantage. Thus, he began by offering an amendment to strike a portion of the bill and insert new text (amendment number 1258). His strike-and-insert perfecting amendment triggered application of chart III.

To fill the amendment tree set forth in chart III, Lott offered first- and second-degree amendments to the text he proposed to insert (amendment numbers 1259 and 1260). He also offered first- and second-degree amendments to the McCain-Feingold language he proposed to strike out (amendment numbers 1261 and 1262). Lott filled the amendment tree to prevent opponents from securing the first vote on an amendment of their choosing.

Because consideration of a motion to recommit takes priority over disposition of amendments, Lott also proffered a motion to recommit with instructions to report back with an amendment. He did so to stop opponents from using the motion to recommit to supersede the amendment tree he had just filled. The motion to recommit with instructions was designated as amendment number 1263. The amendment language accompanying the motion was treated as original text for the purpose of further amendments, so Lott offered first- and second-degree perfecting amendments to it (amendment numbers 1264 and 1265). On the motion to recommit, the applicable amendment tree was chart I.

The chart III amendment tree as to the bill and the chart I amendment tree as to the motion to recommit having been filled, Lott's opponents were foreclosed from offering any amendments at all.

With the amendment process thus frozen, a cloture motion ripened on amendment number 1258. Cloture was not invoked. A cloture vote followed on the underlying bill, S. 25. That motion also failed. Had cloture on the bill succeeded, Lott's amendment number 1258 would have fallen as nongermane, as would all the other amendments Lott had proposed.

After failure of these cloture motions, maneuvering continued. Lott moved that the Senate proceed to the consideration of S. 1156, the District of Columbia appropriations bill. The Senate previously had that measure under consideration, but action had been interrupted by execution of a unanimous consent order to consider S. 25.

Because McCain-Feingold had been brought before the Senate by unanimous consent, Lott could have returned to the underlying bill, S. 1156, by calling for the regular order. However, such a call would have merely suspended consideration of S. 25 so that the Senate could return to S. 1156. Lott did not want S. 25 suspended, which would allow it to recur before the Senate upon completion of S. 1156; rather, he wanted it displaced back to the calendar. To displace S. 25, he had to bring up a nonprivileged measure, by motion while S. 25 was pending. S. 1156 was a nonprivileged measure and so Lott moved to proceed to it.

Lott's motion to proceed to S. 1156 was debated but never came to a vote. Instead, that bill was brought back before the Senate automatically when a cloture vote ripened on an amendment by Senator Connie Mack (R-FL) that had been proposed when S. 1156 was originally pending. Cloture was invoked, and the amendment was agreed to. Because S. 1156 became pending through the ripening of a cloture motion on the Mack amendment, consideration of S. 25 was suspended, but the bill was not displaced.

While S. 1156 was before the Senate, a cloture motion ripened on S. 25. The motion had been filed when S. 25 was previously pending. Cloture was not invoked, so S. 1156 remained pending. Continuing to be faced with the need to displace S. 25, Lott successfully moved to consider S. 1173, a bill to reauthorize the Intermodal Surface Transportation Act. Both S. 25 and S. 1156 were displaced. Once S. 1173 was before the Senate, Lott filled the amendment tree, meaning that no amendments on campaign finance reform or any other subject could be offered.

MANAGER'S SUBSTITUTE AMENDMENTS

At the conclusion of the amendment process, a bill manager sometimes offers a wraparound substitute amendment. There are two principal reasons why he may do so. First, he may capture certain potential floor amendments in the package, obviating a need to debate and vote on such amendments. Second, his substitute can "clean up" legislative history that exists as a result of previous floor votes. Any language previously adopted that is swept clean by a manager's substitute will not be in the Senate's final work product and will not be subject to conference. If there is not a manager's substitute proffered before third reading, then all amendments the Senate has agreed to can be addressed by conferees, including ones that may be inconsistent with each other.

MODIFICATION AND WITHDRAWAL OF AMENDMENTS

Precedents governing modification or withdrawal of an amendment are similar and are used interchangeably here. When a senator sends an amendment to the desk, he continues to "own" that amendment in the sense that he can modify or withdraw it at will, even if a point of order is pending against the amendment but no ruling has been made.[15] To modify or withdraw an amendment, a senator must have the floor.[16] If an amendment has been withdrawn, it can be offered again in identical form at a later time.[17] If an amendment in the second degree is pending, the first-degree amendment can be withdrawn, carrying with it the second-degree amendment.[18] Committee amendments can be modified or withdrawn only at the direction of the committee or by unanimous consent.[19] After modifying or withdrawing the amendment, a senator retains his right to the floor.

Once "action" is taken on the amendment, that situation changes, and the sponsor can modify or withdraw his amendment only by unanimous consent. In this context, "action" means the ordering of the yeas and the nays on the amendment, entering into a unanimous consent agreement applicable to that specific amendment, a ruling on a point of order, invoking cloture,[20] or adopting an amendment to the language proposed to be modified or withdrawn. For instance, if the amendment is considered under a time agreement, it can no longer be modified or withdrawn.[21] A unanimous consent agreement to set aside a pending amendment so that other amendments can be considered does not constitute "action" for this purpose. Once a sponsor loses his right to modify his amendment, he gains the right to offer a second-degree amendment to his own language.

DIVISION OF THE QUESTION

If a question in a debate includes several points, any member may have the same divided.

—Senate Rule X, 1789

To the extent that a question contains two or more parts that could stand independently of one another, it is subject to a specified division on demand by any senator.[22] Neither a vote nor unanimous consent is required to effect such a division. The specified parts of the question are voted sequentially in the order in which they appear. An important exception to this rule is that strike-and-insert amendments are never divisible in any way.[23]

If the yeas and nays have been ordered on a question and then the question is divided, each part is separately amendable and subject to a roll call vote.[24] Votes occur separately in the sequence in which the divided parts stand, including votes on any amendments proposed to those parts, before a vote on the next divided part.[25]

A division cannot occur once a motion to table an amendment has been made.[26] Questions cannot be divided after cloture.[27] A division cannot be demanded after a roll call has commenced.[28] The question of final passage of a bill cannot be divided.[29]

It is not in order to call for a division of a bill or joint resolution, although there is precedent for division of a simple or concurrent resolution.[30]

DISPOSITION OF AN AMENDMENT

Unless brought down by a successful point of order, an amendment will either be adopted or rejected by an up-or-down vote or be killed by a successful tabling motion.

A motion to table is nondebatable and requires a majority vote. When offered, it immediately supersedes debate on the underlying debatable question. If successful, the tabling action kills the amendment (or motion or other debatable question). In addition, if first- and second-degree amendments are pending, a successful tabling motion offered against the first-degree amendment succeeds in killing both amendments at once.[31]

The motion to table can be offered at any time a senator can obtain the floor to make it, unless the measure is being considered under a time limitation, in which case the motion is in order when all time on the proposition has expired or been yielded back. The same rules apply to points of order.

If an amendment is subject to a time agreement, an up-or-down vote occurs when all time has been used or yielded back. If the agreement specifies a time certain to vote, the vote will happen when that hour arrives.

If there is no consent order, the vote will occur when no amendment to the language is pending and when no senator seeks recognition to speak. At that moment, assuming that the Senate is not in a quorum call, the presiding officer will automatically put the question on the amendment. It is not necessary to move that the amendment be adopted.[32]

REOFFERING A REJECTED AMENDMENT

If an amendment has been defeated or tabled, it cannot be proposed again in identical form. If reoffered, some substantive change will have to have been made. A change in dollar amount or effective date will be sufficient for this purpose.

A second-degree amendment that fell when a first-degree amendment was tabled can be reoffered without change. Even though the language it purported to amend was tabled, the tabling motion was not directed at the second-degree amendment, and that language is not prejudiced.

Further, if a motion to strike and insert is rejected, a simple motion to strike the same material is in order.[33]

NONGERMANE AMENDMENTS:
A DEVICE FOR BRINGING ISSUES TO THE FLOOR

Legislative measures are brought before the Senate either by motion or by unanimous consent. In addition, it is common for senators to raise issues via nongermane amendments. By this mechanism, the Senate has considered many legislative items otherwise trapped in committee or detained without action on the calendar.

The use of nongermane amendments is a potent tool for the minority to put subjects before the Senate that committees would not choose to report or the majority leader would not elect to schedule. Even though such amendments may be tabled or otherwise be deflected by votes on preemptive amendments, they are aired in public debate, and voting records are made when senators address them.

If the number of amendments that senators can offer is unrestricted, as frequently is the case, the minority may insist on a "clean" vote on its amendment, even if a vote is later to occur on a countervailing majority amendment.

In that case, the majority's amendment would not amend the minority's proposal but would stand parallel to it. If the majority does not agree to permit a "clean" vote on the minority's amendment, the minority can offer variations of its original proposal over again indefinitely. This leverage allows the minority to secure a "clean" vote for whatever policy or political implications it may engender.

While the majority leader determines what legislation will be scheduled, through normative command over the "motion to proceed," he cannot control what issues individual senators will raise on the floor through nongermane amendment. A leader may attempt to narrow these issues by insisting on a time agreement before he will bring a measure to the floor, but he is sometimes confronted with bills on which the Senate must act and where a time agreement is elusive.

In general, Senate rules do not require that amendments be germane. This contrasts sharply with the House, which does have an overall germaneness requirement and sometimes imposes even narrower restrictions when adopting procedural resolutions reported from the House Rules Committee. In an overall permissive atmosphere, Senate amendments need be germane in only four possible circumstances:

- When cloture is invoked, Rule XXII requires that amendments must be germane.[34] Invoking cloture is the only time that the Senate actually votes to impose a germaneness mandate. Under the following mentioned circumstances, a germaneness requirement arises by operation of the rules or by unanimous consent.
- On appropriations bills, Rule XVI provides that amendments be germane.[35]
- Many rule-making statutes require that amendments be germane in measures they generate,[36] although sometimes such statutes do not provide for amendments at all.[37]
- A requirement that amendments be germane or at least adhere to a somewhat looser standard of relevance is sometimes a feature of unanimous consent agreements.

One test of germaneness is whether an amendment would restrict or broaden the scope of underlying legislation. On the whole, restrictive amendments are germane. Amendments that broaden the reach of a measure may or may not be germane, depending on whether they venture into new subject matter. For example, suppose that a bill establishes a commission to address agricultural price supports and a senator proposes to exempt programs from the commission's purview. The amendment would restrict the reach of the bill and would likely be germane. If an amendment added a support program to a like list already addressed in the bill, it would likely be germane. Conversely, suppose a senator offered an amendment dealing with farm exports. Assuming such an amendment would add new subject matter not elsewhere addressed in the bill, it would likely be nongermane.

In general, amendments that expand a list of items within a like class are likely to be held germane; those that expand to add a different class rather than adding to a class already addressed in the measure are likely to be held nongermane.

As outlined in *Riddick's Senate Procedure*, additional tests of germaneness include whether the amendment, if offered as a freestanding bill, would be referred to the same committee that reported the underlying bill; whether the amendment adds duties to administrative entities; and, generally, whether the amendment is foreseeable given the legislation it purports to modify.

All amendments that would simply strike out language are inherently restrictive in nature and are germane per se, as are all Sense of the Senate amendments if proposed by the committee of jurisdiction[38] and amendments that change numbers and dates. An amendment that contains verbiage "notwithstanding any other provision of law" is very likely to be considered nongermane.

Committee amendments are considered per se germane under rule-making statutes and unanimous consent agreements, but under cloture and on appropriations bills, committee amendments are not automatically germane.[39]

Multiple cloture motions are sometimes necessary when a committee substitute has been proposed to a pending measure. The substitute would be likely to contain at least some nongermane provisions. If germaneness had been imposed by cloture or Rule XVI, the committee substitute would fail the germaneness test and would fall. To avoid this result, the cloture motion is first filed against the substitute. Once the substitute is agreed to, cloture time restraints and germaneness requirements expire. A filibuster and an open-ended amendment process could break out on the measure as amended. This could necessitate filing a second cloture motion. If this seems inefficient, it is also unavoidable. Filing only one cloture motion, against the underlying bill, could put the substitute in jeopardy.

As suggested earlier, it is common practice for senators, especially those in the minority, to use nongermane amendments in an effort to press legislation and set forth issues for political debate. Unless germaneness is required under one of the four circumstances set out previously, no rule prohibits such a strategy.

Germaneness is a tight standard, and the Senate sometimes operates under a looser requirement, that of "relevance." The relevance standard can be imposed only by unanimous consent. Under consent orders that merely require amendments to be relevant, the test will be whether such amendments relate to the subject of the measure to which they attach and do not contain any significant matter not addressed in that measure. Whether the standard is germaneness or relevance, there must be text to which the amendment relates. For instance, if an amendment were relevant to the underlying statute the bill is set to amend but had no bearing on bill text, the amendment would be ruled not relevant or nongermane.

The presiding officer customarily rules on questions of germaneness. On the other hand, if a germaneness point of order is raised on an amendment to an appropriations bill, the presiding officer does not rule at all. Rule XVI requires him to refer the point of order to the Senate for decision without debate.[40] The general Senate practice of submitting questions of germaneness is subject to two important exceptions established by precedent. One of these concerns the "defense of germaneness," and the other regards treatment of nonbinding language. Discussion of these exceptions follows.

The Defense of Germaneness

If a legislative amendment is proposed to an appropriations bill, and a point of order is raised against it, a defense can be raised that the amendment is germane to legislative language in the House bill. The defense is asserted before the presiding officer rules on the underlying point of order. The theory of this defense is that Rule XVI should not operate on the Senate like a straitjacket. If the House has legislated first, the Senate should be able to respond, with a germane modification of the House provisions.[41]

According to Rule XVI, raising the defense of germaneness will cause the question to be decided by the Senate without debate rather than by the chair. If the Senate holds the amendment germane, the point of order falls. If the Senate holds the amendment is not germane, the amendment falls automatically.

By the late 1970s, it had become common practice for senators to attempt to legislate on appropriations bills. The authorization process had become bogged down with filibusters and holds, while appropriations bills remained "must pass" vehicles. Therefore, senators would seek to amend those vehicles, believing them to be harder to filibuster. Points of order would be asserted against those amendments, and the defense of germaneness would be proffered. Once the presiding officer heard the word "germaneness," he would immediately refer the question for Senate decision per the language of Rule XVI.[42] The amendment's sponsor was thus spared from having to overturn the presiding officer, and Senate judgments about germaneness, without benefit of the presiding officer's and parliamentarian's input, were sometimes subject to more permissive standards than if there had been a ruling.

In 1979, Majority Leader Robert Byrd (D-WV) generated a precedent that somewhat altered this procedure. According to the precedent, if the defense of germaneness is asserted, the presiding officer makes a threshold inquiry as to whether there is any legislative provision in the House bill to which the amendment could possibly be germane. If no such language exists or the Senate language is so extensive that it exceeds the breadth of the germaneness "hook" in the House bill, the presiding officer will ignore the defense and proceed to rule on the underlying point of order.[43] The amendment's sponsor could then appeal the ruling but would be burdened with having to overturn the presiding officer. While this appeal—and, for that matter, appeals of rulings other than on Budget Act points of order—requires a simple majority of senators present, the Senate customarily respects and enforces rulings from its presiding officer.

When the appropriations measure before the Senate is a continuing resolution, there is precedent that on assertion of the defense of germaneness, the presiding officer will automatically refer the question to the Senate for determination without regard to the threshold test.[44]

Germaneness of Nonbinding Provisions to Appropriations Bills

Sense of the Senate or Sense of Congress amendments are subject to special germaneness procedures when offered to appropriations bills.

Troubled by many of these nonbinding provisions being proposed as amendments to appropriations bills, Majority Leader Trent Lott (R-MS) secured a precedent in 2000 that the presiding officer, subject to appeal, would decide germaneness points of order against such provisions.[45] Thus, such language is arguably open to a more strictly interpreted germaneness test than would be applied to binding provisions.

SUMMARY OF THE AMENDMENT PROCESS: A CHECKLIST

In thinking about the procedural situation surrounding an amendment, there are some important questions to consider. Not all questions will apply to every amendment. As the previous discussion will have touched on these issues in some detail, summary comments follow each of these questions:

- *Which amendment chart applies?* One cannot evaluate the possibilities for placing and voting on amendments without knowing the answer to this basic question. Key to the response is knowing which amendment underlies all others. For instance, if a committee reported an original bill and the first proposed amendment was an amendment to insert a new provision in the bill, then the applicable amendment chart would be chart I. If the first amendment were an amendment to strike, chart II would govern. If the first amendment were a perfecting amendment to strike a portion of the bill and insert new language, chart III would operate. If, instead of reporting an original bill, the committee generated a substitute, then that would be the underlying amendment, and chart IV would apply. Thus, a senator wishing to offer a floor amendment to insert would work with either chart I if the committee had reported an original bill or chart IV if the committee had reported a substitute.

- *Can another amendment be offered to take precedence?* Two important principles of precedence govern the sequence in which amendments will be considered. They are that voting on amendments in the second degree takes priority over voting on amendments in the first degree and that voting on an amendment to language proposed to be stricken takes priority over voting on the motion to strike or on a motion to strike and insert. Accordingly, if Senator A has offered a first-degree amendment, Senator B could offer a second-degree amendment, and a vote on his amendment would take priority. Similarly, if a committee has offered a substitute for original bill text, Senator A can offer a first-degree amendment to the language the committee proposes to strike. A vote on his amendment will take precedence over a vote on the substitute.

- *Is the amended language subject to a bigger-bite amendment?* It is not in order to amend previously amended text. An important exception to that rule is the bigger-bite theory, which permits previously amended text to be reopened if the sponsor reaches the underlying text more broadly than did the original amendment. If the new amendment takes a bigger bite than its predecessor and makes a substantive change outside the previously amended language, it can also reopen that language.

- *Can its own sponsor amend the amendment? Can the amendment be modified or withdrawn?* When a senator sends an amendment to the desk, he continues to "own" that amendment in the sense that he retains the right to modify or withdraw the amendment at will. Once "action" is taken on the amendment, the senator loses the ability to modify or withdraw it, except by unanimous consent. Accordingly, he secures the ability to amend his own amendment. "Action" occurs if the Senate orders the yeas and nays on the amendment, enters into a unanimous consent order specific to that amendment, or renders a decision on the amendment, such as ruling on a point of order. Amendments may not be modified or withdrawn after cloture is invoked, except by unanimous consent.

- *Is the amendment properly drafted?* An amendment must be drawn to the provision it purports to amend and not to other portions of the measure. The language of the amendment must be contiguous and not hit the underlying material in multiple places.
- *Is the amendment divisible?* An amendment to insert or an amendment to strike will be divisible on demand of any senator into any component parts that can stand separately from the others. Each part so divided is subject to further amendment, unless the divided amendment is an amendment in the second degree. If a roll call has been ordered before a division is demanded, each of the component parts will be subject to a roll call. A strike-and-insert amendment is never divisible.
- *Can a motion to recommit with instructions to report back forthwith (with or without an amendment) supersede the pending amendment?* Under Rule XXII, paragraph 1, a motion to commit takes priority over a motion to amend. Accordingly, if an amendment is pending and a senator moves to recommit the bill, the Senate will set aside consideration of the amendment and turn to the motion to commit. If the motion to commit carries, the measure is returned to committee, and all pending and agreed-on floor amendments are wiped clean.

  The motion to commit could contain instructions that the committee report a certain amendment. On the floor, the instructions are amendable in two degrees.

  The motion could be structured to have the committee report forthwith, which creates the fiction of a committee meeting, and could carry amendment instructions. The effect would be to eliminate pending and agreed-on amendments and replace them with a "reported" bill that contains provisions pursuant to the instructions.
- *Is the amendment subject to a time limitation?* If the amendment is subject to a time limitation, no point of order may be asserted against it, no second-degree amendment may be offered to it, and no tabling motion may be made until all time has been used or yielded back.
- *Is the amendment subject to unanimous consent or statutory germaneness requirements or other restrictions?* If a consent order or statute requires that the amendment be germane, committee amendments are considered germane per se. In the case of the Budget Act, the germaneness requirement as well as other points of order can be waived, most often with the requirement of sixty votes. Requirements imposed by consent orders or other statutes are not subject to a waiver procedure.
- *Has cloture been invoked? If so, is the amendment germane? Has it been timely filed? Is it dilatory?* After cloture, all amendments must be germane. Committee amendments must meet the same standards as floor amend-

ments and are not considered germane per se. To be considered postcloture, an amendment must also be timely filed. That means that first-degree amendments must be filed by 1:00 P.M. of the intervening session day that separates entering the cloture motion and the arrival of the cloture vote. Second-degree amendments must be filed by one hour before the cloture vote, which occurs two session days after the cloture motion was entered.

Rule XXII also bars dilatory motions or amendments. The presiding officer judges whether a motion or amendment is dilatory, subject to appeal.

- *If the amendment is drawn to an appropriations bill, is it germane? Is it legislation on an appropriations bill? If the amendment is a funding limitation, is it in the proper form?* Rule XVI requires that all amendments to appropriations bills be germane.[46] The rule further provides that there should be no general legislation on an appropriations bill, an effort to separate authorizations from appropriations.[47] Funding limitations are permissible to restrict the purposes for which appropriated dollars may be used, but they cannot be based on a contingency, nor can they limit the expenditure of money in any measure other than in the appropriations bill pending at that moment.[48]

Chapter Seven

Voting in the Senate

A simple majority vote is sufficient to carry most questions before the Senate. If there is a tie vote, the question fails. The vice president is empowered to break ties.

Exceptions to simple majority voting are found in constitutional requirements for passage by two-thirds of senators present in the following situations: impeachment,[1] expulsion of a member,[2] consent to the ratification of a treaty,[3] veto overrides,[4] and constitutional amendments.[5] It would very likely be unconstitutional to burden other final-passage votes with supermajority requirements beyond what the Constitution mandates.

Other supermajority requirements can be found in the text of the Standing Rules[6] and in rule-making statutes.[7] These relate to internal steps in the legislative process prior to final passage and has been considered an exercise of the Senate's power to make rules governing its own proceedings.[8]

Voting in the Senate occurs by either voice vote, division vote, or roll call. Except in rare circumstances when the rules require a roll call, such as in voting on a cloture motion,[9] a voice vote will suffice unless the yeas and nays are requested or a division is demanded. In the instance of a voice vote, the presiding officer will put the question before the Senate, saying, "All those in favor signify by saying, 'aye'; all those opposed signify by saying, 'no.'"

Any senator may call for a division vote, as may the presiding officer. A division vote can be demanded before the result of a voice vote is announced, but the division would no longer be in order once an announcement was made.[10]

During a division vote, senators stand, and the presiding officer counts the number of senators on either side of the proposition. He announces the overall outcome but not the number of votes on each side. As in the case of a voice vote, the presence of a quorum will be presumed. As the specific tally of the division is not announced, the presumption of a quorum is not therefore challenged.[11] The following illustrates the use of a division vote on a series of resolutions of ratification on treaties:

> Mr. SUNUNU: Mr. President, I ask for a division vote on the resolutions of ratification.
> The PRESIDING OFFICER: A division is requested. Senators in favor of the resolutions of ratification will rise and stand until counted. [After a pause.] Those opposed will rise and stand until counted.
> On a division, two-thirds of the Senators present and voting having voted in the affirmative, the resolutions of ratification are agreed to.[12]

Before the result of the division vote is announced, it is in order to request a roll call vote. If the outcome of a division vote is announced, it is too late to request a roll call.[13] As in the illustration just given, division votes are employed to determine the outcome of noncontroversial treaties. Apart from that circumstance, their use is rare.

In the event a senator wishes a roll call, he will ask for the yeas and nays. The presiding officer will inquire if there is a sufficient second. Under article I, section V, of the Constitution, a sufficient second represents one-fifth of all senators, a quorum being present.[14]

In general, the Senate operates on the principle of a presumptive quorum, that being fifty-one senators. One-fifth of that number would mean that the assent of eleven senators would constitute a sufficient second. If a live quorum or roll call has just preceded a request for the yeas and nays, a sufficient second would be one-fifth of the number just disclosed to be present.[15] Most of the time, no one insists on these requirements, and if senators on both sides of the aisle support the request for a roll call, a sufficient second will be declared. If a sufficient second is produced, the roll call will be ordered, with voting to begin at the conclusion of debate.

A roll call begins when the first senator answers to his name.[16] Prior to that moment, it would be in order for a senator to be recognized for further debate, to raise a point of order, to suggest the absence of a quorum, and for other purposes. Once the roll call has commenced, it may not be interrupted.

Traditionally, roll calls are set for fifteen minutes but frequently extend longer. At the beginning of a fifteen-minute vote, one bell will sound. Halfway through the fifteen minutes, five bells will sound. The fifteen minutes serve as a minimum rather than a maximum time because the vote does not conclude until the presiding officer has announced the result. When votes on which roll calls are stacked by consent, orders are sometimes entered to make the second and succeeding roll calls ten minutes in length.

A senator who misses a vote is precluded from adding his name to the tally once the vote is announced. The presiding officer may not entertain a unanimous consent for that purpose.[17] A senator may, however, enter a statement into the *Record*, explaining that he missed the vote and indicating how he would have voted. Such statements do not affect the result of the vote. A senator who voted may also seek consent to change his vote if that will not affect the outcome. For example, on June 10, 2003, Senator Richard Shelby (R-AL) made the following request:

> Mr. SHELBY: Mr. President, on Thursday, June 5, on roll call vote No. 209, I voted yea. It was my intention then to vote nay. Therefore, I ask unanimous consent that I be permitted to change my vote since it will not affect the outcome.[18]

Sometimes a senator will have an impact on the outcome by announcing a pair. A live pair occurs when a senator who is present announces that he would vote on one side of the question, while an absent colleague would vote opposite, and therefore he will withhold his vote.[19] Neither the senator who withholds the vote nor the absent senator is counted in the roll call, but pairing allows an absentee to affect a tally by reducing a vote from the opposite side.[20] Senators who give pairs are excused from the mandatory voting requirements of Rule XII.[21]

VOTING GROUND RULES

Rule XII governs voting procedure. It provides that all senators shall vote, unless excused by the Senate from doing so.[22] At the conclusion of a roll call, a senator may announce that he declines to vote. If he does, Rule XII requires that he state his reasons. Without debate, the presiding officer then puts to the Senate the question, "Shall the Senator for the reasons assigned by him, be excused from voting?"[23] These proceedings are conducted before the outcome of the roll call on the main question is announced.

A senator may decline to vote either in committee or on the floor, without seeking permission of the Senate, relative to any matter on which he believes he has a conflict of interest.[24]

The following case study presents an interesting exercise of Rule XII procedure.

CASE STUDY: A VOTE-WITHIN-A-VOTE

On May 13, 1987, the Senate reconvenes following an adjournment. Majority Leader Robert Byrd (D-WV) attempts during the Morning Hour to move via a nondebatable motion to a Department of Defense authorization bill.[25] In an effort to consume the two-hour-long Morning Hour and thus prevent Byrd from offering his motion, Senate Republicans commence a series of delaying tactics based on Rule XII.

Byrd had asked unanimous consent to approve the *Journal*. Republicans objected. Senator Byrd then moves under Rule IV that the *Journal* be approved.[26] Before the result of the roll call on Byrd's motion is announced, Senator John Warner (R-VA) states that he declines to vote because he has not read the *Journal*. Under Rule XII, the presiding officer initiates a vote to determine whether Senator Warner should be excused from voting. The yeas and nays are sought and granted, and a roll call begins.

Before announcement of the result relative to Senator Warner, Senator Dan Quayle (R-IN) declares that he declines to vote on the basis that a senator should not be compelled to vote. The presiding officer initiates a vote on whether Senator Quayle should be excused. The yeas and nays are again sought and granted, and another roll call begins.

During the vote on whether to excuse Senator Quayle, Senator Steve Symms (R-ID) states that he declines to vote, also on the basis that a senator should not be compelled to vote. The yeas and nays are sought, but before they are ordered, Senator Byrd intervenes with a point of order.

As of that moment, four votes were stacked: the vote on Senator Byrd's original motion to approve the *Journal*; within it, the vote on whether Senator Warner should be excused; within that vote, a vote on whether Senator Quayle should be excused; and within that vote, a vote on whether Senator Symms should be excused. If all these roll calls were insufficient to consume the Morning Hour, the tactic could be employed endlessly until that result was ensured.

Senator Byrd makes a point of order that during a roll call on a motion to approve the *Journal*, repeated requests by senators to be excused from voting are dilatory. After considerable parliamentary wrangling, Byrd prevails. In the course of these events, three unusual and narrow precedents were established that pertain solely to proceedings on a motion to approve the *Journal*:

- It is possible to make a point of order that repeated requests to be excused from voting are dilatory.[27]
- It is possible to make a point of order during a roll call.
- A senator does not have unlimited time to explain his reasons for not voting.

The parliamentary discord on the morning of May 13, 1987, in fact consumed the entire Morning Hour, meaning that Senator Byrd's effort to proceed to the Defense authorization bill was frustrated. Taking a longer view, had Byrd not prevailed in establishing these precedents, the Rule XII vote-within-a-vote could have been replicated to negate totally the right to make a nondebatable motion to proceed during the Morning Hour.

RECONSIDERATION OF THE VOTE

A motion to reconsider a vote may be entered on the day a vote is taken or on either of the following two session days.[28] Anyone who voted on the prevailing side of the question or who did not vote may offer the motion.[29] Very often, a senator will act immediately to force reconsideration of the vote. If the motion to reconsider is successful, the proposition is brought back before the Senate as if the original vote had not occurred.

The motion to reconsider is debatable, unless the underlying question is nondebatable, and requires a simple majority to carry.[30] Customarily, another senator will move to table it. A vote to table a motion to reconsider cannot itself be reconsidered.[31]

The motion to reconsider is used to put the original proposition to rest rather than leaving open the possibility that it might be revisited later. Only one motion to reconsider may be made relative to any vote.[32] However, if the motion to reconsider succeeds, the proposition to which it applies is brought to a second Senate vote. The outcome of that second vote may be reconsidered.

If other business has intervened before the motion to reconsider is made or if there is not a desire to reconsider the vote immediately, a senator may enter a motion to reconsider, which will be placed on the calendar.[33] The motion may be entered while another measure is pending.[34] Once entered, the motion may be reached by unanimous consent or through a motion to proceed to its consideration. Whether a motion to proceed to reconsideration is debatable depends on whether the underlying question was debatable.[35] In any case, the process to bring the underlying question back before the Senate involves two stages:

- A motion is made to proceed to the entered motion to reconsider.
- If the motion to proceed is agreed to, then the Senate addresses the motion to reconsider.

There is no time limit within which the Senate must address an entered motion to reconsider. However, entering the motion will prevent a measure from being messaged to the House until the Senate later acts on the motion.[36] If the measure has already been messaged, it is necessary to pass a resolution seeking a return of the papers to the Senate.[37]

Chapter Eight

Finalizing Legislation to Send to the President's Desk

When one house acts identically to the other on the same legislative vehicle, that measure is ready to be enrolled and sent to the president. If the second house amends the legislation, the measure is returned to the house of origin. If the house of origin concurs in the amendment, full agreement has been reached and the legislative process is concluded. Should the house of origin disagree to the proposed amendment, the stage of disagreement exists between the two houses. A second way to reach the stage of disagreement would be for the amending house to insist on its own amendment. Generally, the houses will agree to go to conference so that their differences can be compromised. The product of a conference is a conference report that concludes the legislation when adopted by both houses. Although this approach is a common method to end intrabranch differences, it is not the only way.

AMENDMENTS BETWEEN HOUSES

Another available mechanism to resolve differences is a procedure known as amendments between houses. In that case, the House and Senate avoid going to conference and, for a time, bounce amendments back and forth between each other. A hypothetical example will be instructive.

Assume that the Senate has passed a bill and sent it to the House. The House amends the Senate-passed measure with a complete substitute and sends it back to the Senate. The question before the Senate is how to address the House amendment.

The Senate could disagree to the House amendment and simply send the measure back to the House, or it could disagree and request a conference with the House to compromise the differences. Of greater priority would be a motion to concur in the House amendment. Should that motion carry, both houses would have acted identically on the same vehicle, and the legislative process is over.

Still higher priority would be given to a motion to concur in the House amendment with a further Senate amendment. If that motion prevailed, the measure would be returned to the House for further disposition. In even higher ascending order of priority would stand motions to refer the House-amended measure to a Senate committee, to postpone its consideration to a day certain, to postpone its consideration indefinitely, or to table it.[1] A motion of greater priority can be offered while a lesser motion is pending.

Each of these motions, other than the motion to table, is debatable and thus potentially subject to filibuster. If the motion is offered to concur with an amendment, the text of that amendment is open to floor amendments in two degrees.

The process of amendments between houses can be extremely useful to avoid the potentially cumbersome circumstance of arranging and/or convening a conference, particularly near the end of a session. For example, suppose that the Senate passes a bill that the House later amends. Rather than move to conference, the Senate and House committee chairmen negotiate informally. They conclude an agreement that the Senate chair brings to the floor in the form of a motion to concur in the House amendment with a further Senate amendment. After the measure has been returned to the House, the House chairman moves to concur in the Senate amendment.[2]

The movement back and forth of amendments between houses cannot continue indefinitely. When each house acts originally on a measure, such language is treated as though it were original text for the purpose of amendments between houses. In the hypothetical just given, the first House amendment to the original Senate language is treated like an amendment in the first degree. The further Senate amendment to the House amendment becomes an amendment in the second degree. No further amendments are possible.[3] If the House does not concur in the Senate amendment, either there would need to be a conference or the Senate would have to recede from its amendment.

House messages are frequently brought before the Senate by unanimous consent. They may be received except when the Senate is voting or ascertaining the presence of a quorum, while the *Journal* is being read, while a point of order is being decided, or while a motion to adjourn is pending.[4]

If objection is heard to the consideration of the House message, a motion to proceed can be offered. The motion is privileged, meaning no debate is in order. It also means that consideration of the House message will suspend but not displace business pending before the Senate.[5]

Once the House message is pending, it is fully debatable. Any amendments proposed via the motion to concur with an amendment need not be germane.

These factors create a potential disincentive to resolve disagreements via amendments between houses because they expose the House message to the prospect of a filibuster and the possibility of an open-ended, uncontrolled amendment process, unless cloture can be invoked on a motion to concur in the House amendment.

Notwithstanding these potential difficulties, the use of amendments between houses can also be highly efficient. Consider this illustration drawn from the closing days of the 98th Congress. On the floor for daily wrap-up were Majority Leader Howard Baker Jr. (R-TN) and Minority Leader Robert Byrd (D-WV). They engaged in a procedure to end bicameral disagreement on a land exchange bill and ready it for enrollment and transmittal to the president:

> Mr. BAKER: Mr. President, I ask if the minority leader is agreeable that the Senate turn to the consideration of Calendar Order 984, H.R. 2475, the Mono County, California bill?
>
> Mr. BYRD: We have no objection.
>
> Mr. BAKER: Mr. President, I ask that the Chair lay before the Senate the following message from the House of Representatives: "*Resolved*, That the House agree to the amendment of the Senate numbered 1 to the bill (H.R. 2475) entitled 'An Act to modify a withdrawal of certain lands in Mono County, California, to facilitate an exchange for certain other lands in Mono County, California, and for other purposes.' *Resolved*, That the House disagree to the amendments of the Senate numbered 2 through 7, inclusive, to the aforesaid bill."
>
> Mr. BAKER: Mr. President, I move that the Senate recede en bloc from the amendments 2 through 7.
>
> Mr. BYRD: I have no objection.
>
> The PRESIDING OFFICER: Without objection, the motion is agreed to.

CONFERENCES AND CONFERENCE REPORTS

A more common way to resolve differences between houses is through the conference process. Even if one body requests a conference, the other body may ignore it and proceed through other means. Nevertheless, the conference mechanism is customarily used to address complex legislation.

A motion to request a conference or to agree to a conference requested by the other house usually follows immediately on final passage of a bill. The process involves joining together three motions, as follows.

In the case where the House has amended a Senate text, a senator would say, "Mr. President, I move that the Senate disagree to the amendment of the House, request a conference with the House on the disagreeing votes of the two houses, and that the chair be authorized to appoint conferees."

In the case where the Senate has amended a House text, a senator would say, "Mr. President, I move that the Senate insist on its amendment, request a conference with the House on the disagreeing votes of the two houses, and that the chair be authorized to appoint conferees."

By moving to disagree to the House amendment or by moving to insist on the Senate amendment, the Senate has arrived at the stage of disagreement. Once that stage has been reached, it is possible to seek a conference to resolve intrabranch differences.

Proceeding to conference usually, but not inevitably, follows the stage of disagreement. For instance, one house may disagree to the amendment of the other house and either not seek a conference or not agree to a conference that has been requested.

After the stage of disagreement, the ascending priority of available motions would be to go to conference, to adhere (either to the Senate's own amendment or to its disagreement to the House amendment), to insist on the Senate amendment, to recede (from its own amendment or to recede and concur in the House amendment, with or without an amendment), to refer, to postpone to a day certain, to postpone indefinitely, or to table.[6]

The three-part motion to arrange a conference needs unanimous consent because it actually is a joining of three separate motions, each of which is debatable and can be filibustered.[7] If there is no controversy, the presiding officer will announce that without objection the three-part motion is agreed to and will appoint conferees.

Authority to appoint conferees, however, vests in the Senate and not in the presiding officer.[8] A senator could offer a motion naming conferees. The motion would be subject to debate and amendment. In addition, it would be extremely rare. As to how it works, consider the following illustration from the *Record* of April 5, 1950:

> Mr. McCARRAN: Mr. President, I move that the Senate insist on its amendments, request a conference with the House of Representatives thereon, and that the Chair appoint the following conferees on the part of the Senate.
>
> The VICE PRESIDENT: The Chair has the right to appoint conferees.[9] He desires to have that right in his own name. . . . The Chair has no information as to the conferees that the Senator from Nevada proposes. . . .
>
> Mr. McCARRAN: Then, Mr. President, I move that the following conferees be appointed on behalf of the Senate and I send the list of names to the desk.
>
> The VICE PRESIDENT: The motion is that the Senate insist on its amendment, request a conference with the House thereon, and that the Chair appoint the Senators whose names are sent to the desk by the Senator from Nevada as conferees on the part of the Senate.[10]

Later, McCarran withdrew the motion and moved instead that the chair be authorized to appoint conferees.

Absent a motion like McCarran's, the chair appoints the senators whose names are sent to the desk by the leadership or the jurisdictional committee. In most cases, the conferees will come from the committee, although this is not required, and members of other committees may be appointed for specialized purposes. Once appointed, conferees serve until they reach agreement or render a report of disagreement or until they are discharged by Senate resolution.[11]

The capacity to filibuster motions creating a conference provides powerful potential leverage for the minority and can mean that conferences are impossible to convene. A story prepared by Helen Dewar in the October 19, 2003, edition of the *Washington Post* illustrates this point. Minority Leader Tom Daschle (D-SD) had argued that minority senators were being excluded from substantive conference negotiations on major bills. To involve themselves in those discussions, the minority might need to assert procedural rights to slow down the formation of unrelated conferences, Daschle said. The article began, "Senate Democrats, complaining that Republicans are trying to squeeze them out of final negotiations on energy, Medicare and other bills, are threatening hardball tactics aimed at forcing the majority party to expand Democrats' role in House-Senate conferences." The story continued,

> In a blunt warning last week to Senate Majority Leader Bill Frist (R-TN), Senate Minority Leader Thomas A. Daschle (D-SD) said Democrats may invoke rules under which they can block formation of future conference committees unless Republicans assure Democrats of broader participation in the negotiations. . . . Daschle did not say what legislation his party might target, saying decisions would be made on a case-by-case basis. Democrats could block—or at least seriously delay—formation of a conference committee by staging filibusters that would take 60 votes to overcome in the 100-member chamber. That would be a high hurdle for the 51-member GOP majority and a potential threat to any legislation caught up in the last days of a congressional session.[12]

Among the tactics a minority could use to frustrate the formation of a conference would include filibustering each of the three motions necessary to convene the conference. The minority could also propose amendments to the list of conferees[13] and offer multiple and endless motions to instruct conferees. A discussion of motions to instruct follows in this chapter.

To avoid these filibusters, the majority may use a strategy of amendments between houses. Although this approach reduces the number of filibuster possibilities, it is not filibuster free. As previously noted, the House message that comes before the Senate is privileged, so there is no debate on the motion to proceed, but it is subject to debate and amendment once it is pending.

Even if the votes are available to invoke cloture to shut down any of these filibusters, the cloture process is slow and difficult. Where multiple filibusters are possible, such as those Daschle suggested, and time is short, the threat of filibuster is still potent leverage even when cloture can be achieved. The political costs of conducting such filibusters, weighed against the benefits in leverage or outcomes, will always be a critical factor in determining whether threats are converted into action.[14]

Even if particular senators are appointed as general conferees and other senators are appointed as conferees to consider particular provisions, the signatures of a majority of all Senate conferees are required before a conference report can be brought back to the Senate. Accordingly, no matter what limitations appear to be put on the authority of one conferee in contrast to another, all conferees stand on equal footing when signing the conference report.

Senate conferees will usually be fewer in number than House conferees, but the disparity is of no consequence. Conferees for each house vote as a unit on behalf of that house, so both the Senate and the House have one vote each in conference.

A motion to instruct conferees may be made after the request for a conference is agreed to but before the conferees are actually named.[15] The motion is debatable, and the text of proposed instructions may be amended in two degrees.[16]

An example of an instruction can be seen relative to a conference on the Americans with Disabilities Act. Senator Jesse Helms (R-NC) proposed to instruct conferees on whether restaurant employers should be able to reassign food handlers who had been found to be HIV positive. A provision on this subject had been included in the House version of the bill, but the Senate had been silent. Helms's motion read,

> The Senator from North Carolina, Mr. Helms, moves that the conferees on the part of the Senate be instructed to include in their report the language contained in the amendment by the Congressman from Texas, Mr. Chapman, which reads as follows: (d) Food Handling Jobs.—It shall not be a violation of this Act for an employer to refuse to assign or continue to assign any employee with an infectious or communicable disease of public health significance to a job involving food handling, provided that the employer shall make reasonable accommodation that would offer an alternative employment opportunity for which the employee is qualified and offer which the employee would sustain no economic damage.[17]

Senator Helms's motion was considered under a consent order providing for ninety minutes of debate, equally divided, and no possibility of amendment. Absent the order, the instruction would have been fully debatable and amendable.

Instructions to Senate conferences are not binding. This means that no point of order will lie against the conference report if it does not reflect the instructions that were given.[18]

Conferees are authorized to consider the subject matter committed to them by either house. If differences between the House and the Senate arise from a series of perfecting amendments, then the conferees are limited to negotiating a narrower range of issues than if one house had substituted its version for that of the other. Any material from one house that was not amended by the other is not subject to conference. Where one house amends with a complete substitute, then everything in both versions is in conference.

In search of a compromise, Senate conferees have substantial latitude. They may include in the conference report provisions that have commonsense textual relevance to material committed to conference by either house. Their great latitude also extends to money issues. For instance, if the Senate authorizes a program at $500 million and the House authorizes it at $300 million, conferees can compromise at any amount of funding and not just between the two authorized levels.

The conferees' flexibility is not unlimited, however. If only a study has been committed to conference, the conferees may perfect or drop the study, but they may not use the study as the foundation for substantive statutory language. Conferees have a license to compromise what exists, not a license to create something out of whole cloth. In general, the question is whether there is a reasonable correlation between the original provisions in either the House or the Senate version and the compromise the conferees produce. Is the conference outcome foreseeable in light of those original provisions and faithful to the reach of those provisions?

If conferees exceed their authority, a Rule XXVIII point of order may be raised once the conference report is pending.[19] If the Senate is the first body to act on the conference report, a successful point of order will result in the report being recommitted to conference.

If the House acts first, its conferees are automatically discharged on agreement to the conference report. When the Senate considers the conference report thereafter, a successful point of order will kill the report.[20] The legislative situation will then stand as if no motion to convene a conference had ever been adopted, meaning that resolution of differences can occur via amendments between houses or through convening a new conference.

In theory, the authority of House conferees is narrower than that of their Senate counterparts. If the conference result exceeds the authority of House conferees, however, a remedy is available. The conferees may seek a rule from the House Rules Committee waiving points of order against the conference report. The rule is adopted before the report is considered on the floor, and, pursuant to the rule, the conference work product is inoculated from points of order.

Conferees may recommend that one house recede from its own amendment or recede from its disagreement to the amendment of the other house. Either step would produce bicameral agreement on the same legislative text. If conferees have agreed on a compromise, the conferees would recommend that one house recede from its disagreement and concur in the amendment of the other house with a further amendment, that being the language of the compromise. Consider this illustration from the 108th Congress relative to a conference report on H.R. 1474, legislation addressing check-clearing practices. Prior to conference, the Senate had amended the bill and requested a conference. The House had disagreed to the Senate amendment and had agreed to the conference. The House agreed to the conference report, which was then taken up in the Senate and which said,

> The Committee of Conference on the disagreeing votes of the two Houses on the amendment of the Senate to the bill (H.R. 1474) . . . having met, have agreed that the House recede from its disagreement to the amendment of the Senate, and agree to the same with an amendment, signed by a majority of the conferees on the part of both Houses.[21]

A conference report is privileged, so a motion to proceed to its consideration is nondebatable. The one-day rule[22] and the two-day rule[23] need not be satisfied prior to the consideration of conference reports. A conference report may be presented at any time other than when the *Journal* is being read, while a point of order is pending, or while the Senate is conducting a quorum call or is voting.[24]

Prior to 2000, any senator could demand that the conference report be read, a well-used filibuster tactic on lengthy conference reports brought to the Senate near the end of a session. Under a Standing Order adopted on December 15 of that year, if the conference report is available in printed form on senators' desks, the reading is waived and can occur only by unanimous consent. Printing the report as part of the *Congressional Record*, as the House customarily does, would satisfy this requirement. If the printed report is unavailable, then any senator can demand that the report be read. The demand is timely after the report has been laid before the Senate and before a motion has been made to proceed to its consideration.

A Joint Explanatory Statement of Managers must accompany conference reports. Rule XXVIII provides that the statement "shall be sufficiently detailed and explicit to inform the Senate as to the effect which the amendments or propositions contained in such report will have upon the measure to which those amendments or propositions relate."[25] The statement will summarize the outcome of conference negotiations and may contain important policy pronouncements or recommendations, such as appropriations earmarks. Unlike Senate committee reports, Statements of Managers cannot contain additional or minority views. Such views would have to be expressed outside the statement, perhaps in floor debate on the conference report.

The house that agrees to the conference almost always acts on conference reports first. This is done as a matter of convention rather than rule. Conference reports are debatable but cannot be amended. A motion to recommit can be made in the Senate if the Senate is the first to act on the conference report. If the House has already acted, its conferees are deemed discharged, so the motion to recommit is not in order.[26] Conference reports may also be referred to committee and are subject to motions to postpone and to table.[27] These motions are seldom made. Generally, the vote is up or down on the conference report, although conference reports have been filibustered.

If a filibuster occurs and if cloture cannot be achieved, then the dilemma is how to eliminate controversial provisions and permit a bicameral accord to go forward. Amendments to the conference report of course are not possible, but there are other options.

If floor consideration of a conference report is stalled, a possible strategy would be to recommit it and reopen the negotiations, but this is in order only if the House has not acted first. If a motion to recommit is not possible, the conference report can be tabled to dispose of it. Once the conference report is no longer pending, motions would be in order to convene a new conference, or disagreements might be resolved through amendments between houses.[28] Yet another option would be to adopt the conference report and then adopt a concurrent resolution to correct the enrollment of the bill to eliminate the provision that had caused the filibuster.[29]

AMENDMENTS BETWEEN HOUSES VERSUS CONFERENCE REPORTS: AN OBSERVATION

Jurisdictional committees exercise great power in developing conference reports. Conferees are largely, if not exclusively, appointed from the jurisdictional committee. Their conference work product is not amendable, which means that they have an exceedingly strong voice in creating the final legislative product. In addition, they have drafted the Explanatory Statement of Managers, a critical element in the legislative history of an enactment.

If the conference process is avoided, the jurisdictional committee's power is potentially reduced. Although the committee may have influenced the content of the House message, the floor process is difficult to control, and the measure is open to amendment. This situation is far less dominated by the jurisdictional committee than a "take it or leave it" vote on a conference report.

AMENDMENTS IN DISAGREEMENT: A HYBRID PROCESS

Assume that a series of perfecting amendments has been subject to conference and that agreement is reached on only some of the outstanding differences. If so, conferees issue a report encompassing their areas of accord and report certain amendments in disagreement. Before the amendments in disagreement can be reached, the conference report must be adopted. Thereafter, the amendments in disagreement are taken up one at a time. As each is reached in sequence, it is open to further amendment. Resolution of the amendments in disagreement is accomplished by procedures applicable to the disposition of amendments between houses and could include motions to convene a second conference.

For instance, suppose that the Senate has amended a House bill in twelve places and that the conferees reach agreement on all the amendments except the one to section 302, on which the House insists on its disagreement. Following adoption of the conference report, the Senate amendment to section 302 is put before the body. In this instance, the Senate's two options are to recede from its amendment to the House text, which will end the matter, or insist on its amendment and perhaps request a further conference with the House. If there is a further conference, the conferees will be limited to the differences between the Senate and House version of the unresolved amendment.

Sometimes, conferees report amendments in technical disagreement. Stanley Bach explains,

> Conferees also report individual amendments in disagreement, rather than as part of the conference report, when they wish to resolve the differences over those amendments with proposals that exceed the scope of their authority. In this case, they report the amendments in technical disagreement to protect the conference report itself against a point of order. Acting in turn, the House and Senate first vote to approve the partial conference report and then act on each amendment in technical disagreement and the conferees' recommendation for disposing of it.[30]

Where the conference has been considering a complete substitute, only one amendment is before it. In such a case, the conferees may come to a complete agreement and issue a conference report. In the alternative, they can agree to disagree. In that case, they issue a conference report of disagreement. Once that conference report is agreed to, resolution of House and Senate differences can proceed via amendments between houses.

ENGROSSMENT AND ENROLLMENT

When either house initially passes a bill or resolution, that measure is engrossed and is sent to the other house under the signature of the secretary of the Senate (or the clerk of the House, as the case may be). Before engrossment, changes are sometimes made by unanimous consent to legislation that has already passed. For instance, on September 10, 2003, the Senate passed H.R. 2660, the fiscal year 2004 Labor–Health and Human Services appropriations bill. Thereafter, the bill was amended by unanimous consent in this way:

> Mr. FRIST: I ask unanimous consent that notwithstanding the passage of H.R. 2660, the Labor-HHS appropriations bill, it be in order to consider the amendment I now send to the desk, that the amendment be considered and agreed to, and the motion to reconsider be laid upon the table without intervening action or debate.
>
> The PRESIDING OFFICER: Without objection, it is so ordered.[31]

Once a bill or joint resolution passes both houses in identical form, it is enrolled. For the Senate, the vice president or the president pro tempore signs the measure, and if the legislation is of Senate origin, the secretary of the Senate will certify it.[32] It is also possible for the Senate to designate another senator to sign it. The Speaker signs for the House, and if the measure is of House origin, the clerk of the House will certify it.

On rare occasions, corrections are necessary in enrolled bills. If so, both houses must adopt a concurrent resolution to make the requisite changes. Such a resolution is privileged for immediate consideration only if the changes are purely technical in nature.[33] Otherwise, the motion to proceed to its consideration is debatable. Any amendments to such concurrent resolutions must be germane. An example of a resolution to correct an enrollment follows:

> Mr. BINGAMAN (for himself and Mr. MURKOWSKI) submitted the following concurrent resolution, which was considered and agreed to:
>
> S. Con. Res. 159
>
> *Resolved by the Senate (the House of Representatives concurring),* That in the enrollment of the bill (S. 1843) to extend certain hydroelectric licenses in the State of Alaska, the Secretary of the Senate is hereby authorized and directed, in the enrollment of the said bill, to make the following corrections, namely:
>
> In subsection (c), delete "three consecutive two-year time periods." and insert "one two-year time period."[34]

A concurrent resolution may also be used to request one house to return a measure to the other house for further action. It can also be used to request that the president return a measure to the house of origin.

PRESIDENTIAL SIGNATURE AND VETO PROCEDURE

Once both chambers have acted identically on the same legislative vehicle, the measure is enrolled and sent to the president. Pursuant to article 1, section 7, clause 2, of the Constitution, the president has ten days in which to sign the bill if he so desires. The ten-day period begins to run at midnight following the president's receipt of the legislation and excludes Sundays.

The Constitution further provides that if Congress is in session and the president does not affix his signature, the measure becomes law.[35]

If Congress has adjourned sine die before the president's ten-day window expires, it can frustrate his ability to consider the legislation fully before returning it. Congress can control when it sends the president legislation and when it adjourns. Therefore, the Constitution provides that if Congress has adjourned and if the president fails to sign the measure, the legislation does not become law. This is known as the pocket veto. By its adjournment, Congress has effectively nullified its own right to override.[36]

There is no doubt that the pocket veto can be exercised after the second session of Congress has adjourned sine die. Substantial controversy exists as to whether legislation has been pocket vetoed if it is unsigned during an intersession adjournment, or an adjournment within a session. To negate the possibility of pocket veto, the Senate will make arrangements via a Standing Order to receive presidential messages during periods of recess or adjournment. Such an order was entered at the convening of the 107th Congress on January 3, 2001:

> ORDERED, That for the duration of the 107th Congress, when the Senate is in recess or adjournment, the Secretary of the Senate is authorized to receive messages from the President of the United States . . .[37]

The concept behind this order is that the president should not be able to claim pocket veto rights by arguing that Congress prevented return of his message. As the Congressional Research Service has reported,

> The Supreme Court in 1938 held that the pocket veto is not available to the President during adjournments of three days or less during a session, if the House in which the measure originated has appointed an agent to receive veto messages. Further *dicta* in more recent lower court rulings suggest that today a pocket veto

would be unconstitutional during any adjournment of either or both Houses within a session (such as the now customary August recess) if Congress appoints an agent to receive veto messages.[38]

In certain cases arising after an agent, such as the secretary of the Senate, has been appointed, presidents have claimed to exercise the pocket veto but have taken the precaution to return a veto message to Congress. Congress has ignored the pocket veto claim and acted on such veto messages.[39] If the president decides not to sign the measure, is unwilling to have it become law absent his signature, and cannot pocket veto it, he returns it to Congress with a veto message.

The veto message is returned to the house of Congress where the measure originated. If that house fails to override the veto, the other house will never address it.

Article 1, section 7, commands that the Senate act on the veto message when received. The veto message is read and is affixed to the Senate *Journal*.[40] Thereafter, the Senate may address the veto message. The message is privileged, meaning that there can be no debate on a motion to proceed to its consideration and that action on the veto message will suspend consideration of other business. This includes measures pending by unanimous consent, unless the consent order specifies that consideration of such measure shall not be interrupted.

The Senate can meet its constitutional obligation for reconsideration in a variety of ways, including immediate disposition but also by referring the veto message to committee, moving to postpone, moving to table, or deferring action by unanimous consent. What matters is that the Senate takes some action on the veto message when received. If they choose to attempt a veto override, the House and Senate may act at any time before the end of the second session of the Congress to which the measure was returned.

An illustration of how the Senate addresses disposition of a veto message can be found in a unanimous consent request propounded on April 26, 2000, by Senator John Kyl (R-AZ). President Clinton had vetoed S. 1287, a nuclear waste bill:

> Mr. KYL: Mr. President, on behalf of the majority leader, I ask consent that when the Senate receives the veto message to accompany the nuclear waste bill, it be considered as read by the clerk and spread in full upon the *Journal* and then temporarily laid aside, with no call for the regular order returning the veto message as the pending business in order.
>
> I further ask consent that at 9:30 A.M. on Tuesday, May 2, the Senate proceed to the veto message and there be 90 minutes under the control of Senator MURKOWSKI and 90 minutes under the control of Senators REID and BRYAN.

I further ask consent that the Senate stand in recess for the weekly party conferences between the hours of 12:30 and 2:15 P.M. on Tuesday, May 2, 2000.

I further ask consent that at 2:15 P.M. on Tuesday, there be an additional 30 minutes under the control of Senators REID and BRYAN and 30 minutes under the control of Senator MURKOWSKI and at 3:15 P.M. the Senate proceed to vote on the question "Shall the bill pass, the objections of the President to the contrary notwithstanding?" all without any intervening action.

The PRESIDING OFFICER: Is there objection? Without objection, it is so ordered. The Chair notes for the record the receipt by the Senate of the President's veto message on S. 1287, which, under the previous order, shall be considered as read and spread in full upon the Journal and shall be laid aside until 9:30 A.M. on Tuesday, May 2, 2000.[41]

On May 2, 2003, pursuant to the consent order, the Senate considered the veto message and, by a vote of 64–35, failed to override President Clinton's veto. Because the Senate was the house of origin for the bill, it acted first on the veto message, and the House of Representatives never got to act at all.

Absent such a consent order, a simple majority can adopt the nondebatable motion to proceed to the consideration of a veto message. Once pending, the message can be debated without limitation, subject to cloture.

An affirmative vote of two-thirds of senators present and voting is required to override a veto.[42] The Constitution mandates that the vote be by roll call.[43] A motion to reconsider the vote by which a veto was not overridden is in order and can be agreed to by a simple majority vote.

Since 1789, there have been slightly fewer than 1,500 veto messages to Congress. Of that total, little more than 7 percent of all messaged vetoes have been overridden.[44]

Chapter Nine

The Appropriations and Budget Processes

Article I, section 9, of the Constitution provides, "No money shall be drawn from the Treasury, but in Consequence of Appropriations made by Law." In addition, article I, section 7, states, "All Bills for raising Revenue shall originate in the House of Representatives; but the Senate may propose or concur with Amendments as on other Bills." On its face, this Revenue clause appears to refer to tax measures, but the House has interpreted it to cover appropriations bills as well.[1] Therefore, the House will not consider an appropriations bill that originates in the Senate.[2]

Rule XVI governs general appropriations bills. A general appropriations bill is any appropriations measure except one that makes appropriations for a single purpose only. The latter is known as a special appropriations bill and is rarely seen. Rule XVI does not apply to special appropriations bills, and they are considered under ordinary Senate procedures.[3]

Rule XVI, paragraph 1, states that no amendment to an appropriations bill is in order that would increase an appropriation already in the bill or add a new item of appropriations unless the following occurs:

- The amendment carries out an existing law, treaty stipulation, or an act or resolution previously passed by the Senate during that current session,[4] or
- It is moved by the Appropriations Committee or the jurisdictional authorizing committee, or
- It is proposed pursuant to a presidential budget estimate required by law

Appropriations are not limited to the level established by authorizations. Authorized programs need not be funded at all.[5] They can be funded within or in excess of an authorization or in the complete absence of an authorization.

Paragraph 3 states that if an amendment is proposed by the jurisdictional authorizing committee to increase an appropriation already in the bill or to add a new item of appropriations, such amendment shall be printed and referred to the Appropriations Committee for at least one day. The purpose of this provision is to allow the Appropriations Committee an opportunity to review the amendment, but the committee cannot prevent the amendment from thereafter being offered on the floor. If the authorizing committee actually proposes such a floor amendment, a point of order will lie against any second-degree amendment that would increase the appropriation.

Paragraph 2 provides that the Appropriations Committee shall not report amendments proposing legislation on an appropriations bill or any funding limitation that would take effect or cease to be effective based on a contingency. Paragraph 6 requires that in judging any point of order against a funding restriction, the Senate construe the rule strictly and, in case of doubt, in favor of the point of order.

A point of order may be raised against the bill as a whole for a violation of paragraph 2. If that point of order is sustained, the bill will be recommitted to the Appropriations Committee.[6] In the alternative, a point of order can be directed at the committee amendment rather than at the bill. If such a point of order is sustained, the committee amendment will fall, but the bill will remain pending.[7]

Paragraph 4 stipulates that no floor amendments are in order that propose legislation on an appropriations bill[8] or propose funding limitations that would take effect or cease to be effective based on a contingency. Here again, paragraph 6 mandates strict construction of any point of order against a funding limitation.

Funding limitations are located within the "General Provisions" section of an appropriations bill. For example, section 304 of S. 1689, an emergency supplemental appropriations bill for Iraq and Afghanistan, contained the following provision:

> Sec. 304. None of the funds available to the Department of Defense may be obligated to implement any action which alters the command responsibility or permanent assignment of forces until 90 days after such plan has been provided to the congressional defense committees.

The theory of funding limitations is that if Congress can decide the objectives for which it wishes to appropriate money, it can also restrict the purposes for which the money should be spent. Rule XVI mandates that the limitation cannot be contingent. This means that the limitation may not impose new duties on federal officials or require the officials to make discretionary judgments or determinations.

A further control on this device is that a funding limitation cannot reach beyond the pending appropriations bill in restricting the use of funds. A funding limitation is in order if it applies only to the specific measure to which it is proposed and does not attempt to go outside that bill to affect other laws.[9] Thus, if a restriction were to say "no funds appropriated by this Act or any other Act," it would be construed as legislation on an appropriations bill and be subject to a point of order under either paragraph 2 or paragraph 4 of Rule XVI.

If a proposed limitation is free of these infirmities, it will not be considered legislative in character but rather a procedurally proper restriction on the use of appropriated funds. An example of a funding limitation that would be subject to a point of order is this amendment, which was filed to the Iraq-Afghanistan supplemental:

> Sec. 2313. (a) Limitation on the Amount of Future Funds Available for Iraq Reconstruction Programs—Notwithstanding any other provision of this Act or any other provision of law, the amount of appropriated funds that may be obligated or expended for Iraq reconstruction programs may not exceed the current appropriated amount for Iraq reconstruction programs unless—
>
> 1) the President certifies to Congress that the amount of appropriated funds to be so obligated and expended for Iraq reconstruction programs is equal to or exceeded by an amount of contributions from the international community for Iraq reconstruction programs. . . .[10]

The proposed amendment is defective on two grounds: it reaches beyond dollars appropriated in the supplemental to cover all appropriated funds ("any other provision by law"), and it makes the funding limitation contingent on a presidential certification. For both reasons, it would be subject to a point of order as legislation on an appropriations bill.

Paragraph 4 also provides that all amendments must be germane, whether originating in the Appropriations Committee or from the floor. Rule XVI mandates that points of order on questions of germaneness be decided by the Senate without debate rather than by the presiding officer.[11] The judgment of the Senate on the question of germaneness is dispositive of the point of order, but the parliamentarian does not accord it precedential value.

The general Senate practice of submitting questions of germaneness is subject to two important exceptions established by precedent. One of these concerns the "defense of germaneness," and the other regards treatment of nonbinding language. Discussion of these exceptions follows in this chapter and was also touched upon in material on germaneness found in chapter 6.

PROCEEDING THROUGH AN APPROPRIATIONS BILL

Over many years, the Senate Appropriations Committee followed the practice of offering a series of perfecting amendments to House-passed appropriations bills. Any portion of the House bill not amended in the Senate, by adoption of committee or floor amendments, would not later be subject to conference. When the committee proposed perfecting amendments, it would customarily seek their adoption en bloc. This meant that committee amendments would not have to be addressed one at a time and that floor amendments could be proposed to any portion of the appropriations bill in two degrees whenever the measure was pending. It was also customary not to waive points of order against the committee amendments.

Sometimes a senator would have exempted from the order an amendment on which he wanted separate consideration. The amendment would stand as an amendment in the first degree, would be open to amendment in one further degree, and would be considered in the sequence in which it amended the underlying bill. Floor amendments to unamended portions of the bill would follow disposition of the committee-reported provisions.

In recent years, the Senate has sometimes worked on "S numbered" original appropriations bills reported from the Senate Appropriations Committee, then married such vehicles to the House companion bills after third reading. This process allows the Senate to act initially without awaiting measures from the House, although last steps cannot be taken until the House vehicle is available. Resort to this procedure also obviates the need to seek en bloc agreement to Senate committee amendments because only one amendment (the substitute) has been proposed. Senate reliance on the use of "S numbered bills" has significantly expanded since 1998.

During Senate floor consideration of "S numbered" appropriations bills, no point of order will lie against legislative language proposed by the Senate Appropriations Committee. Rule XVI bars legislative amendments,[12] but during the stage of initial floor consideration on an "S numbered" vehicle, the Senate is addressing not committee amendments but an original bill. Only later, when the Senate takes up the House bill and the text of the Senate measure is proposed as a substitute, would Senate committee–reported language take the form of an amendment and be open to a point of order. Following this strategy greatly strengthens the hand of the Senate Appropriations Committee since a point of order at the final stages to bring down the entire bill is unlikely to be made.

Points of order against floor amendments that propose legislation will lie at any time. If legislative amendments are proposed to a House bill, and a point of order is raised, a defense of germaneness can be offered, arguing that the amendment is germane to House text and therefore in order. If the Senate holds the amendment to be germane, the point of order falls. The defense of germaneness is not available during consideration of an "S" bill because there is not yet any pending House language to which the amendment could be germane.

The following example illustrates this point. During consideration of S. 1689, the fiscal year 2004 Iraq-Afghanistan supplemental, Senator Dick Durbin (D-IL) proposed an amendment to provide funds for the prevention, treatment, and control of and research on HIV/AIDS. The bill manager, Senator Ted Stevens (R-AK), raised a point of order that the Durbin amendment was legislation on an appropriations bill. Durbin made a parliamentary inquiry, which preceded a ruling from the presiding officer:

> Mr. DURBIN: Could the Chair inform me as to the defense of germaneness and whether it applies in this situation where we are not dealing with a bill already passed by the House and a question as to whether our amendment is germane to that House-passed bill?
>
> The PRESIDING OFFICER: The defense of germaneness does not apply when the Senate is considering a Senate bill.
>
> Mr. DURBIN: Is the Chair prepared to rule on the germaneness question raised by the Senator from Alaska?
>
> The PRESIDING OFFICER: The Chair's understanding is that the Senator from Alaska has challenged the amendment on the grounds that it is legislation on appropriations . . .
>
> Mr. DURBIN: Is that debatable?
>
> The PRESIDING OFFICER: No, the ruling is not debatable. The point of order is sustained. The Chair rules the amendment constitutes legislating on an appropriations bill. The amendment falls.[13]

As with any marriage of Senate and House measures, the Senate substitute for a House vehicle is subject to amendment, creating the opportunity to slow the process and to reopen issues thought to be resolved when the "S" numbered original bill was first before the Senate.[14] These problems may be avoided by securing consent for the automatic substitution of the Senate text for that of the House and the arrangement of a conference. Sometimes consent is forthcoming, but sometimes it is not, and the minority may find leverage and other benefits in not easing legislative movement.

APPROPRIATIONS: ADDITIONAL CONSIDERATIONS

The Appropriations Committee has thirteen subcommittees, each with a companion subcommittee in the House. Each subcommittee reports a separate appropriations bill that, in theory, must be taken through the floor and conference and be signed by the president before the new fiscal year begins on October 1. This ambitious schedule is seldom achieved, meaning that both houses will pass one or more continuing resolutions to keep the government functioning while unfinished appropriations bills are processed. As each of the remaining freestanding bills is completed, it supersedes provisions in the continuing resolution. Sometimes, it is considered neither possible nor desirable to complete all thirteen bills, in which case Congress will fold unfinished measures into an omnibus bill that passes before sine die adjournment.

Appropriations Committee report language and Statements of Managers to accompany appropriations conference reports often contain "soft earmarks," which are directive provisions to agencies on how appropriated funds shall be spent. These report provisions are technically advisory, inasmuch as only statutory language is binding, but agencies generally pay close attention to them. In a sense, earmarks have something in common with funding limitations, is that both restrict agency discretion in spending appropriated funds. Less frequently, earmarks will appear in bill provisions.

Report language is an important part of the legislative history of a bill, particularly at the conference stage. Report language cannot be amended on the floor, nor is it subject to a point of order. Therefore, an opponent of a report provision, such as an earmark, is burdened with generating offsetting legislative history. Reforms have been proposed in the Senate to increase the difficulty of generating earmarks, but these measures have not been enacted.

THE APPROPRIATIONS PROCESS AND THE BUDGET ACT

The 1974 Congressional Budget and Impoundment Control Act, as amended, has a significant impact on the appropriations process. No appropriations bill can be considered on the floor before a concurrent budget resolution for that fiscal year has been adopted.[15]

In the budget resolution, the Appropriations Committee is granted an overall spending allocation.[16] A Budget Act point of order under section 311(a)(2) prevents this total allocation from being exceeded. In addition, the act provides that the committee shall subdivide its allocation among its thirteen subcommittees[17] and shall report such subcommittee allocations to the full Senate as soon as practicable. The Appropriations Committee can revise these subcommittee allocations throughout the year, repositioning money to ease passage of the individual bills, so long as the overall allocation is not exceeded.[18]

Pursuant to section 302(c), no appropriations bill can be considered until the subcommittee allocations have been made. A point of order under section 302(f) prevents consideration of any appropriations bill that exceeds its subcommittee allocation.

A practical effect of this fiscal discipline is that most floor amendments to appropriations bills will require a Budget Act waiver because the amendments will cause the spending allocations to be exceeded. As noted by James Saturno of the Congressional Research Service:

Because the Appropriations Committees typically report measures that spend at the level of the subcommittee allocation, any amendment that would increase spending would be likely to cause that sub-allocation to be breached, and thus subject to a point of order. This rule, in combination with other rules of procedure, frequently makes it difficult to rearrange spending priorities within an appropriations bill through amendments on the floor.[19]

The appropriations bill manager can be expected to raise a 302(f) point of order and the amendment's sponsor is likely to seek a waiver, which requires sixty votes. If the waiver is agreed to, the point of order falls. If the waiver is not agreed to, the amendment falls.

For example, during consideration of S. 1689, the Iraq-Afghanistan supplemental appropriations bill, Senator Jon Corzine (D-NJ) proposed an amendment to shift funds from Iraq reconstruction into military retirement accounts. This would have caused spending for accounts under the jurisdiction of the Defense appropriations subcommittee to exceed that subcommittee's 302(b) allocation.

Senator Ted Stevens (R-AK), who was managing the bill, made a point of order, as follows:

I am constrained to point out that the pending amendment 1811 offered by the Senator from New Jersey, Mr. Corzine, increases spending by $2.3 billion in fiscal year 2004. This additional spending would cause the underlying bill to exceed the Defense subcommittee's section 302(b) allocation. Therefore, I raise a point of order against the amendment pursuant to section 302(f) of the Budget Act.

Senator Corzine then moved under section 904 of the act to waive the applicable point of order. The vote was forty-seven in favor of the waiver and forty-nine against, well short of the sixty votes required to waive, so the amendment fell.

It is important to note that the 302(f) point of order lay because the Defense appropriations bill had been signed into public law, and the spending it contained relative to the subcommittee's 302(b) allocation was therefore measurable. If the bill had not been signed, then the spending for fiscal year 2004 would not have yet been fixed. Accordingly, it would not have been possible to claim that the Corzine amendment would breach the subcommittee's allocation, and no point of order could have been asserted.

A budget resolution may set forth other fiscal controls on appropriations. For example, the fiscal year 2004 budget resolution conference report contained several important constraints. For instance, section 504 stipulated discretionary budget authority and outlay spending[20] limits for fiscal years 2003, 2004, and 2005, with further specified limits on highway and mass transit spending. The conference report established a sixty-vote point of order to enforce these limits.

In addition, section 501 of the conference report restricted advance appropriations to no more than $23.158 billion in each of fiscal year 2004 and 2005. Advance appropriations are dollars that become available one or more fiscal years after the fiscal year covered by that appropriations bill.

Section 502 of the conference report set out restrictions on emergency spending as well as tax changes designed as an emergency. These restrictions were proven necessary because of the readiness of earlier Congresses to categorize certain spending as emergencies in order to obviate spending controls discussed. For example, the conference report set out criteria to be met before an expenditure or tax adjustment can be declared an emergency. Those criteria were the following:

A) IN GENERAL—The criteria to be considered in determining whether a proposed expenditure or tax change is an emergency requirement are that the expenditure or tax change is—
   (i) necessary, essential, or vital (not merely useful or beneficial);
   (ii) sudden, quickly coming into being, and not building up over time;
   (iii) an urgent, pressing, and compelling need requiring immediate action;
   (iv) subject to subparagraph (B), unforeseen, unpredictable, and unanticipated; and
   (v) not permanent, temporary in nature.
B) UNFORESEEN—An emergency that is part of an aggregate level of anticipated emergencies, particularly when normally estimated in advance, is not unforeseen.

If a point of order is raised against an emergency designation, the emergency designation is automatically stripped, but a waiver motion may be offered to retain it. If the motion is agreed to by at least sixty votes, the emergency designation may be maintained.[21] Otherwise, the item is deprived of its emergency designation, making it subject to points of order for exceeding overall spending limitations (or subcommittee allocations) or revenue floors. Under the fiscal year 2004 budget resolution, discretionary defense appropriations were exempt from this procedure on emergency designations. Pursuant to section 314 of the act, the Budget Committee chairman is obligated to revise budget authority and outlays to reflect emergency spending.

THE BUDGET ACT

In 1973, a constitutional confrontation was brewing between the legislative and executive branches over presidential impoundment of appropriated funds. President Richard Nixon took the position that appropriated amounts represented a spending ceiling. While the ceiling could not be exceeded, Nixon asserted, the president has the discretion to withhold spending appropriated dollars. Not surprisingly, Congress took the opposite view, claiming that appropriated funds had to be spent. The issue was resolved through passage of the Congressional Budget and Impoundment Control Act of 1974.

The Budget Act established a mechanism to address impoundments and funding rescissions as part of a broad overhaul of congressional fiscal procedures. Within that overhaul, Congress created the Congressional Budget Office, established the budget process, and changed the starting date for the federal fiscal year from July 1 to October 1. The Act set timetables for the consideration of the budget resolution and spending legislation. The current timetable, revised from the original, is located at section 300 of the Budget Act:

On or Before	Action to Be Completed
First Monday in February	President submits his budget
February 15	Congressional Budget Office submits report to Budget Committees
February 25	Committees submit views and estimates to Budget Committees
April 1	Senate Budget Committee reports concurrent resolution on the budget
April 15	Congress completes action on concurrent resolution on the budget
May 15	Annual appropriations bills may be considered in the House
June 10	House Appropriations Committee reports last annual appropriation bill
June 15	Congress completes action on reconciliation legislation
June 30	House completes action on annual appropriation bills
October 1	Fiscal year begins

It is common for Congress to miss the deadlines for adopting a budget resolution. For instance, only twice since 1974 has Congress adopted a budget resolution before the April 15 deadline.

The Act set out various points of order to enforce orderly budget procedures and fiscal discipline.[22] It afforded Congress an opportunity to rectify an imbalance with the Executive over fiscal matters that had existed at least since enactment of the Budget and Accounting Act of 1921.[23] Beyond question, the Act was one of the most important laws related to congressional powers and operations enacted in the twentieth century.

Central to the Act was its provision for two privileged budget resolutions, the first of which was to pass in May and be advisory; to be followed by a

binding resolution passed in September. By the early 1980s, the budget workload had become so overwhelming and timetable deadlines missed so frequently that Congress started passing only the first resolution and deeming it
to count for both. Later, the act was amended to require only one budget resolution, although revised resolutions thereafter are permitted.

Budget Resolutions: Development and Floor Considerations

At the heart of the budget process is the budget resolution, which is Congress' fiscal blueprint. It is a concurrent resolution rather than a joint resolution. As such, it makes no changes in law and is not signed by the president.

Development of the budget resolution begins on submission of the president's budget and, theoretically, is completed through conference by the April
15 statutory deadline.[24] The Budget Committee in each house drafts the budget
resolution after reviewing the president's recommendations and receiving the
views and estimates of other committees, as well as data and testimony through
budget hearings.[25] The resolution sets forth aggregate totals of new budget authority and outlays. Budget authority is the legal authority for agencies to enter
into obligations, and outlays are the actual disbursement of funds. Spending is
broken down into twenty functional areas. These functions are as follows:

Function 050—National Defense
Function 100—International Affairs
Function 250—General Science, Space, and Technology
Function 270—Energy
Function 300—Natural Resources and the Environment
Function 350—Agriculture
Function 370—Commerce and Housing Credit
Function 400—Transportation
Function 450—Community and Regional Development
Function 500—Education, Training, and Social Services
Function 550—Health
Function 570—Medicare
Function 600—Income Security
Function 650—Social Security
Function 700—Veterans Benefits and Services
Function 750—Administration of Justice
Function 800—General Government
Function 900—Net Interest
Function 920—Allowances
Function 950—Undistributed Offsetting Receipts

These budget functions are a useful way to prioritize spending, but they do not correspond to committee jurisdictions. To distribute spending among committees, a reallocation of these functional divisions is made pursuant to section 302(a) of the budget resolution. This process is known as cross-walking and is normally set forth in the explanatory statement of managers that accompanies the budget resolution conference report.[26]

The budget resolution establishes the appropriate total levels of federal revenues, budget authority and outlays, budgetary surplus or deficit, and the overall level of public debt. It also sets forth the revenues and outlays of the Social Security program.[27] The resolution may contain budget discipline enforcement mechanisms, such as the appropriations restraints mentioned previously and an extension of PAYGO rules.[28] Authority for these procedures is found in an important and widely used elastic clause located at section 301(b)(4) of the act. This section provides that the budget resolution may "set forth such other matters, and require such other procedures, relating to the budget, as may be appropriate to carry out the purposes of this Act."

The budget resolution also uses reserve funds, provisions that grant the chairs of the Senate and House Budget Committees authority to revise committee spending allocations and other budget levels if certain conditions are met. By using reserve funds, Congress can ensure that money available under 302(a) allocations is used for specified purposes. Without the constraint of a reserve fund, dollars made available to a committee under a section 302(a) cross-walk could be used for any purpose within that committee's jurisdiction. By creating a reserve fund, the budget resolution ensures that a committee can only access those dollars to meet mandated objectives.

The conference report to accompany H. Con. Res. 95, the concurrent resolution on the budget for fiscal year 2004, contained six reserve funds. An illustration follows:

SEC. 401. RESERVE FUND FOR MEDICARE MODERNIZATION AND PRESCRIPTION DRUGS.

(b) IN THE SENATE—If the Committee on Finance of the Senate reports a bill or joint resolution, or an amendment is offered thereto or a conference report thereon is submitted, that strengthens and enhances the Medicare Program under title XVIII of the Social Security Act (42 U.S.C. 1395 et seq.) and improves the access of beneficiaries under that program to prescription drugs or promotes geographic equity payments, the chairman of the Committee on the Budget may revise appropriate budgetary aggregates and committee allocations of new budget authority and outlays provided by that measure for that purpose, but not to exceed $7,000,000,000 for fiscal year 2004 and $400,000,000,000 for the period of fiscal years 2004 through 2013.

Most years, the budget resolution contains reconciliation instructions.[29] These are directives to committees to make changes in law within their jurisdiction to achieve certain fiscal objectives. The object is to harmonize revenue and entitlement laws to the fiscal policies set forth in the budget resolution. Without such adjustments, taxation and spending patterns would continue according to existing law, and the budget resolution would be a toothless document.

Budget reconciliation instructions may effect changes in spending, meaning budget authority, entitlement authority, and credit authority. A reconciliation bill may also effect adjustments to revenues. Finally, the reconciliation process may be used to adjust the level of public debt. All three of these categories (or some combination of them) may be included in one reconciliation bill. The Parliamentarian has construed that one budget resolution can trigger a maximum of one reconciliation bill per category. Accordingly, to have multiple reconciliation bills in a given year, Congress must adopt an equivalent number of budget resolutions.

On the fiscal year 2004 budget resolution, a House committee was instructed to produce a higher level of revenue reductions than the level given to a Senate committee, the first time such a disparity occurred. The Senate parliamentarian took the position that the Senate was bound to observe the Senate-instructed level through initial floor consideration. Any committee-generated language or floor amendment that exceeded the Senate level would be subject to a point of order.[30] In conference, Senate conferees could agree to revenue reductions higher than the Senate level but no greater than the House level.

An example of reconciliation instructions included in the fiscal year 2004 concurrent resolution on the budget follows:

SEC. 104. RECONCILIATION IN THE SENATE.
    (b) COMMITTEE ON FINANCE—The Senate Committee on Finance shall report a reconciliation bill not later than April 8, 2003, that consists of changes in laws within its jurisdiction sufficient to reduce revenues by not more than $698,294,000,000 and increase the total level of outlays by not more than $27,476,000,000 for the period of fiscal years 2003 through 2013.

Committees are instructed as to overall dollar targets only and have great flexibility as to how they make statutory adjustments to meet their objections. Reconciliation instructions are not proposed in a policy vacuum. When dollar totals are stated, Congress has a reasonable sense of what statutory changes will be proposed to achieve the goal. Nothing but jurisdictional boundaries, however, limits a committee's discretion in responding to the instruction.

By a date specified in the budget resolution, instructed committees report such changes to their respective house's budget panel, which bundles the material together into its version of an omnibus reconciliation bill without making substantive changes.[31] As it bundles, the Budget Committee cannot make substantive changes in the legislative recommendations received from other committees. If only one committee is instructed to reconcile, it reports directly to the Senate.

The Congressional Budget Office estimates the economic value of proposed spending adjustments, a process known as "scorekeeping," to determine whether a committee has complied with its instructions. The Joint Committee on Taxation "scores" revenue provisions. "Scoring" is essential to determine whether a committee has complied with its instructions.

Beyond its effect on reconciliation, scoring has a central and significant relationship to every fiscal issue Congress confronts throughout the year. Through scoring, the fiscal effect of any proposed provision can be measured and its impact on the budget determined. Budget enforcement depends on scoring, without which the effect that given provisions would have on spending and revenue levels would be unknown.[32]

The budget resolution is also likely to contain statements of budgetary policy that take the form of Sense of the Senate declarations. These statements can be construed as policy guidance and/or political rhetoric, but they have no statutory effect and are not binding on later acts of Congress. In the fiscal year 2004 budget resolution, sixteen Sense of the Senate statements were included.[33] An illustration of a Sense of the Senate provision, drawn from the fiscal year 2004 budget resolution, follows:

SEC. 609. SENSE OF THE SENATE CONCERNING AN EXPANSION IN HEALTH CARE COVERAGE.
It is the sense of the Senate that the functional totals in this resolution assume that—
(1) expanded access to health care coverage throughout the United States is a top priority for national policymaking; and
(2) to the extent that additional funds are made available, a significant portion of such funds should be dedicated to expanding access to health care coverage so that fewer individuals are uninsured and fewer individuals are likely to become uninsured.

When the budget resolution is brought to the Senate floor, it is privileged. Although the Budget Act does not specify that motions to proceed to budget resolutions are nondebatable, the presiding officer has construed this to be the case. The theory of this construction is that if debate on the motion to proceed were not restricted, the fast-track debate provisions applicable to the underlying vehicle would be frustrated.

Once on the floor, the budget resolution is subject to a fifty-hour time limit on debate, equally divided, between the two leaders or their designees. Within the overall time limitation, there are sublimits, including a two-hour cap on any first-degree amendment and a one-hour limit on any second-degree amendment, debatable motion, or appeal. Time can be yielded from the overall allocation to expand the time for debate on an amendment, a tactic commonly used by the bill managers.[34] If time is yielded back, then both sides share equally in the time that remains.

All amendments to the budget resolution must be germane. Amendments that are germane per se include any that strike language, such as a motion to strike a reconciliation instruction, or any that change dollar levels or dates. Germane amendments to the nonbinding Sense of the Senate language reported by the Budget Committee are in order, but new and unrelated provisions of this nature are not.

Customarily, language that has previously been amended may not be reopened, and amendments may not be drawn to more than one place in a bill.[35] Under the Budget Act, however, mathematically consistent amendments are always in order, so totals once amended can be readjusted in the course of later amendments.[36]

Budget Act points of order and appeals from rulings of the presiding officer are subject to unique procedures. Even though appeals from rulings on points of order are customarily decided by a simple majority of senators present, most points of order created by the Budget Act require sixty votes to overturn the presiding officer on appeal. Moreover, section 904(b) of the Budget Act provides that any of the act's procedural provisions can be waived. The voting requirement for the waiver is equivalent to the vote needed to appeal a ruling successfully, which usually means sixty votes.

Nowhere else in Senate procedure does there exist a formal waiver process. To "waive" points of order arising outside the Budget Act, a senator would need unanimous consent or a two-thirds vote to adopt a motion to suspend the rules.[37] A waiver motion may be offered at any time prior to a ruling on a point of order, even before the point of order is lodged.[38] The waiver motion can propose to inoculate a provision against any Budget Act point of order that would lie at any stage of the legislative process. For instance, a motion to waive the Byrd Rule,[39] offered when a provision is initially before the Senate, can include language that would immunize against a point of order even through the presentation of the conference report. Waiver motions can be amended in two degrees, such amendments proposing to expand or restrict the scope of the waiver.

An example of the use of a waiver motion can be found in the 2003 debate on prescription drug legislation. Democratic Leader Tom Daschle (D-SD) made a point of order against the prescription drug conference report, as Majority Leader Bill Frist (R-TN) moved to waive.

Mr. DASCHLE: Mr. President, I make a point of order that H.R. 1, the pending conference report, violates section 311(a)(2) and section 302(f) of the Congressional Budget Act of 1974, among other reasons, because of the provisions related to premium support and health savings accounts.

The PRESIDING OFFICER: The Majority Leader.

Mr. FRIST: Mr. President, on behalf of myself and Senators GRASSLEY, BAUCUS, and BREAUX, pursuant to section 904 of the Congressional Budget Act of 1974, I move to waive the applicable sections of that act and the budget resolution for the consideration of the conference report.[40]

Budget Resolution: The "vote-a-rama"

In theory, once all debate time has been used or yielded back, a vote should occur on adoption of the budget resolution or passage of the reconciliation bill. The Budget Act time restrictions, however, represent a limit on debate only and not on overall consideration.[41] Beginning in the middle 1990s, a practice developed that has come to be known as the "vote-a-rama." After all debate time has elapsed, senators continue to offer further amendments. No debate is in order, but roll call votes can be taken.[42] In this situation, dozens of votes occur on amendments and waiver motions with little explanation.[43] Notwithstanding the expedited procedures set forth in the Budget Act, there is essentially no end to this process except for cloture, if it could be achieved, or exhaustion.

Those who defend the vote-a-rama argue that it ensures that minority party amendments can be offered. Otherwise, they contend, the majority party can continue to yield time off the budget resolution to prolong debate on a handful of amendments until time expires, fill the amendment tree and lock out minority amendments until the time expires, or yield back time to consume portions of the fifty-hour limit so that amendments could not be offered under the cap. Various reforms have been suggested to modify or end the vote-a-rama, but none has yet been adopted.

Budget resolution conference reports are privileged and subject to a ten-hour time limitation on debate, equally divided and controlled by the two leaders or their designees. A ten-hour debate limit also applies to any amendments in disagreement. Debatable motions or appeals in connection with the conference report or any amendments in disagreement are limited to one hour each.[44] If a motion to proceed to a budget resolution conference report is defeated, a further motion to the same effect may subsequently be made.

If a conference report is defeated, a motion to request a new conference and to appoint conferees is limited to one hour. Motions to instruct conferees may be debated for thirty minutes, and any amendment to the instructions is debatable for twenty minutes. Instructions may be amended in two degrees. Amendments in disagreement may be debated for thirty minutes each.

Reconciliation Bills

A motion to proceed to a reconciliation bill is privileged.[45] When such a bill is brought to the floor, it is debated for twenty hours, with sublimits of two hours on amendments in the first degree and one hour on amendments in the second degree, debatable motions, and appeals. All amendments must be germane.

Except when a declaration of war is in effect, no amendment to a reconciliation bill may be offered that would increase the deficit assumed in the budget resolution. Section 310(d)(2) states that it shall not be in order to consider an amendment to a reconciliation bill that would either decrease budget outlay reductions or reduce federal revenue increases beyond the instructions provided in the budget resolution for the fiscal years it covers. This means that proposed spending increases or revenue cuts must be offset either with spending cuts or with tax increases to ensure deficit neutrality. Notwithstanding this requirement, a motion to strike is always in order.[46]

The reconciliation process cannot be used to propose changes in the old-age, survivors, and disability program in Title II of the Social Security Act. A point of order under section 310(g) lies against this, as does a Byrd Rule point of order at section 313(b) (1) (F).

Section 310(c) allows a certain degree of flexibility in complying with reconciliation instructions. For instance, in the fiscal year 2004 budget resolution, the Senate Finance Committee was instructed to make revenue decreases of $323 billion and outlay increases of $27 billion, totaling $350 billion. Section 310(c) permits up to 20 percent of the aggregate amount to be added to either the outlay increases or tax cuts, so long as the aggregate ceiling is not breached. Accordingly, the committee could have reported $70 billion in outlay increases (20 percent of the total of $350 billion) and reduced the tax cuts to $280 billion. In the alternative, the committee could have enlarged tax cuts to $350 billion, leaving nothing for spending increases.[47]

If a committee is not in compliance with its reconciliation instructions, a remedy exists on the Senate floor. A motion will be in order to commit the bill to the errant committee with instructions to report back forthwith to include an amendment. The amendment would contain language to bring the committee into compliance, as if the committee had actually met and reported the provision itself. The amendment will not be subject to a germaneness point of order because if the committee had complied, the provision would have been part of the base bill in the first place.[48]

Reconciliation rules also place a huge premium on accomplishing legislative objectives in committee, procedurally strengthening a committee's hand beyond the subject matter deference normally accorded to them. For example, suppose a tax on distilled spirits were being considered as part of a reconciliation bill. A senator wishes to propose a floor amendment to cut the tax increase by five cents a gallon. He must proffer a revenue offset or else face a point of order that he can waive or successfully appeal only by a three-fifths vote.[49] To replace the revenue, the senator would propose to increase beer taxes, but no language on beer taxes is in the reported bill. The senator's beer provision is therefore nongermane and subject to a point of order that may be waived or successfully appealed only by sixty votes. To avoid a point of order on germaneness, the senator's offset may increase only taxes that were otherwise set forth in the bill.

Budget Reconciliation and the Byrd Rule

The reconciliation process provides an expedited means to change federal spending programs, revenues, and public debt levels. It does so under parliamentary rules that substantially diminish the procedural rights normally enjoyed by senators. Reconciliation therefore invites the possibility of abuse as senators attempt to include in a fast-track vehicle provisions that would otherwise be subject to traditional debate and amendment rules.

To prevent senators' rights from being unduly infringed, Senator Robert Byrd (D-WV) amended the 1974 act to bar extraneous matter from reconciliation bills. Although Byrd was initially successful in 1985, his effort began four years earlier.

The first major use of budget reconciliation occurred in 1981, when a Republican majority sat for the first time in twenty-six years. Anxious to avoid filibusters and to force the Democrat-dominated House to conference on major issues, Senate Republicans aggressively shaped that year's reconciliation bill. Included in the measure were provisions that were clearly responsive to reconciliation instructions. Included as well were provisions that did not appear to relate to those instructions.

Senator Byrd, then minority leader, inquired informally of the parliamentarian as to whether nonresponsive provisions would contaminate the entire bill to the end that the legislation would no longer be considered a reconciliation bill. If so, the bill would no longer carry Budget Act protections and would be wide open to amendments and filibuster. The parliamentarian responded that so long as a preponderance of the material was responsive to the instructions, the entire vehicle would enjoy reconciliation protection.

To rid the bill of nonresponsive provisions, Senator Byrd could have proposed a motion to strike. Motions to strike, however, are resolved on a simple majority vote. A determined majority could simply table such motions and maintain the integrity of the bill. No other curative motion or point of order was available in 1981.

Senator Byrd and Majority Leader Howard Baker Jr. (R-TN) reached an accord identifying provisions that both could agree were extraneous to the instructions, and these provisions were stricken from the bill. Afterward, Byrd addressed the Senate, claiming that the two leaders had done all they could do but not all they should do. Four years later, the Senate, as part of the 1985 budget resolution, adopted the first Byrd Rule point of order against extraneous provisions. Several additional iterations passed in the years that followed, culminating in 1990 in its formal incorporation into the Budget Act.

In 1985, Senator Byrd explained the rationale for creating a point of order against extraneous material in reconciliation bills. Speaking with reference to the reconciliation bill then pending, Byrd said,

> There are 122 items in the reconciliation bill that are extraneous. Henceforth, if the majority on a committee should wish to include in reconciliation recommendations to the Budget Committee any measure, no matter how controversial, it can be brought to the Senate under an ironclad built-in time agreement that limits debate, plus time on amendments and motions, to no more than 20 hours.
>
> It was never foreseen that the Budget Reform Act would be used in that way. So if the budget reform process is going to be preserved, and more importantly if we are going to preserve the deliberative process in this U.S. Senate—which is the outstanding, unique element with respect to the U.S. Senate, action must be taken now to stop this abuse of the budget process.[50]

Codified at section 313 of the Act, the Byrd Rule creates points of order against extraneous language found in Senate committee–reported provisions, Senate floor amendments, or conference reports. Congressional Research Service analyst Robert Keith explains,

> In general, a point of order authorized under the Byrd Rule may be raised in order to strike extraneous matter already in the bill as reported or discharged (or in the conference report), or to prevent the incorporation of extraneous matter through the adoption of amendments or motions, A point of order may be raised against a single provision or two or more provisions (as designated by title or section number, or by page or line number) and may be raised against a single amendment or two or more amendments or only some of them.[51]

If the presiding officer upholds a Byrd Rule point of order, sixty votes are required to overturn his decision. Under section 313 of the act, a provision will be deemed extraneous and will therefore violate the Byrd Rule if it does the following:

- Has no budgetary effect (as scored by the Congressional Budget Office) because it does not produce a change in outlays or revenues. 313(b)(1)(A)[52]
- Loses revenue or increases spending, if reported by a committee that has failed to meet its reconciliation instructions. 313(b)(1)(B)
- Falls within the jurisdiction of a committee other than the committee that reported it. 313(b)(1)(C)

- Produces savings that are merely incidental to the nonbudgetary effects of the provision. 313(b)(1)(D)
- Loses revenue or increases spending in a year beyond the reach of the budget resolution in excess of other savings in that year. 313(b)(1)(E)[53]
- Proposes changes in the Social Security program 313(b)(1)(F)[54]

Each of these provisions is objectively measurable, with the exception of the "merely incidental" language of section 313(b)(1)(D). A provision may survive only if its nonbudgetary spillover effects are merely incidental to its budgetary purposes.[55] Thus, if a provision is predominantly fiscal in its purpose and if any nonbudgetary spillover effect is both minimal and integral to the provision as a whole, such language may pass Byrd Rule muster. However, no matter how minor the nonfiscal effect may be, it must still be stricken if it is possible to do so without undermining the provision's fiscal impact.

In the event the point of order is successfully made against a conference report, the offending language is stricken. The Byrd Rule provides that, on material being stricken from the conference report, the Senate proceeds immediately, and without any intervening action or motion, to consider whether it shall recede from its own amendment and concur with a further amendment or concur in the House amendment with a further amendment. In either case, the content of that further amendment is restricted to the language of the conference agreement that has not survived. No amendments are in order.[56]

As to conference reports, a useful distinction can be drawn between making a point of order under the Byrd Rule and the more traditional point of order under Rule XXVIII. Both points of order lie because the conferees exceeded their authority. In the case of Rule XXVIII, the conferees acted on material not committed to them by either house. In the case of the Byrd Rule, the conferees may have acted on material in one of the bills[57] but such material was nonetheless extraneous to the purposes of budget reconciliation. Senators who would use a Rule XXVIII point of order must be able to command a majority either to defend or to overturn the presiding officer's ruling. Senators who would use the Byrd Rule need to command only forty-one votes to defend the ruling or avert a waiver.

Reconciliation is a unique Senate procedure in that it sets timetables, permits the coalescing of disparate legislation into one vehicle, and tends to neutralize the filibuster. By limiting debate, imposing germaneness requirements, and mandating deficit neutrality for amendments, reconciliation significantly intrudes on the normal exercise of senators' rights and is especially burdensome to whichever party happens to be in the minority at the moment. The Byrd Rule is an important exception to the overall character of this process and is a critical protection for the minority.

The Byrd Rule has profoundly affected the reconciliation process for some two decades. Some of this effect can be measured. In a study of the use of the Byrd Rule between 1985 and 2002, the Congressional Research Service reported,

> The Byrd Rule has been applied to 13 reconciliation measures considered by the Senate from 1985 to 2002. In 41 of the 54 actions involving the Byrd Rule, opponents were able to strike extraneous matter from legislation (18 cases) or bar the consideration of extraneous amendments (23 bases) by raising points of order. Nine of 40 motions to waive the Byrd Rule, in order to retain or add extraneous matter, were successful. The Byrd Rule has been used only four times during consideration of a conference report on a reconciliation measure (twice in 1993, once in 1995, and once in 1997).[58]

These statistics are impressive but do not begin to disclose the full impact of the rule, especially as to conference reports. Unreported are instances when a jurisdictional committee does not include language, a floor amendment is not offered, or a provision is not brought back to the Senate from conference because it will be subject to the Byrd Rule and the votes to waive are not available.

Budget Act procedures make the Senate more closely resemble the House. The Act has had an immense effect on major fiscal legislation passed since 1981, when the budget reconciliation process was first fully employed.

Chapter Ten

Executive Business and the Executive Calendar

Article 2, section 2, of the Constitution vests unicameral power in the Senate to address nominations and treaties. From the very first United States Senate in 1789, consideration of executive business has been kept separate from the legislative agenda. The Senate honors this tradition by keeping two calendars, one for legislative business and the other for executive business. The executive calendar covers solely nominations and treaties. The Senate does not do executive business in legislative session, nor does it do legislative business in executive session.[1]

A motion to proceed to executive business, like a motion to return to legislative business, is nondebatable. Only a motion to adjourn, a motion to adjourn to a day certain, and a motion to recess may supersede it.[2]

In offering this motion, it is in order to specify that the Senate consider a particular nomination or treaty. As a practical matter, this procedural nuance means that a motion to proceed to an item on the executive calendar is not debatable. If no such item is specified, then when the Senate proceeds to executive business, the first item on the calendar is automatically made pending. On adoption of a motion to go into executive session, action on the legislative business that had been pending is suspended until the Senate again returns to legislative session.[3]

NOMINATIONS

The president's constitutional power to nominate, with the advice and consent of the Senate, is found at article 2, section 2. Rule XXXI is the principal Senate rule governing the confirmation process.

It is not in order to consider a nomination on the calendar day it is received. Instead, the nomination is to be referred to committee.[4] Once reported, a nomination must lie over one calendar day.[5] A motion to proceed to the consideration of a nomination is not debatable when the motion is phrased as proceeding to executive business for the purpose of considering a particular nominee.[6] Once the nomination is pending, it can be debated. In a relatively rare number of instances, nominations have been filibustered.[7]

More typical of the treatment most nominees receive is the following unanimous consent order:

> Mr. FRIST: I ask unanimous consent that the Senate immediately proceed to executive session to consider the following nominations on today's Executive Calendar: Calendar nos. 406, 407, 408 and 409. I further ask unanimous consent that the nominations be confirmed, that the motions to reconsider be laid upon the table, the President be immediately notified of the Senate's action, and that the Senate then return to legislative session.[8]
>
> The PRESIDING OFFICER: Without objection, it is so ordered.

Confirmation of a nominee requires a simple majority of senators present, which is also the voting requirement for most motions that may be made in connection with the nomination. These include a motion to recommit, a motion to postpone to a date certain, a motion to postpone indefinitely, a motion to table, and a motion to reconsider.

When a nominee is confirmed or rejected, the Senate notifies the president. The motion to reconsider may be made by any senator voting in the majority on the day the vote was taken or on either of the next two days of actual executive session. Customarily, the motion to reconsider is made immediately after the confirmation vote and is tabled.[9] If the notice to the president has been sent prior to a vote on reconsideration and if that motion to reconsider is successful, the motion to reconsider must be accompanied by a request to the president to return the nomination to the Senate.[10] The president is free, however, to ignore the request.[11]

Nominations not acted on during a session or prior to a recess or adjournment of more than thirty days will lapse and are returned to the president unless unanimous consent is obtained to hold them over.[12] For example,

> Mr. REID: Mr. President, I ask unanimous consent that all nominations received by the Senate during the 107th Congress, first session, remain in status quo notwithstanding the adjournment of the Senate and the provisions of rule XXXI, paragraph 6, of the Standing Rules of the Senate, with the following exceptions: PN850, Otto Reich, to be Assistant Secretary of State; PN983-4, Colonel David R. Leffarge, to be Brigadier General.
>
> The PRESIDENT pro tempore: Without objection, it is so ordered.[13]

If nominations are returned to the president, the Senate does not consider them further unless such individuals are renominated.[14] This non-retention of nominations contrasts with the way legislation is handled under Rule XVIII. That rule provides that at the second or any subsequent session of a Congress, business carrying over from the previous session shall automatically be continued. Also contrast the rule on nominations with procedure on treaties under Rule XXX, which permits treaties to remain before the Senate from one Congress to the next.[15]

The Constitution gives the president the power to make recess appointments.[16] Recess appointees nominated during an intrasession recess in one session can serve to the end of the sine die adjournment of the Senate's next session, but the appointment will expire sooner if someone is confirmed for the position.[17] It is unclear how short a recess can be for purposes of making recess appointments, this being an obvious point of tension between the president, who wishes to fill vacancies, and the Senate, who does not want to see its confirmation power eroded. It is rare for recess appointments to be made during recesses of fewer than twenty days, although one such appointment was made during a ten-day recess.[18]

A federal statutory provision on pay[19] bars compensation to a recess appointee to a vacancy that existed when the Senate was in session. This prohibition does not apply if the vacancy occurred within thirty days of sine die adjournment of that session. It also does not apply if a nomination to fill the vacancy was pending at the time of the recess and the nominee was other than the recess appointee, or if a nomination for the position was rejected within thirty days of sine die adjournment and the recess appointee is not the rejected nominee. Even if a recess appointee is paid because he or she meets one of these criteria, the Senate still jealously guards its confirmation power. Thus, the statute mandates that the president submit a nomination to fill the vacancy no later than forty days after the next session of the Senate begins.

If the Senate rejects a recess appointee, he may continue to serve out the term of his recess appointment. However, under an annually renewed provision in the appropriations bill governing the Department of the Treasury, his pay will cease after the Senate has voted to reject him.[20] For example, a provision in S. 1589, 108th Congress, reads as follows:

> SEC. 609. No part of any appropriation for the current fiscal year contained in this or any other Act shall be paid to any person for the filling of any position for which he or she has been nominated after the Senate has voted not to approve the nomination of said person.

TREATIES

Treaty procedure is set forth at Rule XXX. The rule provides that when a treaty is received by the Senate, it shall be read a first time and that no motions be in order except to remove the injunction of secrecy,[21] to print it in confidence for Senate use, or to refer it to committee.

Disposition of treaty documents is made while the Senate is in executive session, unless consent is granted to process treaties whenever they are received. Treaties are referred to the Committee on Foreign Relations. An illustration of this procedure follows:

> Mr. DeWINE: Mr. President, as in executive session, I ask unanimous consent that the injunction of secrecy be removed from the following protocol transmitted to the Senate on September 2, 2003, by the President of the United States: Protocol to Treaty of Friendship, Commerce, and Navigation with Denmark, treaty document 108-8.
>
> I further ask that the protocol be considered as having been read the first time; that it be referred, with accompanying papers, to the Committee on Foreign Relations and ordered to be printed; and that the President's message be printed in the *Record*.
>
> The PRESIDING OFFICER: Without objection, it is so ordered.[22]

Following report by a committee, a treaty must lie over for one calendar day. When the treaty is put before the Senate, second reading occurs.[23] The reading will be done in its entirety and not simply by title, unless shortened by unanimous consent.[24]

Once the treaty is pending, it is open to amendment. Committee amendments will be considered amendments in the first degree, unless consent is given to treat them as original text for purpose of further amendment.[25] Prior to a 1986 rules change, treaties were considered article by article, first in a committee of the whole and then in the full Senate. This procedure no longer operates. The Committee of the Whole has been abolished, and all unamended portions of the treaty are open to amendment at any time.

When all amendments to the text have been dispensed with and after a layover of one calendar day, the resolution of ratification will be presented.[26] Thereafter, amendments to the treaty text are not in order.[27] While the resolution of ratification is pending, reservations, statements, understandings, and declarations may be proposed to it.[28] Depending on the nature of the Senate's declaration, the president may communicate such to other treaty parties, and this may force the renegotiation of the treaty. An example of advice and consent to a treaty, subject to a reservation, follows:

> The Senate advises and consents to the ratification of the Convention for the Unification of Certain Rules for International Carriage by Air, done at Montreal

May 28, 1999 (T. Doc. 106-45, in this resolution referred to as the "Convention"), subject to the reservation in section 2.

Sec. 2. Reservation.

The advice and consent of the Senate to the ratification of the Convention is subject to the following reservation, which shall be included in the instrument of ratification:

Pursuant to Article 57 of the Convention, the United States of America declares that the Convention shall not apply to international carriage by air performed and operated directly by the United States of America for noncommercial purposes in respect to the functions and duties of the United States of America as a sovereign State.[29]

In his Senate history, Senator Robert Byrd (D-WV) speaks to the somewhat confusing distinctions between amendments, reservations, declarations, and so on, each of which conditions the Senate's consent:

Although the labeling of the Senate's expression may be relatively unimportant in determining its legal effect, the most significant actions, in order of their effect, are amendments; reservations; understandings; interpretations, declarations; and statements. . . .

Regardless of what an action is called, the substance determines the legal effect. For example, language would constitute a reservation (or an amendment) when it would exclude or vary the legal effect of one or more of the provisions of the treaty. On the other hand, language which merely explains or clarifies the meaning of treaty provisions but which does not exclude or vary the legal effect of such provisions, would properly constitute an understanding or interpretation.[30]

All amendments agreed to at any stage of treaty proceedings require only a simple majority of senators present. Adoption of a motion to postpone indefinitely requires a two-thirds vote.[31] The vote to concur in the resolution of ratification is also subject to a two-thirds vote.[32] While the Constitution does not specify that this vote must be by roll call, this is now the general practice of the Senate. Consent has been given to the ratification of minor treaties by division vote.

For noncontroversial treaties, floor procedure is substantially simplified. On March 2, 2003, the Senate considered three such treaties en bloc, under the following process:

Mr. BENNETT: Mr. President, I ask unanimous consent that the Senate proceed to executive session to consider the following treaties on today's Executive Calendar: Nos. 2, 3, and 4.

I further ask unanimous consent that the treaties be considered as having passed through their various parliamentary stages up to and including the presentation of the resolutions of ratification; that any statements be inserted in the *Record* as if read; and that the Senate take one vote on the resolutions of ratification to be considered as separate votes; further, that when the resolutions of ratification are voted upon, the motion to reconsider be laid upon the table, the President be notified of the Senate's action, and that following the disposition of the treaties the Senate return to legislative session.

The PRESIDING OFFICER: Without objection, it is so ordered. The treaties will be considered to have passed through their various parliamentary stages up to and including the presentation of the resolutions of ratification.

The three treaties were agreed to by a division vote.

Unlike nominations, treaties not acted on remain with the Senate unless the Senate votes to return them to the president. A treaty that is held over from one Congress to the next is treated as though no proceedings had ever occurred on it. Thus, a treaty that was reported from committee and is pending on the executive calendar when the second session adjourns sine die will start the following Congress back in committee, and the process will resume from the beginning.[33]

Senator Byrd summarizes the Senate's role in the treaty process:

The Senate itself does not ratify treaties—actual ratification only takes place when the instruments of ratification are formally exchanged between the parties. When a treaty is submitted to the Senate for approval, it has several options for action. Depending on whether or not a two-thirds majority votes in favor, the Senate may approve or reject the treaty as it has been submitted. It may make its approval conditional by including in the resolution amendments to the text of the treaty, reservations, understandings, interpretations, declarations or other statements. The president and the other countries involved must then decide whether to accept the conditions and changes in the legislation, renegotiate the provisions, or abandon the treaty.[34]

CLOSING AND OPENING THE DOORS

Although the Senate operates in open session, a procedure exists to close the doors and clear the galleries if a senator believes there is a need for the Senate to proceed in secrecy.

Pursuant to Rule XXI, a senator may at any time move that the Senate's doors be closed. To close the doors, it is sufficient if one other senator seconds the motion.[35] The motion is highly privileged, meaning that it can interrupt other business and even a senator who is speaking and is not debated or voted on.[36] Staff access is limited to persons described in Rule XXIX,[37] and strict rules of confidentiality apply, unless the Senate votes to waive them. A senator violating these rules is subject to disciplinary action that could include expulsion from the Senate.[38] Staff violations may result in dismissal from Senate service and punishment for contempt.[39]

Before 1794, all Senate business was conducted behind closed doors. For legislative discussions, the doors were thereafter opened. However, closed session continued for executive business until 1929. Since then, consideration of matters on the executive calendar is done in open session, subject to being closed under Rule XXI procedures. Rule XXXI permits lifting the injunction of secrecy by majority vote for all or part of proceedings undertaken in closed executive session and further provides that any senator may disclose his vote in such a closed session.[40] Once the closed session commences, it is in order to make a nondebatable motion to open the doors.[41]

IMPEACHMENT

The Senate derives its impeachment power from the Constitution, as follows:

> The Senate shall have the sole Power to try all Impeachments. When sitting for that Purpose, they shall be on Oath or Affirmation. When the President of the United States is tried, the Chief Justice shall preside: And no Person shall be convicted without the Concurrence of two-thirds of the Members present.
>
> Judgment in Cases of Impeachments shall not extend further than to removal from Office, and disqualification to hold or enjoy any Office of honor, Trust or Profit under the United States: but the Party convicted shall nevertheless be liable and subject to Indictment, Trial, Judgment and Punishment, according to Law.[42]

Impeachment proceedings may be brought against the president, the vice president, and all civil officers of the United States. They may be impeached and convicted for "Treason, Bribery, or other High Crimes and Misdemeanors."[43] Impeachment proceedings begun in one Congress may carry over until the next, as was the case in the Clinton impeachment trial and the trials of several federal judges.[44]

To implement its powers, the Senate has adopted twenty-six special rules of procedure that apply when it is sitting as a court of impeachment. The rules were last revised in 1986, pursuant to S. Res. 479, 99th Congress. A lengthy and detailed discussion of these procedures can be found in a document titled *Procedure and Guidelines for Impeachment Trials in the United States Senate*, authored in 1986 by Floyd Riddick and Robert Dove.[45] Their study contains precedents from impeachment trials other than the trial of President Clinton. It is the best single document available to study the Senate's impeachment process. The essence of that process follows.

The House of Representatives transmits a message to the Senate, stating that the House has voted articles of impeachment and requesting that the Senate receive a delegation of managers on the part of the House. The secretary of the Senate notifies the House that the Senate is prepared to receive the managers.[46]

When the managers first appear at the bar of the Senate, the sergeant at arms makes a proclamation that he will repeat at the opening of each day the trial is in session: "All persons are commanded to keep silence, on pain of imprisonment, while the House of Representatives is exhibiting to the Senate of the United States articles of impeachment against _____ _____."[47]

The managers present the articles of impeachment and ask the Senate to convene the trial. The presiding officer then indicates that the Senate will advise the House when it is ready to commence the trial, and the managers leave the Senate and return to the House.[48]

After the articles are presented, the Senate begins the trial, starting at 1 P.M. of the following day (except for Sunday), unless the Senate enters an order to start at a different time. The trial continues without interruption until a verdict is rendered on the articles or the Senate adjourns the trial sine die.[49]

At the commencement of the trial, the presiding officer takes and administers an oath.[50] If the president of the United States is on trial, the chief justice presides.[51] Otherwise, the presiding officer is the vice president, the president pro tempore, or the president pro tempore's designee. During the trial, the presiding officer rules on all questions of evidence, subject to appeals to the Senate. The appeals are decided without debate.[52]

The oath that senators take reads, "I solemnly swear (or affirm) that in all things appertaining to the trial of the impeachment of _____ _____, now pending, I will do impartial justice according to the Constitution and laws: So help me God." Thereafter, a summons is issued to the person impeached, so that he may answer the charges set forth in the articles. The requirement for the summons and procedures for its execution and return are set forth in Impeachment Rules VIII and IX.

In the impeachment trial of President William Jefferson Clinton, the Senate unanimously adopted S. Res. 16, 106th Congress, on January 8, 1999. The resolution authorized a summons to the president and set forth a procedure for the conduct of the impeachment trial. The resolution reads as follows:

> Resolved, that summons be issued in the usual form provided, that the president may have until 12 noon on Monday, January 11, to file his answer with the secretary of the Senate and the House have until 12 noon on January 13 to file its replication with the secretary of the Senate, together with the record, which will consist of those publicly available materials that have been submitted to or produced by the House Judiciary Committee, including transcripts of public hear-

ings or mark-ups and any materials printed by the House of Representatives or House Judiciary Committee pursuant to House Resolutions 525 and 581. Such record will be admitted into evidence, printed and made available to Senators. If the House wishes to file a trial brief it shall be filed by 5 P.M. on January 11.

The president and the House shall have until 5 P.M. on January 11 to file any motions permitted under the rules of impeachment except for motions to subpoena witnesses or to present any evidence not in the record. Responses to any such motion shall be filed no later than 10 A.M. on January 13. The president may file a trial brief at or before that time. The House may file a rebuttal brief no later than 10 A.M. on January 14.

Arguments on such motions shall begin at 1 P.M. on January 13, and each side may determine the number of persons to make its presentation, following which the Senate shall deliberate and vote on any such motions. Following the disposition of these motions, or if no motions occur, then at 1 P.M. on January 14th, the House shall make its presentation in support of the Articles of Impeachment for a period of time not to exceed 24 hours. Each side may determine the number of persons to make its presentation. The presentation shall be limited to argument from the record. Following the House presentation, the president shall make his presentation for a period not to exceed 24 hours, as outlined in the paragraph above with reference to the House presentation.

Upon the conclusion of the president's presentation, senators may question the parties for a period of time not to exceed 16 hours.

After the conclusion of questioning by the Senate, it shall be in order to consider and debate a motion to dismiss as outlined by the impeachment rules. Following debate, it shall be in order to make a motion to subpoena witnesses and to present any evidence not in the record, with debate time on that motion limited to 6 hours, to be equally divided between the two parties. Following debate and any deliberation as provided in the impeachment rules, the Senate will proceed to vote on the motion to dismiss, and if defeated, an immediate vote on the motion to subpoena witnesses and to present any evidence not in the record, all without any intervening action, motion, amendment or debate.

If the Senate agrees to allow either the House or the president to call witnesses, the witnesses shall first be deposed and the Senate shall decide after deposition which witnesses shall testify pursuant to the impeachment rules. Further, the time for deposition shall be agreed to by both leaders. No testimony shall be admissible in the Senate unless the parties have had an opportunity to depose such witnesses.

If the Senate fails to dismiss the case, the parties will proceed to present evidence. At the conclusion of the deliberations by the Senate, the Senate shall proceed to vote on each article of impeachment.

Impeachment Rule XI permits appointment of a committee to receive evidence rather than the full Senate having to sit through the evidentiary phase. This procedure was used to prepare for the impeachment trials of several federal judges impeached and convicted in the late 1980s. Two of the impeached judges, Walter Nixon and Alcee Hastings, challenged their convictions on the basis that using a Rule XI committee for evidentiary purposes had deprived them of an appropriate Senate trial. The courts rejected these challenges.[53] During the Clinton impeachment trial, evidence was presented to the Senate as a whole, and no there was use of a Rule XI committee.

The presiding officer convenes the impeachment trial each day. The Senate chaplain delivers a prayer, the sergeant at arms makes his proclamation, and the *Journal* of impeachment proceedings is approved. That journal is separate from the legislative, executive, and confidential executive journals the Senate otherwise keeps.[54]

During trial, all procedural questions are addressed to the presiding officer, and either he or any senator may require them to be submitted in writing.[55] Questions to a witness or to one of the parties must be reduced to writing and will be propounded orally by the presiding officer.[56] In the Clinton trial, senators submitted fifty questions, either to the managers or to counsel for the president.

Throughout an impeachment trial, senators are not permitted to debate.[57] These restrictions can be altered by unanimous consent.

Proceedings in impeachment trials are conducted in open session, although a nondebatable roll call motion is in order to close the doors.[58] Actual deliberations on the verdict are conducted in closed session. During the Clinton trial, the Senate rejected a motion proposed by Senator Tom Harkin (D-IA) to suspend the rules in order to open the deliberations on Senator Robert Byrd's motion to dismiss the proceedings. The vote was 43–57, and with all senators present, sixty-seven votes would have been the two-thirds necessary to suspend the rules.[59] A later motion by Senator Harkin and Senator Kay Bailey Hutchison (R-TX) to open deliberations on the articles received fifty-nine affirmative votes but failed because sixty-seven were needed.[60]

At the conclusion of each day of trial, the Senate adjourns as an impeachment court and resumes its executive or legislative business, which has been suspended during the impeachment proceedings.[61] The impeachment trial has no effect on such other business.

The House of Representatives both opens and closes the impeachment trial.[62] Articles of impeachment are not divisible.[63] During the closed proceeding for deliberations, each senator may speak once and for no more than ten minutes on any interlocutory question and once for a total of fifteen minutes on the final question. The final question embraces all articles of impeachment, so senators may not speak for fifteen minutes on each individual article.[64]

After deliberations are complete, the Senate returns to open session. Each article is voted on separately, the question being, "Senators, how say you? Is the respondent, _____ _____, guilty or not guilty?" Given the solemnity of the occasion and the requirements of the rules, senators vote from their desks.[65]

Voting on the articles can be terminated before all are addressed through adoption of a motion to adjourn the impeachment trial sine die. This motion was used to end the impeachment trial of President Andrew Johnson after the president had been acquitted on several articles and before remaining articles were considered.

It is not in order to reconsider the vote on any article of impeachment. The Senate's verdict is communicated to the secretary of state and to the House of Representatives.[66]

The Senate has adopted resolutions permitting its members the right to file written opinions on the impeachment articles after the vote. Although the vote is public, the debate and deliberations occurred in closed session, so senators may avail themselves of this chance to go on the public record with their views. As to the Clinton trial, seventy-two senators publicly issued statements of their views.

Conviction of any article of impeachment requires a two-thirds vote of senators present. In certain impeachment trials, senators have been excused from voting, and they are not counted as part of the denominator against which the two-thirds is tallied. Both the Constitution and impeachment precedents are clear that conviction on any article results in automatic removal from office. A separate Senate vote, needing only a simple majority, is required to make a convicted person ineligible to again hold an office of "honor, trust or profit under the United States."[67] As noted in a Congressional Research Service Report,

> The Senate also has a unique role to play in the impeachment process. It alone has the authority and responsibility to try an impeachment brought by the House. The final decision as to whether to convict on any of the articles of impeachment is one that only the Senate can make. As to each article, a conviction must rest upon a two-thirds majority vote of the Senators present. In addition, should an individual be convicted on any of the articles, the Senate must determine the appropriate judgment: either removal from office alone, or, alternatively, removal and disqualification from holding further offices of "honor, Trust or Profit under the United States." The precedents in impeachment suggest that removal can flow automatically from conviction, but that the Senate must vote to prohibit the individual from holding future offices of public trust under the United States, if that judgment is also deemed appropriate. A simple majority vote is required on a judgment. The Constitution precludes the President from extending executive clemency to anyone to preclude their impeachment by the House of Representatives or trial by the Senate.[68]

Thus far, there have been fifteen impeachment trials in the Senate, twelve involving federal judges plus the trials of President Andrew Johnson and President William Clinton, and an early impeachment trial of Senator William Blount of Tennessee. In these trials, seven judges have been convicted. Senator Blount was acquitted when the Senate decided that sitting senators did not represent "civil officers" subject to impeachment proceedings.[69] The appropriate remedy against Blount would be use of the Senate's power to expel on a two-thirds vote.[70]

Appendix A

The Standing Rules of the Senate

Rules I through XXXIV

RULE I: APPOINTMENT OF A SENATOR TO THE CHAIR

1. In the absence of the Vice President, the Senate shall choose a President pro tempore, who shall hold the office and execute the duties thereof during the pleasure of the Senate and until another is elected or his term of office as a Senator expires.

2. In the absence of the Vice President, and pending the election of a President pro tempore, the Acting President pro tempore or the Secretary of the Senate, or in his absence the Assistant Secretary, shall perform the duties of the Chair.

3. The President pro tempore shall have the right to name in open Senate or, if absent, in writing, a Senator to perform the duties of the Chair, including the signing of duly enrolled bills and joint resolutions but such substitution shall not extend beyond an adjournment, except by unanimous consent; and the Senator so named shall have the right to name in open session, or, if absent, in writing, a Senator to perform the duties of the Chair, but not to extend beyond an adjournment, except by unanimous consent.

RULE II: PRESENTATION OF CREDENTIALS AND QUESTIONS OF PRIVILEGE

1. The presentation of the credentials of Senators elect or of Senators designate and other questions of privilege shall always be in order, except during the reading and correction of the Journal, while a question of order or a

motion to adjourn is pending, or while the Senate is voting or ascertaining the presence of a quorum; and all questions and motions arising or made upon the presentation of such credentials shall be proceeded with until disposed of.

2. The Secretary shall keep a record of the certificates of election and certificates of appointment of Senators by entering in a wellbound book kept for that purpose the date of the election or appointment, the name of the person elected or appointed, the date of the certificate, the name of the governor and the secretary of state signing and countersigning the same, and the State from which such Senator is elected or appointed.

3. The Secretary of the Senate shall send copies of the following recommended forms to the governor and secretary of state of each State wherein an election is about to take place or an appointment is to be made so that they may use such forms if they see fit.

THE RECOMMENDED FORMS FOR CERTIFICATE OF ELECTION AND CERTIFICATE OF APPOINTMENT ARE AS FOLLOWS:

CERTIFICATE OF ELECTION FOR SIX-YEAR TERM
To the President of the Senate of the United States:

This is to certify that on the __ day of __, 19__, A__ B__ was duly chosen by the qualified electors of the State of __ a Senator from said State to represent said State in the Senate of the United States for the term of six years, beginning on the 3d day of January, 19__.

Witness: His excellency our governor __, and our seal hereto affixed at __ this __ day of __, in the year of our Lord 19__.

By the governor:
C__ D__,
Governor.

E__ F__,
Secretary of State.

CERTIFICATE OF ELECTION FOR UNEXPIRED TERM
To the President of the Senate of the United States:

This is to certify that on the __ day of __, 19__, A__ B__ was duly chosen by the qualified electors of the State of __ a Senator for the unexpired term ending at noon on the 3d day of January, 19__, to fill the vacancy in the representation from said State in the Senate of the United States caused by the __ of C__ D__.

Witness: His excellency our governor __, and our seal hereto affixed at ____ this __ day of __, in the year of our Lord 19__.
By the governor:
E__ F__,
Governor.

G__ H__,
Secretary of State.

CERTIFICATE OF APPOINTMENT
To the President of the Senate of the United States:

This is to certify that, pursuant to the power vested in me by the Constitution of the United States and the laws of the State of __, I, A__ B__, the governor of said State, do hereby appoint C__ D__ a Senator from said State to represent said State in the Senate of the United States until the vacancy therein caused by the __ of E__ F__, is filled by election as provided by law.
Witness: His excellency our governor __, and our seal hereto affixed at ____ this __ day of __, in the year of our Lord 19__.
By the governor:
G__ H__,
Governor.

I__ J__,
Secretary of State.

RULE III: OATHS

The oaths or affirmations required by the Constitution and prescribed by law shall be taken and subscribed by each Senator, in open Senate, before entering upon his duties.

OATH REQUIRED BY THE CONSTITUTION AND BY LAW TO BE TAKEN BY SENATORS
"I, A__ B__, do solemnly swear (or affirm) that I will support and defend the Constitution of the United States against all enemies, foreign and domestic; that I will bear true faith and allegiance to the same; that I take this obligation freely, without any mental reservation or purpose of evasion; and that I will well and faithfully discharge the duties of the office on which I am about to enter: So help me God." (5 U.S.C. 3331.)

RULE IV: COMMENCEMENT OF DAILY SESSIONS

1. (a) The Presiding Officer having taken the chair, following the prayer by the Chaplain, and after the Presiding Officer, or a Senator designated by the Presiding Officer, leads the Senate from the dias in reciting the Pledge of Allegiance to the Flag of the United States, and a quorum being present, the Journal of the preceding day shall be read unless by nondebatable motion the reading shall be waived, the question being, "Shall the Journal stand approved to date?", and any mistake made in the entries corrected. Except as provided in subparagraph (b) the reading of the Journal shall not be suspended unless by unanimous consent; and when any motion shall be made to amend or correct the same, it shall be deemed a privileged question, and proceeded with until disposed of.

(b) Whenever the Senate is proceeding under paragraph 2 of rule XXII, the reading of the Journal shall be dispensed with and shall be considered approved to date.

(c) The proceedings of the Senate shall be briefly and accurately stated on the Journal. Messages of the President in full; titles of bills and resolutions, and such parts as shall be affected by proposed amendments; every vote, and a brief statement of the contents of each petition, memorial, or paper presented to the Senate, shall be entered.

(d) The legislative, the executive, the confidential legislative proceedings, and the proceedings when sitting as a Court of Impeachment, shall each be recorded in a separate book.

2. During a session of the Senate when that body is in continuous session, the Presiding Officer shall temporarily suspend the business of the Senate at noon each day for the purpose of having the customary daily prayer by the Chaplain.

RULE V: SUSPENSION AND AMENDMENT OF THE RULES

1. No motion to suspend, modify, or amend any rule, or any part thereof, shall be in order, except on one day's notice in writing, specifying precisely the rule or part proposed to be suspended, modified, or amended, and the purpose thereof. Any rule may be suspended without notice by the unanimous consent of the Senate, except as otherwise provided by the rules.

2. The rules of the Senate shall continue from one Congress to the next Congress unless they are changed as provided in these rules.

RULE VI: QUORUM—ABSENT SENATORS MAY BE SENT FOR

1. A quorum shall consist of a majority of the Senators duly chosen and sworn.

2. No Senator shall absent himself from the service of the Senate without leave.

3. If, at any time during the daily sessions of the Senate, a question shall be raised by any Senator as to the presence of a quorum, the Presiding Officer shall forthwith direct the Secretary to call the roll and shall announce the result, and these proceedings shall be without debate.

4. Whenever upon such roll call it shall be ascertained that a quorum is not present, a majority of the Senators present may direct the Sergeant at Arms to request, and, when necessary, to compel the attendance of the absent Senators, which order shall be determined without debate; and pending its execution, and until a quorum shall be present, no debate nor motion, except to adjourn, or to recess pursuant to a previous order entered by unanimous consent, shall be in order.

RULE VII: MORNING BUSINESS

1. On each legislative day after the Journal is read, the Presiding Officer on demand of any Senator shall lay before the Senate messages from the President, reports and communications from the heads of Departments, and other communications addressed to the Senate, and such bills, joint resolutions, and other messages from the House of Representatives as may remain upon his table from any previous day's session undisposed of. The Presiding Officer on demand of any Senator shall then call for, in the following order:

The presentation of petitions and memorials.

Reports of committees.

The introduction of bills and joint resolutions.

The submission of other resolutions.

All of which shall be received and disposed of in such order, unless unanimous consent shall be otherwise given, with newly offered resolutions being called for before resolutions coming over from a previous legislative day are laid before the Senate.

2. Until the morning business shall have been concluded, and so announced from the Chair, or until one hour after the Senate convenes at the beginning of a new legislative day, no motion to proceed to the consideration of any bill, resolution, report of a committee, or other subject upon the Calendar shall be entertained by the Presiding Officer, unless by unanimous consent: Provided, however, That on Mondays which are the beginning of a legislative day the

Calendar shall be called under rule VIII, and until two hours after the Senate convenes no motion shall be entertained to proceed to the consideration of any bill, resolution, or other subject upon the Calendar except the motion to continue the consideration of a bill, resolution, or other subject against objection as provided in rule VIII, or until the call of the Calendar has been completed.

3. The Presiding Officer may at any time lay, and it shall be in order at any time for a Senator to move to lay, before the Senate, any bill or other matter sent to the Senate by the President or the House of Representatives for appropriate action allowed under the rules and any question pending at that time shall be suspended for this purpose. Any motion so made shall be determined without debate.

4. Petitions or memorials shall be referred, without debate, to the appropriate committee according to subject matter on the same basis as bills and resolutions, if signed by the petitioner or memorialist. A question of receiving or reference may be raised and determined without debate. But no petition or memorial or other paper signed by citizens or subjects of a foreign power shall be received, unless the same be transmitted to the Senate by the President.

5. Only a brief statement of the contents of petitions and memorials shall be printed in the Congressional Record; and no other portion of any petition or memorial shall be printed in the Record unless specifically so ordered by vote of the Senate, as provided for in paragraph 4 of rule XI, in which case the order shall be deemed to apply to the body of the petition or memorial only; and names attached to the petition or memorial shall not be printed unless specially ordered, except that petitions and memorials from the legislatures or conventions, lawfully called, of the respective States, Territories, and insular possessions shall be printed in full in the Record whenever presented.

6. Senators having petitions, memorials, bills, or resolutions to present after the morning hour may deliver them in the absence of objection to the Presiding Officer's desk, endorsing upon them their names, and with the approval of the Presiding Officer, they shall be entered on the Journal with the names of the Senators presenting them and in the absence of objection shall be considered as having been read twice and referred to the appropriate committees, and a transcript of such entries shall be furnished to the official reporter of debates for publication in the Congressional Record, under the direction of the Secretary of the Senate.

RULE VIII: ORDER OF BUSINESS

1. At the conclusion of the morning business at the beginning of a new legislative day, unless upon motion the Senate shall at any time otherwise order,

the Senate shall proceed to the consideration of the Calendar of Bills and Resolutions, and shall continue such consideration until 2 hours after the Senate convenes on such day (the end of the morning hour); and bills and resolutions that are not objected to shall be taken up in their order, and each Senator shall be entitled to speak once and for five minutes only upon any question; and an objection may be interposed at any stage of the proceedings, but upon motion the Senate may continue such consideration; and this order shall commence immediately after the call for "other resolutions," or after disposition of resolutions coming "over under the rule," and shall take precedence of the unfinished business and other special orders. But if the Senate shall proceed on motion with the consideration of any matter notwithstanding an objection, the foregoing provisions touching debate shall not apply.

2. All motions made during the first two hours of a new legislative day to proceed to the consideration of any matter shall be determined without debate, except motions to proceed to the consideration of any motion, resolution, or proposal to change any of the Standing Rules of the Senate shall be debatable. Motions made after the first two hours of a new legislative day to proceed to the consideration of bills and resolutions are debatable.

RULE IX: MESSAGES

1. Messages from the President of the United States or from the House of Representatives may be received at any stage of proceedings, except while the Senate is voting or ascertaining the presence of a quorum, or while the Journal is being read, or while a question of order or a motion to adjourn is pending.

2. Messages shall be sent to the House of Representatives by the Secretary, who shall previously certify the determination of the Senate upon all bills, joint resolutions, and other resolutions which may be communicated to the House, or in which its concurrence may be requested; and the Secretary shall also certify and deliver to the President of the United States all resolutions and other communications which may be directed to him by the Senate.

RULE X: SPECIAL ORDERS

1. Any subject may, by a vote of two-thirds of the Senators present, be made a special order of business for consideration and when the time so fixed for its consideration arrives the Presiding Officer shall lay it before the Senate, unless there be unfinished business in which case it takes its place on the Calendar of Special Orders in the order of time at which it was made special, to

be considered in that order when there is no unfinished business.

2. All motions to change such order, or to proceed to the consideration of other business, shall be decided without debate.

RULE XI: PAPERS—WITHDRAWAL, PRINTING, READING OF, AND REFERENCE

1. No memorial or other paper presented to the Senate, except original treaties finally acted upon, shall be withdrawn from its files except by order of the Senate.

2. The Secretary of the Senate shall obtain at the close of each Congress all the noncurrent records of the Senate and of each Senate committee and transfer them to the National Archives and Records Administration for preservation, subject to the orders of the Senate.

3. When the reading of a paper is called for, and objected to, it shall be determined by a vote of the Senate, without debate.

4. Every motion or resolution to print documents, reports, and other matter transmitted by the executive departments, or to print memorials, petitions, accompanying documents, or any other paper, except bills of the Senate or House of Representatives, resolutions submitted by a Senator, communications from the legislatures or conventions, lawfully called, of the respective States, shall, unless the Senate otherwise order, be referred to the Committee on Rules and Administration. When a motion is made to commit with instructions, it shall be in order to add thereto a motion to print.

5. Motions or resolutions to print additional numbers shall also be referred to the Committee on Rules and Administration; and when the committee shall report favorably, the report shall be accompanied by an estimate of the probable cost thereof; and when the cost of printing such additional numbers shall exceed the sum established by law, the concurrence of the House of Representatives shall be necessary for an order to print the same.

6. Every bill and joint resolution introduced or reported from a committee, and all bills and joint resolutions received from the House of Representatives, and all reports of committees, shall be printed, unless, for the dispatch of the business of the Senate, such printing may be dispensed with.

RULE XII: VOTING PROCEDURE

1. When the yeas and nays are ordered, the names of Senators shall be called alphabetically; and each Senator shall, without debate, declare his assent or

dissent to the question, unless excused by the Senate; and no Senator shall be permitted to vote after the decision shall have been announced by the Presiding Officer, but may for sufficient reasons, with unanimous consent, change or withdraw his vote. No motion to suspend this rule shall be in order, nor shall the Presiding Officer entertain any request to suspend it by unanimous consent.

2. When a Senator declines to vote on call of his name, he shall be required to assign his reasons therefor, and having assigned them, the Presiding Officer shall submit the question to the Senate: "Shall the Senator for the reasons assigned by him, be excused from voting?" which shall be decided without debate; and these proceedings shall be had after the roll call and before the result is announced; and any further proceedings in reference thereto shall be after such announcement.

3. A Member, notwithstanding any other provisions of this rule, may decline to vote, in committee or on the floor, on any matter when he believes that his voting on such a matter would be a conflict of interest.

4. No request by a Senator for unanimous consent for the taking of a final vote on a specified date upon the passage of a bill or joint resolution shall be submitted to the Senate for agreement thereto until after a quorum call ordered for the purpose by the Presiding Officer, it shall be disclosed that a quorum of the Senate is present; and when a unanimous consent is thus given the same shall operate as the order of the Senate, but any unanimous consent may be revoked by another unanimous consent granted in the manner prescribed above upon one day's notice.

RULE XIII: RECONSIDERATION

1. When a question has been decided by the Senate, any Senator voting with the prevailing side or who has not voted may, on the same day or on either of the next two days of actual session thereafter, move a reconsideration; and if the Senate shall refuse to reconsider such a motion entered, or if such a motion is withdrawn by leave of the Senate, or if upon reconsideration the Senate shall affirm its first decision, no further motion to reconsider shall be in order unless by unanimous consent. Every motion to reconsider shall be decided by a majority vote, and may be laid on the table without affecting the question in reference to which the same is made, which shall be a final disposition of the motion.

2. When a bill, resolution, report, amendment, order, or message, upon which a vote has been taken, shall have gone out of the possession of the Senate and been communicated to the House of Representatives, the motion to

reconsider shall be accompanied by a motion to request the House to return the same; which last motion shall be acted upon immediately, and without debate, and if determined in the negative shall be a final disposition of the motion to reconsider.

RULE XIV: BILLS, JOINT RESOLUTIONS, RESOLUTIONS, AND PREAMBLES THERETO

1. Whenever a bill or joint resolution shall be offered, its introduction shall, if objected to, be postponed for one day.

2. Every bill and joint resolution shall receive three readings previous to its passage which readings on demand of any Senator shall be on three different legislative days, and the Presiding Officer shall give notice at each reading whether it be the first, second, or third: Provided, That each reading may be by title only, unless the Senate in any case shall otherwise order.

3. No bill or joint resolution shall be committed or amended until it shall have been twice read, after which it may be referred to a committee; bills and joint resolutions introduced on leave, and bills and joint resolutions from the House of Representatives, shall be read once, and may be read twice, if not objected to, on the same day for reference, but shall not be considered on that day nor debated, except for reference, unless by unanimous consent.

4. Every bill and joint resolution reported from a committee, not having previously been read, shall be read once, and twice, if not objected to, on the same day, and placed on the Calendar in the order in which the same may be reported; and every bill and joint resolution introduced on leave, and every bill and joint resolution of the House of Representatives which shall have received a first and second reading without being referred to a committee, shall, if objection be made to further proceeding thereon, be placed on the Calendar.

5. All bills, amendments, and joint resolutions shall be examined under the supervision of the Secretary of the Senate before they go out of the possession of the Senate, and all bills and joint resolutions which shall have passed both Houses shall be examined under the supervision of the Secretary of the Senate, to see that the same are correctly enrolled, and, when signed by the Speaker of the House and the President of the Senate, the Secretary of the Senate shall forthwith present the same, when they shall have originated in the Senate, to the President of the United States and report the fact and date of such presentation to the Senate.

6. All other resolutions shall lie over one day for consideration, if not referred, unless by unanimous consent the Senate shall otherwise direct. When

objection is heard to the immediate consideration of a resolution or motion when it is submitted, it shall be placed on the Calendar under the heading of "Resolutions and Motions over, under the Rule," to be laid before the Senate on the next legislative day when there is no further morning business but before the close of morning business and before the termination of the morning hour.

7. When a bill or joint resolution shall have been ordered to be read a third time, it shall not be in order to propose amendments, unless by unanimous consent, but it shall be in order at any time before the passage of any bill or resolution to move its commitment; and when the bill or resolution shall again be reported from the committee it shall be placed on the Calendar.

8. When a bill or resolution is accompanied by a preamble, the question shall first be put on the bill or resolution and then on the preamble, which may be withdrawn by a mover before an amendment of the same, or ordering of the yeas and nays; or it may be laid on the table without prejudice to the bill or resolution, and shall be a final disposition of such preamble.

9. Whenever a private bill, except a bill for a pension, is under consideration, it shall be in order to move the adoption of a resolution to refer the bill to the Chief Commissioner of the Court of Claims for a report in conformity with section 2509 of title 28, United States Code.

10. No private bill or resolution (including so-called omnibus claims or pension bills), and no amendment to any bill or resolution, authorizing or directing (1) the payment of money for property damages, personal injuries, or death, for which a claim may be filed under chapter 171 of title 28, United States Code, or for a pension (other than to carry out a provision of law or treaty stipulation); (2) the construction of a bridge across a navigable stream; or (3) the correction of a military or naval record, shall be received or considered.

RULE XV: AMENDMENTS AND MOTIONS

1. All motions and amendments shall be reduced to writing, if desired by the Presiding Officer or by any Senator, and shall be read before the same shall be debated.

2. Any motion, amendment, or resolution may be withdrawn or modified by the mover at any time before a decision, amendment, or ordering of the yeas and nays, except a motion to reconsider, which shall not be withdrawn without leave.

3. If the question in debate contains several propositions, any Senator may have the same divided, except a motion to strike out and insert, which shall not be divided; but the rejection of a motion to strike out and insert one

proposition shall not prevent a motion to strike out and insert a different proposition; nor shall it prevent a motion simply to strike out; nor shall the rejection of a motion to strike out prevent a motion to strike out and insert. But pending a motion to strike out and insert, the part to be stricken out and the part to be inserted shall each be regarded for the purpose of amendment as a question, and motions to amend the part to be stricken out shall have precedence.

4. When an amendment proposed to any pending measure is laid on the table, it shall not carry with it, or prejudice, such measure.

5. It shall not be in order to consider any proposed committee amendment (other than a technical, clerical, or conforming amendment) which contains any significant matter not within the jurisdiction of the committee proposing such amendment.

RULE XVI: APPROPRIATIONS AND AMENDMENTS TO GENERAL APPROPRIATIONS BILLS

1. On a point of order made by any Senator, no amendments shall be received to any general appropriation bill the effect of which will be to increase an appropriation already contained in the bill, or to add a new item of appropriation, unless it be made to carry out the provisions of some existing law, or treaty stipulation, or act or resolution previously passed by the Senate during that session; or unless the same be moved by direction of the Committee on Appropriations or of a committee of the Senate having legislative jurisdiction of the subject matter, or proposed in pursuance of an estimate submitted in accordance with law.

2. The Committee on Appropriations shall not report an appropriation bill containing amendments to such bill proposing new or general legislation or any restriction on the expenditure of the funds appropriated which proposes a limitation not authorized by law if such restriction is to take effect or cease to be effective upon the happening of a contingency, and if an appropriation bill is reported to the Senate containing amendments to such bill proposing new or general legislation or any such restriction, a point of order may be made against the bill, and if the point is sustained, the bill shall be recommitted to the Committee on Appropriations.

3. All amendments to general appropriation bills moved by direction of a committee having legislative jurisdiction of the subject matter proposing to increase an appropriation already contained in the bill, or to add new items of appropriation, shall, at least one day before they are considered, be referred to the Committee on Appropriations, and when actually proposed to the bill

no amendment proposing to increase the amount stated in such amendment shall be received on a point of order made by any Senator.

4. On a point of order made by any Senator, no amendment offered by any other Senator which proposes general legislation shall be received to any general appropriation bill, nor shall any amendment not germane or relevant to the subject matter contained in the bill be received; nor shall any amendment to any item or clause of such bill be received which does not directly relate thereto; nor shall any restriction on the expenditure of the funds appropriated which proposes a limitation not authorized by law be received if such restriction is to take effect or cease to be effective upon the happening of a contingency; and all questions of relevancy of amendments under this rule, when raised, shall be submitted to the Senate and be decided without debate; and any such amendment or restriction to a general appropriation bill may be laid on the table without prejudice to the bill.

5. On a point of order made by any Senator, no amendment, the object of which is to provide for a private claim, shall be received to any general appropriation bill, unless it be to carry out the provisions of an existing law or a treaty stipulation, which shall be cited on the face of the amendment.

6. When a point of order is made against any restriction on the expenditure of funds appropriated in a general appropriation bill on the ground that the restriction violates this rule, the rule shall be construed strictly and, in case of doubt, in favor of the point of order.

7. Every report on general appropriation bills filed by the Committee on Appropriations shall identify with particularity each recommended amendment which proposes an item of appropriation which is not made to carry out the provisions of an existing law, a treaty stipulation, or an act or resolution previously passed by the Senate during that session.

8. On a point of order made by any Senator, no general appropriation bill or amendment thereto shall be received or considered if it contains a provision reappropriating unexpended balances of appropriations; except that this provision shall not apply to appropriations in continuation of appropriations for public works on which work has commenced.

RULE XVII: REFERENCE TO COMMITTEES; MOTIONS TO DISCHARGE; REPORTS OF COMMITTEES; AND HEARINGS AVAILABLE

1. Except as provided in paragraph 3, in any case in which a controversy arises as to the jurisdiction of any committee with respect to any proposed legislation, the question of jurisdiction shall be decided by the presiding officer, without

debate, in favor of the committee which has jurisdiction over the subject matter which predominates in such proposed legislation; but such decision shall be subject to an appeal.

2. A motion simply to refer shall not be open to amendment, except to add instructions.

3. (a) Upon motion by both the majority leader or his designee and the minority leader or his designee, proposed legislation may be referred to two or more committees jointly or sequentially. Notice of such motion and the proposed legislation to which it relates shall be printed in the Congressional Record. The motion shall be privileged, but it shall not be in order until the Congressional Record in which the notice is printed has been available to Senators for at least twenty-four hours. No amendment to any such motion shall be in order except amendments to any instructions contained therein. Debate on any such motion, and all amendments thereto and debatable motions and appeals in connection therewith, shall be limited to not more than two hours, the time to be equally divided between, and controlled by, the majority leader and the minority leader or their designees.

(b) Proposed legislation which is referred to two or more committees jointly may be reported only by such committees jointly and only one report may accompany any proposed legislation so jointly reported.

(c) A motion to refer any proposed legislation to two or more committees sequentially shall specify the order of referral.

(d) Any motion under this paragraph may specify the portion or portions of proposed legislation to be considered by the committees, or any of them, to which such proposed legislation is referred, and such committees or committee shall be limited, in the consideration of such proposed legislation, to the portion or portions so specified.

(e) Any motion under this subparagraph may contain instructions with respect to the time allowed for consideration by the committees, or any of them, to which proposed legislation is referred and the discharge of such committees, or any of them, from further consideration of such proposed legislation.

4. (a) All reports of committees and motions to discharge a committee from the consideration of a subject, and all subjects from which a committee shall be discharged, shall lie over one day for consideration, unless by unanimous consent the Senate shall otherwise direct.

(b) Whenever any committee (except the Committee on Appropriations) has reported any measure, by action taken in conformity with the requirements of paragraph 7 of rule XXVI, no point of order shall lie with respect to that measure on the ground that hearings upon that measure by the committee were not conducted in accordance with the provisions of paragraph 4 of rule XXVI.

5. Any measure or matter reported by any standing committee shall not be considered in the Senate unless the report of that committee upon that measure or matter has been available to Members for at least two calendar days (excluding Sundays and legal holidays) prior to the consideration of that measure or matter. If hearings have been held on any such measure or matter so reported, the committee reporting the measure or matter shall make every reasonable effort to have such hearings printed and available for distribution to the Members of the Senate prior to the consideration of such measure or matter in the Senate. This paragraph

(1) may be waived by joint agreement of the Majority Leader and the Minority Leader of the Senate; and

(2) shall not apply to

(A) any measure for the declaration of war, or the declaration of a national emergency, by the Congress, and

(B) any executive decision, determination, or action which would become, or continue to be, effective unless disapproved or otherwise invalidated by one or both Houses of Congress.

RULE XVIII: BUSINESS CONTINUED FROM SESSION TO SESSION

At the second or any subsequent session of a Congress the legislative business of the Senate which remained undetermined at the close of the next preceding session of that Congress shall be resumed and proceeded with in the same manner as if no adjournment of the Senate had taken place.

RULE XIX: DEBATE

1. (a) When a Senator desires to speak, he shall rise and address the Presiding Officer, and shall not proceed until he is recognized, and the Presiding Officer shall recognize the Senator who shall first address him. No Senator shall interrupt another Senator in debate without his consent, and to obtain such consent he shall first address the Presiding Officer, and no Senator shall speak more than twice upon any one question in debate on the same legislative day without leave of the Senate, which shall be determined without debate.

(b) At the conclusion of the morning hour at the beginning of a new legislative day or after the unfinished business or any pending business has first been laid before the Senate on any calendar day, and until after the duration of three hours of actual session after such business is laid down except as determined to the contrary by unanimous consent or on motion without debate, all debate shall be germane and confined to the specific question then pending before the Senate.

2. No Senator in debate shall, directly or indirectly, by any form of words impute to another Senator or to other Senators any conduct or motive unworthy or unbecoming a Senator.

3. No Senator in debate shall refer offensively to any State of the Union.

4. If any Senator, in speaking or otherwise, in the opinion of the Presiding Officer transgress the rules of the Senate the Presiding Officer shall, either on his own motion or at the request of any other Senator, call him to order; and when a Senator shall be called to order he shall take his seat, and may not proceed without leave of the Senate, which, if granted, shall be upon motion that he be allowed to proceed in order, which motion shall be determined without debate. Any Senator directed by the Presiding Officer to take his seat, and any Senator requesting the Presiding Officer to require a Senator to take his seat, may appeal from the ruling of the Chair, which appeal shall be open to debate.

5. If a Senator be called to order for words spoken in debate, upon the demand of the Senator or of any other Senator, the exceptionable words shall be taken down in writing, and read at the table for the information of the Senate.

6. Whenever confusion arises in the Chamber or the galleries, or demonstrations of approval or disapproval are indulged in by the occupants of the galleries, it shall be the duty of the Chair to enforce order on his own initiative and without any point of order being made by a Senator.

7. No Senator shall introduce to or bring to the attention of the Senate during its sessions any occupant in the galleries of the Senate. No motion to suspend this rule shall be in order, nor may the Presiding Officer entertain any request to suspend it by unanimous consent.

8. Former Presidents of the United States shall be entitled to address the Senate upon appropriate notice to the Presiding Officer who shall thereupon make the necessary arrangements.

RULE XX: QUESTIONS OF ORDER

1. A question of order may be raised at any stage of the proceedings, except when the Senate is voting or ascertaining the presence of a quorum, and, unless submitted to the Senate, shall be decided by the Presiding Officer without debate, subject to an appeal to the Senate. When an appeal is taken, any subsequent question of order which may arise before the decision of such appeal shall be decided by the Presiding Officer without debate; and every appeal therefrom shall be decided at once, and without debate; and any appeal

may be laid on the table without prejudice to the pending proposition, and thereupon shall be held as affirming the decision of the Presiding Officer.

2. The Presiding Officer may submit any question of order for the decision of the Senate.

RULE XXI: SESSION WITH CLOSED DOORS

1. On a motion made and seconded to close the doors of the Senate, on the discussion of any business which may, in the opinion of a Senator, require secrecy, the Presiding Officer shall direct the galleries to be cleared; and during the discussion of such motion the doors shall remain closed.

2. When the Senate meets in closed session, any applicable provisions of rules XXIX and XXXI, including the confidentiality of information shall apply to any information and to the conduct of any debate transacted.

RULE XXII: PRECEDENCE OF MOTIONS

1. When a question is pending, no motion shall be received but
    To adjourn.
    To adjourn to a day certain, or that when the Senate adjourn it shall be to a day certain.
    To take a recess.
    To proceed to the consideration of executive business.
    To lay on the table.
    To postpone indefinitely.
    To postpone to a day certain.
    To commit.
    To amend.
Which several motions shall have precedence as they stand arranged; and the motions relating to adjournment, to take a recess, to proceed to the consideration of executive business, to lay on the table, shall be decided without debate.

2. Notwithstanding the provisions of rule II or rule IV or any other rule of the Senate, at any time a motion signed by sixteen Senators, to bring to a close the debate upon any measure, motion, other matter pending before the Senate, or the unfinished business, is presented to the Senate, the Presiding Officer, or clerk at the direction of the Presiding Officer, shall at once state the motion to the Senate, and one hour after the Senate meets on the following calendar day but one, he shall lay the motion before the Senate and direct that

the clerk call the roll, and upon the ascertainment that a quorum is present, the Presiding Officer shall, without debate, submit to the Senate by a yea-and-nay vote the question:

"Is it the sense of the Senate that the debate shall be brought to a close?" And if that question shall be decided in the affirmative by three-fifths of the Senators duly chosen and sworn—except on a measure or motion to amend the Senate rules, in which case the necessary affirmative vote shall be two-thirds of the Senators present and voting—then said measure, motion, or other matter pending before the Senate, or the unfinished business, shall be the unfinished business to the exclusion of all other business until disposed of.

Thereafter no Senator shall be entitled to speak in all more than one hour on the measure, motion, or other matter pending before the Senate, or the unfinished business, the amendments thereto, and motions affecting the same, and it shall be the duty of the Presiding Officer to keep the time of each Senator who speaks. Except by unanimous consent, no amendment shall be proposed after the vote to bring the debate to a close, unless it had been submitted in writing to the Journal Clerk by 1 o'clock P.M. on the day following the filing of the cloture motion if an amendment in the first degree, and unless it had been so submitted at least one hour prior to the beginning of the cloture vote if an amendment in the second degree. No dilatory motion, or dilatory amendment, or amendment not germane shall be in order. Points of order, including questions of relevancy, and appeals from the decision of the Presiding Officer, shall be decided without debate.

After no more than thirty hours of consideration of the measure, motion, or other matter on which cloture has been invoked, the Senate shall proceed, without any further debate on any question, to vote on the final disposition thereof to the exclusion of all amendments not then actually pending before the Senate at that time and to the exclusion of all motions, except a motion to table, or to reconsider and one quorum call on demand to establish the presence of a quorum (and motions required to establish a quorum) immediately before the final vote begins. The thirty hours may be increased by the adoption of a motion, decided without debate, by a three-fifths affirmative vote of the Senators duly chosen and sworn, and any such time thus agreed upon shall be equally divided between and controlled by the Majority and Minority Leaders or their designees. However, only one motion to extend time, specified above, may be made in any one calendar day.

If, for any reason, a measure or matter is reprinted after cloture has been invoked, amendments which were in order prior to the reprinting of the measure or matter will continue to be in order and may be conformed and reprinted at the request of the amendment's sponsor. The conforming changes must be limited to lineation and pagination.

No Senator shall call up more than two amendments until every other Senator shall have had the opportunity to do likewise.

Notwithstanding other provisions of this rule, a Senator may yield all or part of his one hour to the majority or minority floor managers of the measure, motion, or matter or to the Majority or Minority Leader, but each Senator specified shall not have more than two hours so yielded to him and may in turn yield such time to other Senators.

Notwithstanding any other provision of this rule, any Senator who has not used or yielded at least ten minutes, is, if he seeks recognition, guaranteed up to ten minutes, inclusive, to speak only.

After cloture is invoked, the reading of any amendment, including House amendments, shall be dispensed with when the proposed amendment has been identified and has been available in printed form at the desk of the Members for not less than twenty-four hours.

RULE XXIII: PRIVILEGE OF THE FLOOR

Other than the Vice President and Senators, no person shall be admitted to the floor of the Senate while in session, except as follows:

The President of the United States and his private secretary.

The President elect and Vice President elect of the United States.

Ex-Presidents and ex–Vice Presidents of the United States.

Judges of the Supreme Court.

Ex-Senators and Senators elect.

The officers and employees of the Senate in the discharge of their official duties.

Ex-Secretaries and ex–Sergeants at Arms of the Senate.

Members of the House of Representatives and Members elect.

Ex-Speakers of the House of Representatives.

The Sergeant at Arms of the House and his chief deputy and the Clerk of the House and his deputy.

Heads of the Executive Departments.

Ambassadors and Ministers of the United States.

Governors of States and Territories.

Members of the Joint Chiefs of Staff.

The General Commanding the Army.

The Senior Admiral of the Navy on the active list.

Members of National Legislatures of foreign countries and Members of the European Parliament.

Judges of the Court of Claims.

The Mayor of the District of Columbia.

The Librarian of Congress and the Assistant Librarian in charge of the Law Library.

The Architect of the Capitol.

The Chaplain of the House of Representatives.

The Secretary of the Smithsonian Institution.

The Parliamentarian Emeritus of the Senate.

Members of the staffs of committees of the Senate and joint committees of the Congress when in the discharge of their official duties and employees in the office of a Senator when in the discharge of their official duties (but in each case subject to such rules or regulations as may be prescribed by the Committee on Rules and Administration). Senate committee staff members and employees in the office of a Senator must be on the payroll of the Senate and members of joint committee staffs must be on the payroll of the Senate or the House of Representatives.

RULE XXIV: APPOINTMENT OF COMMITTEES

1. In the appointment of the standing committees, or to fill vacancies thereon, the Senate, unless otherwise ordered, shall by resolution appoint the chairman of each such committee and the other members thereof. On demand of any Senator, a separate vote shall be had on the appointment of the chairman of any such committee and on the appointment of the other members thereof. Each such resolution shall be subject to amendment and to division of the question.

2. On demand of one-fifth of the Senators present, a quorum being present, any vote taken pursuant to paragraph 1 shall be by ballot.

3. Except as otherwise provided or unless otherwise ordered, all other committees, and the chairmen thereof, shall be appointed in the same manner as standing committees.

4. When a chairman of a committee shall resign or cease to serve on a committee, action by the Senate to fill the vacancy in such committee, unless specially otherwise ordered, shall be only to fill up the number of members of the committee, and the election of a new chairman.

RULE XXV: STANDING COMMITTEES

1. The following standing committees shall be appointed at the commencement of each Congress, and shall continue and have the power to act until

their successors are appointed, with leave to report by bill or otherwise on matters within their respective jurisdictions:

(a)(1) Committee on Agriculture, Nutrition, and Forestry, to which committee shall be referred all proposed legislation, messages, petitions, memorials, and other matters relating primarily to the following subjects:

1. Agricultural economics and research.
2. Agricultural extension services and experiment stations.
3. Agricultural production, marketing, and stabilization of prices.
4. Agriculture and agricultural commodities.
5. Animal industry and diseases.
6. Crop insurance and soil conservation.
7. Farm credit and farm security.
8. Food from fresh waters.
9. Food stamp programs.
10. Forestry, and forest reserves and wilderness areas other than those created from the public domain.
11. Home economics.
12. Human nutrition.
13. Inspection of livestock, meat, and agricultural products.
14. Pests and pesticides.
15. Plant industry, soils, and agricultural engineering.
16. Rural development, rural electrification, and watersheds.
17. School nutrition programs.

(2) Such committee shall also study and review, on a comprehensive basis, matters relating to food, nutrition, and hunger, both in the United States and in foreign countries, and rural affairs, and report thereon from time to time.

(b) Committee on Appropriations, to which committee shall be referred all proposed legislation, messages, petitions, memorials, and other matters relating to the following subjects:

1. Appropriation of the revenue for the support of the Government, except as provided in subparagraph (e).
2. Rescission of appropriations contained in appropriation acts (referred to in section 105 of title 1, United States Code).
3. The amount of new spending authority described in section 401(c)(2) (A) and (B) of the Congressional Budget Act of 1974 which is to be effective for a fiscal year.
4. New spending authority described in section 401(c)(2)(C) of the Congressional Budget Act of 1974 provided in bills and resolutions referred to the committee under section 401(b)(2) of that Act (but subject to the provisions of section 401(b)(3) of that Act).

(c)(1) Committee on Armed Services, to which committee shall be referred all proposed legislation, messages, petitions, memorials, and other matters relating to the following subjects:

1. Aeronautical and space activities peculiar to or primarily associated with the development of weapons systems or military operations.

2. Common defense.

3. Department of Defense, the Department of the Army, the Department of the Navy, and the Department of the Air Force, generally.

4. Maintenance and operation of the Panama Canal, including administration, sanitation, and government of the Canal Zone.

5. Military research and development.

6. National security aspects of nuclear energy.

7. Naval petroleum reserves, except those in Alaska.

8. Pay, promotion, retirement, and other benefits and privileges of members of the Armed Forces, including overseas education of civilian and military dependents.

9. Selective service system.

10. Strategic and critical materials necessary for the common defense.

(2) Such committee shall also study and review, on a comprehensive basis, matters relating to the common defense policy of the United States, and report thereon from time to time.

(d)(1) Committee on Banking, Housing, and Urban Affairs, to which committee shall be referred all proposed legislation, messages, petitions, memorials, and other matters relating to the following subjects:

1. Banks, banking, and financial institutions.

2. Control of prices of commodities, rents, and services.

3. Deposit insurance.

4. Economic stabilization and defense production.

5. Export and foreign trade promotion.

6. Export controls.

7. Federal monetary policy, including Federal Reserve System.

8. Financial aid to commerce and industry.

9. Issuance and redemption of notes.

10. Money and credit, including currency and coinage.

11. Nursing home construction.

12. Public and private housing (including veterans' housing).

13. Renegotiation of Government contracts.

14. Urban development and urban mass transit.

(2) Such committee shall also study and review, on a comprehensive basis, matters relating to international economic policy as it affects United States monetary affairs, credit, and financial institutions; economic growth, urban affairs, and credit, and report thereon from time to time.

(e)(1) Committee on the Budget, to which committee shall be referred all concurrent resolutions on the budget (as defined in section 3(a)(4) of the Congressional Budget Act of 1974) and all other matters required to be referred to that committee under titles III and IV of that Act, and messages, petitions, memorials, and other matters relating thereto.

(2) Such committee shall have the duty

(A) to report the matters required to be reported by it under titles III and IV of the Congressional Budget Act of 1974;

(B) to make continuing studies of the effect on budget outlays of relevant existing and proposed legislation and to report the results of such studies to the Senate on a recurring basis;

(C) to request and evaluate continuing studies of tax expenditures, to devise methods of coordinating tax expenditures, policies, and programs with direct budget outlays, and to report the results of such studies to the Senate on a recurring basis; and

(D) to review, on a continuing basis, the conduct by the Congressional Budget Office of its functions and duties.

(f)(1) Committee on Commerce, Science, and Transportation, to which committee shall be referred all proposed legislation, messages, petitions, memorials, and other matters relating to the following subjects:

1. Coast Guard.

2. Coastal zone management.

3. Communications.

4. Highway safety.

5. Inland waterways, except construction.

6. Interstate commerce.

7. Marine and ocean navigation, safety, and transportation, including navigational aspects of deepwater ports.

8. Marine fisheries.

9. Merchant marine and navigation.

10. Nonmilitary aeronautical and space sciences.

11. Oceans, weather, and atmospheric activities.

12. Panama Canal and interoceanic canals generally, except as provided in subparagraph (c).

13. Regulation of consumer products and services, including testing related to toxic substances, other than pesticides, and except for credit, financial services, and housing.

14. Regulation of interstate common carriers, including railroads, buses, trucks, vessels, pipelines, and civil aviation.

15. Science, engineering, and technology research and development and policy.

16. Sports.

17. Standards and measurement.

18. Transportation.

19. Transportation and commerce aspects of Outer Continental Shelf lands.

(2) Such committee shall also study and review, on a comprehensive basis, all matters relating to science and technology, oceans policy, transportation, communications, and consumer affairs, and report thereon from time to time.

(g)(1) Committee on Energy and Natural Resources, to which committee shall be referred all proposed legislation, messages, petitions, memorials, and other matters relating to the following subjects:

1. Coal production, distribution, and utilization.

2. Energy policy.

3. Energy regulation and conservation.

4. Energy related aspects of deepwater ports.

5. Energy research and development.

6. Extraction of minerals from oceans and Outer Continental Shelf lands.

7. Hydroelectric power, irrigation, and reclamation.

8. Mining education and research.

9. Mining, mineral lands, mining claims, and mineral conservation.

10. National parks, recreation areas, wilderness areas, wild and scenic rivers, historical sites, military parks and battlefields, and on the public domain, preservation of prehistoric ruins and objects of interest.

11. Naval petroleum reserves in Alaska.

12. Nonmilitary development of nuclear energy.

13. Oil and gas production and distribution.

14. Public lands and forests, including farming and grazing thereon, and mineral extraction therefrom.

15. Solar energy systems.

16. Territorial possessions of the United States, including trusteeships.

(2) Such committee shall also study and review, on a comprehensive basis, matters relating to energy and resources development, and report thereon from time to time.

(h)(1) Committee on Environment and Public Works, to which committee shall be referred all proposed legislation, messages, petitions, memorials, and other matters relating to the following subjects:

1. Air pollution.

2. Construction and maintenance of highways.

3. Environmental aspects of Outer Continental Shelf lands.

4. Environmental effects of toxic substances, other than pesticides.

5. Environmental policy.

6. Environmental research and development.

7. Fisheries and wildlife.

8. Flood control and improvements of rivers and harbors, including environmental aspects of deepwater ports.

9. Noise pollution.

10. Nonmilitary environmental regulation and control of nuclear energy.

11. Ocean dumping.

12. Public buildings and improved grounds of the United States generally, including Federal buildings in the District of Columbia.

13. Public works, bridges, and dams.

14. Regional economic development.

15. Solid waste disposal and recycling.

16. Water pollution.

17. Water resources.

(2) Such committee shall also study and review, on a comprehensive basis, matters relating to environmental protection and resource utilization and conservation, and report thereon from time to time.

(i) Committee on Finance, to which committee shall be referred all proposed legislation, messages, petitions, memorials, and other matters relating to the following subjects:

1. Bonded debt of the United States, except as provided in the Congressional Budget Act of 1974.

2. Customs, collection districts, and ports of entry and delivery.

3. Deposit of public moneys.

4. General revenue sharing.

5. Health programs under the Social Security Act and health programs financed by a specific tax or trust fund.

6. National social security.

7. Reciprocal trade agreements.

8. Revenue measures generally, except as provided in the Congressional Budget Act of 1974.

9. Revenue measures relating to the insular possessions.

10. Tariffs and import quotas, and matters related thereto.

11. Transportation of dutiable goods.

(j)(1) Committee on Foreign Relations, to which committee shall be referred all proposed legislation, messages, petitions, memorials, and other matters relating to the following subjects:

1. Acquisition of land and buildings for embassies and legations in foreign countries.

2. Boundaries of the United States.

3. Diplomatic service.

4. Foreign economic, military, technical, and humanitarian assistance.

5. Foreign loans.

6. International activities of the American National Red Cross and the International Committee of the Red Cross.

7. International aspects of nuclear energy, including nuclear transfer policy.

8. International conferences and congresses.

9. International law as it relates to foreign policy.

10. International Monetary Fund and other international organizations established primarily for international monetary purposes (except that, at the request of the Committee on Banking, Housing, and Urban Affairs, any proposed legislation relating to such subjects reported by the Committee on Foreign Relations shall be referred to the Committee on Banking, Housing, and Urban Affairs).

11. Intervention abroad and declarations of war.

12. Measures to foster commercial intercourse with foreign nations and to safeguard American business interests abroad.

13. National security and international aspects of trusteeships of the United States.

14. Oceans and international environmental and scientific affairs as they relate to foreign policy.

15. Protection of United States citizens abroad and expatriation.

16. Relations of the United States with foreign nations generally.

17. Treaties and executive agreements, except reciprocal trade agreements.

18. United Nations and its affiliated organizations.

19. World Bank group, the regional development banks, and other international organizations established primarily for development assistance purposes.

(2) Such committee shall also study and review, on a comprehensive basis, matters relating to the national security policy, foreign policy, and international economic policy as it relates to foreign policy of the United States, and matters relating to food, hunger, and nutrition in foreign countries, and report thereon from time to time.

(k)(1) Committee on Governmental Affairs, to which committee shall be referred all proposed legislation, messages, petitions, memorials, and other matters relating to the following subjects:

1. Archives of the United States.

2. Budget and accounting measures, other than appropriations, except as provided in the Congressional Budget Act of 1974.

3. Census and collection of statistics, including economic and social statistics.

4. Congressional organization, except for any part of the matter that amends the rules or orders of the Senate.

5. Federal Civil Service.

6. Government information.

7. Intergovernmental relations.

8. Municipal affairs of the District of Columbia, except appropriations therefor.

9. Organization and management of United States nuclear export policy.

10. Organization and reorganization of the executive branch of the Government.

11. Postal Service.

12. Status of officers and employees of the United States, including their classification, compensation, and benefits.

(2) Such committee shall have the duty of

(A) receiving and examining reports of the Comptroller General of the United States and of submitting such recommendations to the Senate as it deems necessary or desirable in connection with the subject matter of such reports;

(B) studying the efficiency, economy, and effectiveness of all agencies and departments of the Government;

(C) evaluating the effects of laws enacted to reorganize the legislative and executive branches of the Government; and

(D) studying the intergovernmental relationships between the United States and the States and municipalities, and between the United States and international organizations of which the United States is a member.

(l) Committee on the Judiciary, to which committee shall be referred all proposed legislation, messages, petitions, memorials, and other matters relating to the following subjects:

1. Apportionment of Representatives.

2. Bankruptcy, mutiny, espionage, and counterfeiting.

3. Civil liberties.

4. Constitutional amendments.

5. Federal courts and judges.

6. Government information.

7. Holidays and celebrations.

8. Immigration and naturalization.

9. Interstate compacts generally.

10. Judicial proceedings, civil and criminal, generally.

11. Local courts in the territories and possessions.

12. Measures relating to claims against the United States.

13. National penitentiaries.

14. Patent Office.

15. Patents, copyrights, and trademarks.

16. Protection of trade and commerce against unlawful restraints and monopolies.

17. Revision and codification of the statutes of the United States.

18. State and territorial boundary lines.

(m)(1) Committee on Health, Education, Labor and Pensions, to which committee shall be referred all proposed legislation, messages, petitions, memorials, and other matters relating to the following subjects:

1. Measures relating to education, labor, health, and public welfare.

2. Aging.

3. Agricultural colleges.

4. Arts and humanities.

5. Biomedical research and development.

6. Child labor.

7. Convict labor and the entry of goods made by convicts into interstate commerce.

8. Domestic activities of the American National Red Cross.

9. Equal employment opportunity.

10. Gallaudet College, Howard University, and Saint Elizabeth's Hospital.

11. Individuals with disabilities.

12. Labor standards and labor statistics.

13. Mediation and arbitration of labor disputes.

14. Occupational safety and health, including the welfare of miners.

15. Private pension plans.

16. Public health.

17. Railway labor and retirement.

18. Regulation of foreign laborers.

19. Student loans.

20. Wages and hours of labor.

(2) Such committee shall also study and review, on a comprehensive basis, matters relating to health, education and training, and public welfare, and report thereon from time to time.

(n)(1) Committee on Rules and Administration, to which committee shall be referred all proposed legislation, messages, petitions, memorials, and other matters relating to the following subjects:

1. Administration of the Senate Office Buildings and the Senate wing of the Capitol, including the assignment of office space.

2. Congressional organization relative to rules and procedures, and Senate rules and regulations, including floor and gallery rules.

3. Corrupt practices.

4. Credentials and qualifications of Members of the Senate, contested elections, and acceptance of incompatible offices.

5. Federal elections generally, including the election of the President, Vice President, and Members of the Congress.

6. Government Printing Office, and the printing and correction of the Congressional Record, as well as those matters provided for under rule XI.

7. Meetings of the Congress and attendance of Members.

8. Payment of money out of the contingent fund of the Senate or creating a charge upon the same (except that any resolution relating to substantive matter within the jurisdiction of any other standing committee of the Senate shall be first referred to such committee).

9. Presidential succession.

10. Purchase of books and manuscripts and erection of monuments to the memory of individuals.

11. Senate Library and statuary, art, and pictures in the Capitol and Senate Office Buildings.

12. Services to the Senate, including the Senate restaurant.

13. United States Capitol and congressional office buildings, the Library of Congress, the Smithsonian Institution (and the incorporation of similar institutions), and the Botanic Gardens.

(2) Such committee shall also

(A) make a continuing study of the organization and operation of the Congress of the United States and shall recommend improvements in such organization and operation with a view toward strengthening the Congress, simplifying its operations, improving its relationships with other branches of the United States Government, and enabling it better to meet its responsibilities under the Constitution of the United States;

(B) identify any court proceeding or action which, in the opinion of the Committee, is of vital interest to the Congress as a constitutionally established institution of the Federal Government and call such proceeding or action to the attention of the Senate; and develop, implement, and update as necessary a strategy planning process and a strategic plan for the functional and technical infrastructure support of the Senate and provide oversight over plans developed by Senate officers and others in accordance with the strategic planning process.

(o)(1) Committee on Small Business, to which committee shall be referred all proposed legislation, messages, petitions, memorials, and other matters relating to the Small Business Administration.

(2) Any proposed legislation reported by such committee which relates to matters other than the functions of the Small Business Administration shall, at the request of the chairman of any standing committee having jurisdiction over the subject matter extraneous to the functions of the Small Business Administration, be considered and reported by such standing committee prior to its consideration by the Senate; and likewise measures reported by other committees directly relating to the Small Business Administration shall, at

the request of the chairman of the Committee on Small Business, be referred to the Committee on Small Business for its consideration of any portions of the measure dealing with the Small Business Administration, and be reported by this committee prior to its consideration by the Senate.

(3) Such committee shall also study and survey by means of research and investigation all problems of American small business enterprises, and report thereon from time to time.

(p) Committee on Veterans' Affairs, to which committee shall be referred all proposed legislation, messages, petitions, memorials, and other matters relating to the following subjects:

1. Compensation of veterans.

2. Life insurance issued by the Government on account of service in the Armed Forces.

3. National cemeteries.

4. Pensions of all wars of the United States, general and special.

5. Readjustment of servicemen to civil life.

6. Soldiers' and sailors' civil relief.

7. Veterans' hospitals, medical care and treatment of veterans.

8. Veterans' measures generally.

9. Vocational rehabilitation and education of veterans.

2. Except as otherwise provided by paragraph 4 of this rule, each of the following standing committees shall consist of the number of Senators set forth in the following table on the line on which the name of that committee appears:

Committee / Members
Agriculture, Nutrition, and Forestry / 18
Appropriations / 28
Armed Services / 18
Banking, Housing, and Urban Affairs / 18
Commerce, Science, and Transportation / 20
Energy and Natural Resources / 20
Environment and Public Works / 18
Finance / 20
Foreign Relations / 18
Governmental Affairs / 16
Judiciary / 18
H.E.L.P. / 18

3. (a) Except as otherwise provided by paragraph 4 of this rule, each of the following standing committees shall consist of the number of Senators set forth in the following table on the line on which the name of that committee appears:

Committee / Members
Budget / 22
Rules and Administration / 16
Veterans' Affairs / 12
Small Business / 18

(b) Each of the following committees and joint committees shall consist of the number of Senators (or Senate members, in the case of a joint committee) set forth in the following table on the line on which the name of that committee appears:

Committee / Members
Aging / 18
Intelligence / 19
Joint Economic Committee / 10

(c) Each of the following committees and joint committees shall consist of the number of Senators (or Senate members, in the case of a joint committee) set forth in the following table on the line on which the name of that committee appears:

Committee / Members
Ethics / 6
Indian Affairs / 14
Joint Committee on Taxation / 5

4. (a) Except as otherwise provided by this paragraph

(1) each Senator shall serve on two and no more committees listed in paragraph 2; and

(2) each Senator may serve on only one committee listed in paragraph 3 (a) or (b).

(b)(1) Each Senator may serve on not more than three subcommittees of each committee (other than the Committee on Appropriations) listed in paragraph 2 of which he is a member.

(2) Each Senator may serve on not more than two subcommittees of a committee listed in paragraph 3 (a) or (b) of which he is a member.

(3) Notwithstanding subparagraphs (1) and (2), a Senator serving as chairman or ranking minority member of a standing, select, or special committee of the Senate or joint committee of the Congress may serve ex officio, without vote, as a member of any subcommittee of such committee or joint committee.

(4) No committee of the Senate may establish any subunit of that committee other than a subcommittee, unless the Senate by resolution has given permission therefor. For purposes of this subparagraph, any subunit of a joint committee shall be treated as a subcommittee.

(c) By agreement entered into by the majority leader and the minority leader, the membership of one or more standing committees may be increased temporarily from time to time by such number or numbers as may be required to accord to the majority party a majority of the membership of all standing committees. When any such temporary increase is necessary to accord to the majority party a majority of the membership of all standing committees, members of the majority party in such number as may be required for that purpose may serve as members of three standing committees listed in paragraph 2. No such temporary increase in the membership of any standing committee under this subparagraph shall be continued in effect after the need therefor has ended. No standing committee may be increased in membership under this subparagraph by more than two members in excess of the number prescribed for that committee by paragraph 2 or 3(a).

(d) A Senator may serve as a member of any joint committee of the Congress the Senate members of which are required by law to be appointed from a standing committee of the Senate of which he is a member, and service as a member of any such joint committee shall not be taken into account for purposes of subparagraph (a)(2).

(e)(1) No Senator shall serve at any time as chairman of more than one standing, select, or special committee of the Senate or joint committee of the Congress, except that a Senator may serve as chairman of any joint committee of the Congress having jurisdiction with respect to a subject matter which is directly related to the jurisdiction of a standing committee of which he is chairman.

(2) No Senator shall serve at any time as chairman of more than one subcommittee of each standing, select, or special committee of the Senate or joint committee of the Congress of which he is a member.

(3) A Senator who is serving as the chairman of a committee listed in paragraph 2 may serve at any time as the chairman of only one subcommittee of all committees listed in paragraph 2 of which he is a member and may serve at any time as the chairman of only one subcommittee of each committee listed in paragraph 3 (a) or (b) of which he is a member. A Senator who is serving as the chairman of a committee listed in paragraph 3 (a) or (b) may not serve as the chairman of any subcommittee of that committee, and may serve at any time as the chairman of only one subcommittee of each committee listed in paragraph 2 of which he is a member. Any other Senator may serve as the chairman of only one subcommittee of each committee listed in paragraph 2, 3(a), or 3(b) of which he is a member.

(f) A Senator serving on the Committee on Rules and Administration may not serve on any joint committee of the Congress unless the Senate members thereof are required by law to be appointed from the Committee on Rules and

Administration, or unless such Senator served on the Committee on Rules and Administration and the Joint Committee on Taxation on the last day of the Ninety-eighth Congress.

(g) A Senator who on the day preceding the effective date of title I of the Committee System Reorganization Amendments of 1977 was serving as the chairman or ranking minority member of the Committee on the District of Columbia or the Committee on Post Office and Civil Service may serve on the Committee on Governmental Affairs in addition to serving on two other standing committees listed in paragraph 2. At the request of any such Senator, he shall be appointed to serve on such committee but, while serving on such committee and two other standing committees listed in paragraph 2, he may not serve on any committee listed in paragraph 3 (a) or (b) other than the Committee on Rules and Administration. The preceding provisions of this subparagraph shall apply with respect to any Senator only so long as his service as a member of the Committee on Governmental Affairs is continuous after the date on which the appointment of the majority and minority members of the Committee on Governmental Affairs is initially completed.

RULE XXVI: COMMITTEE PROCEDURE

1. Each standing committee, including any subcommittee of any such committee, is authorized to hold such hearings, to sit and act at such times and places during the sessions, recesses, and adjourned periods of the Senate, to require by subpoena or otherwise the attendance of such witnesses and the production of such correspondence, books, papers, and documents, to take such testimony and to make such expenditures out of the contingent fund of the Senate as may be authorized by resolutions of the Senate. Each such committee may make investigations into any matter within its jurisdiction, may report such hearings as may be had by it, and may employ stenographic assistance at a cost not exceeding the amount prescribed by the Committee on Rules and Administration. The expenses of the committee shall be paid from the contingent fund of the Senate upon vouchers approved by the chairman.

2. Each committee shall adopt rules (not inconsistent with the Rules of the Senate) governing the procedure of such committee. The rules of each committee shall be published in the Congressional Record not later than March 1 of the first year of each Congress, except that if any such committee is established on or after February 1 of a year, the rules of that committee during the year of establishment shall be published in the Congressional Record not later than sixty days after such establishment. Any amendment to the rules of a committee shall not take effect until the amendment is published in the Congressional Record.

3. Each standing committee (except the Committee on Appropriations) shall fix regular weekly, biweekly, or monthly meeting days for the transaction of business before the committee and additional meetings may be called by the chairman as he may deem necessary. If at least three members of any such committee desire that a special meeting of the committee be called by the chairman, those members may file in the offices of the committee their written request to the chairman for that special meeting. Immediately upon the filing of the request, the clerk of the committee shall notify the chairman of the filing of the request. If, within three calendar days after the filing of the request, the chairman does not call the requested special meeting, to be held within seven calendar days after the filing of the request, a majority of the members of the committee may file in the offices of the committee their written notice that a special meeting of the committee will be held, specifying the date and hour of that special meeting. The committee shall meet on that date and hour. Immediately upon the filing of the notice, the clerk of the committee shall notify all members of the committee that such special meeting will be held and inform them of its date and hour. If the chairman of any such committee is not present at any regular, additional, or special meeting of the committee, the ranking member of the majority party on the committee who is present shall preside at that meeting.

4. (a) Each committee (except the Committee on Appropriations and the Committee on the Budget) shall make public announcement of the date, place, and subject matter of any hearing to be conducted by the committee on any measure or matter at least one week before the commencement of that hearing unless the committee determines that there is good cause to begin such hearing at an earlier date.

(b) Each committee (except the Committee on Appropriations) shall require each witness who is to appear before the committee in any hearing to file with the clerk of the committee, at least one day before the date of the appearance of that witness, a written statement of his proposed testimony unless the committee chairman and the ranking minority member determine that there is good cause for noncompliance. If so requested by any committee, the staff of the committee shall prepare for the use of the members of the committee before each day of hearing before the committee a digest of the statements which have been so filed by witnesses who are to appear before the committee on that day.

(c) After the conclusion of each day of hearing, if so requested by any committee, the staff shall prepare for the use of the members of the committee a summary of the testimony given before the committee on that day. After approval by the chairman and the ranking minority member of the committee, each such summary may be printed as a part of the committee hearings if such hearings are ordered by the committee to be printed.

(d) Whenever any hearing is conducted by a committee (except the Committee on Appropriations) upon any measure or matter, the minority on the committee shall be entitled, upon request made by a majority of the minority members to the chairman before the completion of such hearing, to call witnesses selected by the minority to testify with respect to the measure or matter during at least one day of hearing thereon.

5. (a) Notwithstanding any other provision of the rules, when the Senate is in session, no committee of the Senate or any subcommittee thereof may meet, without special leave, after the conclusion of the first two hours after the meeting of the Senate commenced and in no case after two o'clock postmeridian unless consent therefor has been obtained from the majority leader and the minority leader (or in the event of the absence of either of such leaders, from his designee). The prohibition contained in the preceding sentence shall not apply to the Committee on Appropriations or the Committee on the Budget. The majority leader or his designee shall announce to the Senate whenever consent has been given under this subparagraph and shall state the time and place of such meeting. The right to make such announcement of consent shall have the same priority as the filing of a cloture motion.

(b) Each meeting of a committee, or any subcommittee thereof, including meetings to conduct hearings, shall be open to the public, except that a meeting or series of meetings by a committee or a subcommittee thereof on the same subject for a period of no more than fourteen calendar days may be closed to the public on a motion made and seconded to go into closed session to discuss only whether the matters enumerated in clauses (1) through (6) would require the meeting to be closed, followed immediately by a record vote in open session by a majority of the members of the committee or subcommittee when it is determined that the matters to be discussed or the testimony to be taken at such meeting or meetings

(1) will disclose matters necessary to be kept secret in the interests of national defense or the confidential conduct of the foreign relations of the United States;

(2) will relate solely to matters of committee staff personnel or internal staff management or procedure;

(3) will tend to charge an individual with crime or misconduct, to disgrace or injure the professional standing of an individual, or otherwise to expose an individual to public contempt or obloquy, or will represent a clearly unwarranted invasion of the privacy of an individual;

(4) will disclose the identity of any informer or law enforcement agent or will disclose any information relating to the investigation or prosecution of a criminal offense that is required to be kept secret in the interests of effective law enforcement;

(5) will disclose information relating to the trade secrets of financial or commercial information pertaining specifically to a given person if

(A) an Act of Congress requires the information to be kept confidential by Government officers and employees; or

(B) the information has been obtained by the Government on a confidential basis, other than through an application by such person for a specific Government financial or other benefit, and is required to be kept secret in order to prevent undue injury to the competitive position of such person; or

(6) may divulge matters required to be kept confidential under other provisions of law or Government regulations.

(c) Whenever any hearing conducted by any such committee or subcommittee is open to the public, that hearing may be broadcast by radio or television, or both, under such rules as the committee or subcommittee may adopt.

(d) Whenever disorder arises during a committee meeting that is open to the public, or any demonstration of approval or disapproval is indulged in by any person in attendance at any such meeting, it shall be the duty of the Chair to enforce order on his own initiative and without any point of order being made by a Senator. When the Chair finds it necessary to maintain order, he shall have the power to clear the room, and the committee may act in closed session for so long as there is doubt of the assurance of order.

(e) Each committee shall prepare and keep a complete transcript or electronic recording adequate to fully record the proceeding of each meeting or conference whether or not such meeting or any part thereof is closed under this paragraph, unless a majority of its members vote to forgo such a record.

6. Morning meetings of committees and subcommittees thereof shall be scheduled for one or both of the periods prescribed in this paragraph. The first period shall end at eleven o'clock antemeridian. The second period shall begin at eleven o'clock antemeridian and end at two o'clock postmeridian.

7. (a)(1) Except as provided in this paragraph, each committee, and each subcommittee thereof is authorized to fix the number of its members (but not less than one-third of its entire membership) who shall constitute a quorum thereof for the transaction of such business as may be considered by said committee, except that no measure or matter or recommendation shall be reported from any committee unless a majority of the committee were physically present.

(2) Each such committee, or subcommittee, is authorized to fix a lesser number than one-third of its entire membership who shall constitute a quorum thereof for the purpose of taking sworn testimony.

(3) The vote of any committee to report a measure or matter shall require the concurrence of a majority of the members of the committee who are present. No vote of any member of any committee to report a measure or matter may be cast by proxy if rules adopted by such committee forbid the casting of votes for that purpose by proxy; however, proxies may not be voted when the absent committee member has not been informed of the matter on which he is

being recorded and has not affirmatively requested that he be so recorded. Action by any committee in reporting any measure or matter in accordance with the requirements of this subparagraph shall constitute the ratification by the committee of all action theretofore taken by the committee with respect to that measure or matter, including votes taken upon the measure or matter or any amendment thereto, and no point of order shall lie with respect to that measure or matter on the ground that such previous action with respect thereto by such committee was not taken in compliance with such requirements.

(b) Each committee (except the Committee on Appropriations) shall keep a complete record of all committee action. Such record shall include a record of the votes on any question on which a record vote is demanded. The results of roll call votes taken in any meeting of any committee upon any measure, or any amendment thereto, shall be announced in the committee report on that measure unless previously announced by the committee, and such announcement shall include a tabulation of the votes cast in favor of and the votes cast in opposition to each such measure and amendment by each member of the committee who was present at that meeting.

(c) Whenever any committee by roll call vote reports any measure or matter, the report of the committee upon such measure or matter shall include a tabulation of the votes cast by each member of the committee in favor of and in opposition to such measure or matter. Nothing contained in this subparagraph shall abrogate the power of any committee to adopt rules (2) providing in accordance with subparagraph (a) for a lesser number as a quorum for any action other than the reporting of a measure or matter.

8. (a) In order to assist the Senate in—

(1) its analysis, appraisal, and evaluation of the application, administration, and execution of the laws enacted by the Congress, and

(2) its formulation, consideration, and enactment of such modifications of or changes in those laws, and of such additional legislation, as may be necessary or appropriate, each standing committee (except the Committees on Appropriations and the Budget) shall review and study, on a continuing basis the application, administration, and execution of those laws, or parts of laws, the subject matter of which is within the legislative jurisdiction of that committee. Such committees may carry out the required analysis, appraisal, and evaluation themselves, or by contract, or may require a Government agency to do so and furnish a report thereon to the Senate. Such committees may rely on such techniques as pilot testing, analysis of costs in comparison with benefits, or provision for evaluation after a defined period of time.

(b) In each odd-numbered year, each such committee shall submit, not later than March 31, to the Senate, a report on the activities of that committee under this paragraph during the Congress ending at noon on January 3 of such year.

9. (a) Except as provided in subparagraph (b), each committee shall report one authorization resolution each year authorizing the committee to make expenditures out of the contingent fund of the Senate to defray its expenses, including the compensation of members of its staff and agency contributions related to such compensation, during the period beginning on March 1 of such year and ending on the last day of February of the following year. Such annual authorization resolution shall be reported not later than January 31 of each year, except that, whenever the designation of members of standing committees of the Senate occurs during the first session of a Congress at a date later than January 20, such resolution may be reported at any time within thirty days after the date on which the designation of such members is completed. After the annual authorization resolution of a committee for a year has been agreed to, such committee may procure authorization to make additional expenditures out of the contingent fund of the Senate during that year only by reporting a supplemental authorization resolution. Each supplemental authorization resolution reported by a committee shall amend the annual authorization resolution of such committee for that year and shall be accompanied by a report specifying with particularity the purpose for which such authorization is sought and the reason why such authorization could not have been sought at the time of the submission by such committee of its annual authorization resolution for that year.

(b) In lieu of the procedure provided in subparagraph (a), the Committee on Rules and Administration may

(1) direct each committee to report an authorization resolution for a two-year budget period beginning on March 1 of the first session of a Congress; and

(2) report one authorization resolution containing more than one committee authorization resolution for a one-year or two-year budget period.

10. (a) All committee hearings, records, data, charts, and files shall be kept separate and distinct from the congressional office records of the Member serving as chairman of the committee; and such records shall be the property of the Senate and all members of the committee and the Senate shall have access to such records. Each committee is authorized to have printed and bound such testimony and other data presented at hearings held by the committee.

(b) It shall be the duty of the chairman of each committee to report or cause to be reported promptly to the Senate any measure approved by his committee and to take or cause to be taken necessary steps to bring the matter to a vote. In any event, the report of any committee upon a measure which has been approved by the committee shall be filed within seven calendar days (exclusive of days on which the Senate is not in session) after the day on which there has been filed with the clerk of the committee a written and signed request of a majority of the committee for the reporting of that measure. Upon the filing of any such request, the clerk of the committee shall transmit immediately to the chairman of the committee notice of the filing of that request. This subparagraph does not apply to the Committee on Appropriations.

(c) If at the time of approval of a measure or matter by any committee (except for the Committee on Appropriations), any member of the committee gives notice of intention to file supplemental, minority, or additional views, that member shall be entitled to not less than three calendar days in which to file such views, in writing, with the clerk of the committee. All such views so filed by one or more members of the committee shall be included within, and shall be a part of, the report filed by the committee with respect to that measure or matter. The report of the committee upon that measure or matter shall be printed in a single volume which

(1) shall include all supplemental, minority, or additional views which have been submitted by the time of the filing of the report, and

(2) shall bear upon its cover a recital that supplemental, minority, or additional views are included as part of the report.

This subparagraph does not preclude

(A) the immediate filing and printing of a committee report unless timely request for the opportunity to file supplemental, minority, or additional views has been made as provided by this subparagraph; or

(B) the filing by any such committee of any supplemental report upon any measure or matter which may be required for the correction of any technical error in a previous report made by that committee upon that measure or matter.

11. (a) The report accompanying each bill or joint resolution of a public character reported by any committee (except the Committee on Appropriations and the Committee on the Budget) shall contain

(1) an estimate, made by such committee, of the costs which would be incurred in carrying out such bill or joint resolution in the fiscal year in which it is reported and in each of the five fiscal years following such fiscal year (or for the authorized duration of any program authorized by such bill or joint resolution, if less than five years), except that, in the case of measures affecting the revenues, such reports shall require only an estimate of the gain or loss in revenues for a one-year period; and

(2) a comparison of the estimate of costs described in subparagraph (1) made by such committee with any estimate of costs made by any Federal agency; or

(3) in lieu of such estimate or comparison, or both, a statement of the reasons why compliance by the committee with the requirements of subparagraph (1) or (2), or both, is impracticable.

(b) Each such report (except those by the Committee on Appropriations) shall also contain

(1) an evaluation, made by such committee, of the regulatory impact which would be incurred in carrying out the bill or joint resolution. The evaluation shall include (A) an estimate of the numbers of individuals and businesses who would be regulated and a determination of the groups and classes of such individuals and businesses, (B) a determination of the economic impact of such regulation on the individuals, consumers, and businesses affected, (C) a determination of the impact on the personal privacy of the individuals affected, and (D) a determination of the amount of additional paperwork that will result from the regulations to be promulgated pursuant to the bill or joint resolution, which determination may include, but need not be limited to, estimates of the amount of time and financial costs required of affected parties, showing whether the effects of the bill or joint resolution could be substantial, as well as reasonable estimates of the record-keeping requirements that may be associated with the bill or joint resolution; or

(2) in lieu of such evaluation, a statement of the reasons why compliance by the committee with the requirements of clause (1) is impracticable.

(c) It shall not be in order for the Senate to consider any such bill or joint resolution if the report of the committee on such bill or joint resolution does not comply with the provisions of subparagraphs (a) and (b) on the objection of any Senator.

12. Whenever a committee reports a bill or a joint resolution repealing or amending any statute or part thereof it shall make a report thereon and shall include in such report or in an accompanying document (to be prepared by the staff of such committee) (a) the text of the statute or part thereof which is proposed to be repealed; and (b) a comparative print of that part of the bill or joint resolution making the amendment and of the statute or part thereof proposed to be amended, showing by stricken-through type and italics, parallel columns, or other appropriate typographical devices the omissions and insertions which would be made by the bill or joint resolution if enacted in the form recommended by the committee. This paragraph shall not apply to any such report in which it is stated that, in the opinion of the committee, it is necessary to dispense with the requirements of this subsection to expedite the business of the Senate.

13. (a) Each committee (except the Committee on Appropriations) which has legislative jurisdiction shall, in its consideration of all bills and joint resolutions of a public character within its jurisdiction, endeavor to insure that

(1) all continuing programs of the Federal Government and of the government of the District of Columbia, within the jurisdiction of such committee or joint committee, are designed; and

(2) all continuing activities of Federal agencies, within the jurisdiction of such committee or joint committee, are carried on; so that, to the extent con-

sistent with the nature, requirements, and objectives of those programs and activities, appropriations therefor will be made annually.

(b) Each committee (except the Committee on Appropriations) shall with respect to any continuing program within its jurisdiction for which appropriations are not made annually, review such program, from time to time, in order to ascertain whether such program could be modified so that appropriations therefore would be made annually.

RULE XXVII: COMMITTEE STAFF

1. Staff members appointed to assist minority members of committees pursuant to authority of a resolution described in paragraph 9 of rule XXVI or other Senate resolution shall be accorded equitable treatment with respect to the fixing of salary rates, the assignment of facilities, and the accessibility of committee records.

2. The minority shall receive fair consideration in the appointment of staff personnel pursuant to authority of a resolution described in paragraph 9 of rule XXVI.

3. The staffs of committees (including personnel appointed pursuant to authority of a resolution described in paragraph 9 of rule XXVI or other Senate resolution) should reflect the relative number of majority and minority members of committees. A majority of the minority members of any committee may, by resolution, request that at least one-third of all funds of the committee for personnel (other than those funds determined by the chairman and ranking minority member to be allocated for the administrative and clerical functions of the committee as a whole) be allocated to the minority members of such committee for compensation of minority staff as the minority members may decide. The committee shall thereafter adjust its budget to comply with such resolution. Such adjustment shall be equitably made over a four-year period, commencing July 1, 1977, with not less than one-half being made in two years. Upon request by a majority of the minority members of any committee by resolution, proportionate space, equipment, and facilities shall be provided for such minority staff.

4. No committee shall appoint to its staff any experts or other personnel detailed or assigned from any department or agency of the Government, except with the written permission of the Committee on Rules and Administration.

RULE XXIX: EXECUTIVE SESSIONS

1. When the President of the United States shall meet the Senate in the Senate Chamber for the consideration of Executive business, he shall have a seat

on the right of the Presiding Officer. When the Senate shall be convened by the President of the United States to any other place, the Presiding Officer of the Senate and the Senators shall attend at the place appointed, with the necessary officers of the Senate.

2. When acting upon confidential or Executive business, unless the same shall be considered in open Executive session, the Senate Chamber shall be cleared of all persons except the Secretary, the Assistant Secretary, the Principal Legislative Clerk, the Parliamentarian, the Executive Clerk, the Minute and Journal Clerk, the Sergeant at Arms, the Secretaries to the Majority and the Minority, and such other officers as the Presiding Officer shall think necessary; and all such officers shall be sworn to secrecy.

3. All confidential communications made by the President of the United States to the Senate shall be by the Senators and the officers of the Senate kept secret; and all treaties which may be laid before the Senate, and all remarks, votes, and proceedings thereon shall also be kept secret, until the Senate shall, by their resolution, take off the injunction of secrecy.

4. Whenever the injunction of secrecy shall be removed from any part of the proceedings of the Senate in closed Executive or legislative session, the order of the Senate removing the same shall be entered in the Legislative Journal as well as in the Executive Journal, and shall be published in the Congressional Record under the direction of the Secretary of the Senate.

5. Any Senator, officer, or employee of the Senate who shall disclose the secret or confidential business or proceedings of the Senate, including the business and proceedings of the committees, subcommittees, and offices of the Senate, shall be liable, if a Senator, to suffer expulsion from the body; and if an officer or employee, to dismissal from the service of the Senate, and to punishment for contempt.

6. Whenever, by the request of the Senate or any committee thereof, any documents or papers shall be communicated to the Senate by the President or the head of any department relating to any matter pending in the Senate, the proceedings in regard to which are secret or confidential under the rules, said documents and papers shall be considered as confidential, and shall not be disclosed without leave of the Senate.

RULE XXX: EXECUTIVE SESSION—PROCEEDINGS ON TREATIES

1. (a) When a treaty shall be laid before the Senate for ratification, it shall be read a first time; and no motion in respect to it shall be in order, except to refer it to a committee, to print it in confidence for the use of the Senate, or to remove the injunction of secrecy.

(b) When a treaty is reported from a committee with or without amendment, it shall, unless the Senate unanimously otherwise directs, lie over one day for consideration; after which it may be read a second time, after which amendments may be proposed. At any stage of such proceedings the Senate may remove the injunction of secrecy from the treaty.

(c) The decisions thus made shall be reduced to the form of a resolution of ratification, with or without amendments, as the case may be, which shall be proposed on a subsequent day, unless, by unanimous consent, the Senate determine otherwise, at which stage no amendment to the treaty shall be received unless by unanimous consent; but the resolution of ratification when pending shall be open to amendment in the form of reservations, declarations, statements, or understandings.

(d) On the final question to advise and consent to the ratification in the form agreed to, the concurrence of two-thirds of the Senators present shall be necessary to determine it in the affirmative; but all other motions and questions upon a treaty shall be decided by a majority vote, except a motion to postpone indefinitely, which shall be decided by a vote of two-thirds.

2. Treaties transmitted by the President to the Senate for ratification shall be resumed at the second or any subsequent session of the same Congress at the stage in which they were left at the final adjournment of the session at which they were transmitted; but all proceedings on treaties shall terminate with the Congress, and they shall be resumed at the commencement of the next Congress as if no proceedings had previously been had thereon.

RULE XXXI: EXECUTIVE SESSION—PROCEEDINGS ON NOMINATIONS

1. When nominations shall be made by the President of the United States to the Senate, they shall, unless otherwise ordered, be referred to appropriate committees; and the final question on every nomination shall be, "Will the Senate advise and consent to this nomination?" which question shall not be put on the same day on which the nomination is received, nor on the day on which it may be reported by a committee, unless by unanimous consent.

2. All business in the Senate shall be transacted in open session, unless the Senate as provided in rule XXI by a majority vote shall determine that a particular nomination, treaty, or other matter shall be considered in closed executive session, in which case all subsequent proceedings with respect to said nomination, treaty, or other matter shall be kept secret: Provided, That the injunction of secrecy as to the whole or any part of proceedings in closed

executive session may be removed on motion adopted by a majority vote of the Senate in closed executive session: Provided further, That any Senator may make public his vote in closed executive session.

3. When a nomination is confirmed or rejected, any Senator voting in the majority may move for a reconsideration on the same day on which the vote was taken, or on either of the next two days of actual executive session of the Senate; but if a notification of the confirmation or rejection of a nomination shall have been sent to the President before the expiration of the time within which a motion to reconsider may be made, the motion to reconsider shall be accompanied by a motion to request the President to return such notification to the Senate. Any motion to reconsider the vote on a nomination may be laid on the table without prejudice to the nomination, and shall be a final disposition of such motion.

4. Nominations confirmed or rejected by the Senate shall not be returned by the Secretary to the President until the expiration of the time limited for making a motion to reconsider the same, or while a motion to reconsider is pending unless otherwise ordered by the Senate.

5. When the Senate shall adjourn or take a recess for more than thirty days, all motions to reconsider a vote upon a nomination which has been confirmed or rejected by the Senate, which shall be pending at the time of taking such adjournment or recess, shall fall; and the Secretary shall return all such nominations to the President as confirmed or rejected by the Senate, as the case may be.

6. Nominations neither confirmed nor rejected during the session at which they are made shall not be acted upon at any succeeding session without being again made to the Senate by the President; and if the Senate shall adjourn or take a recess for more than thirty days, all nominations pending and not finally acted upon at the time of taking such adjournment or recess shall be returned by the Secretary to the President, and shall not again be considered unless they shall again be made to the Senate by the President.

7. (a) The Official Reporters shall be furnished with a list of nominations to office after the proceedings of the day on which they are received, and a like list of all confirmations and rejections.

(b) All nominations to office shall be prepared for the printer by the Official Reporter, and printed in the Congressional Record, after the proceedings of the day in which they are received, also nominations recalled, and confirmed.

(c) The Secretary shall furnish to the press, and to the public upon request, the names of nominees confirmed or rejected on the day on which a final vote shall be had, except when otherwise ordered by the Senate.

RULE XXXII: THE PRESIDENT FURNISHED WITH COPIES OF RECORDS OF EXECUTIVE SESSIONS

The President of the United States shall, from time to time, be furnished with an authenticated transcript of the public executive records of the Senate, but no further extract from the Executive Journal shall be furnished by the Secretary, except by special order of the Senate; and no paper, except original treaties transmitted to the Senate by the President of the United States, and finally acted upon by the Senate, shall be delivered from the office of the Secretary without an order of the Senate for that purpose.

RULE XXXIV: SENATE CHAMBER—SENATE WING OF THE CAPITOL

1. The Senate Chamber shall not be granted for any other purpose than for the use of the Senate; no smoking shall be permitted at any time on the floor of the Senate, or lighted cigars, cigarettes, or pipes be brought into the Chamber.

2. It shall be the duty of the Committee on Rules and Administration to make all rules and regulations respecting such parts of the Capitol, its passages and galleries, including the restaurant and the Senate Office Buildings, as are or may be set apart for the use of the Senate and its officers, to be enforced under the direction of the Presiding Officer. The Committee shall make such regulations respecting the reporters' galleries of the Senate, together with the adjoining rooms and facilities, as will confine their occupancy and use to bona fide reporters of newspapers and periodicals, and of news or press associations for daily news dissemination through radio, television, wires, and cables, and similar media of transmission. These regulations shall so provide for the use of such space and facilities as fairly to distribute their use to all such media of news dissemination.

Appendix B

Other Standing Rules

Rules XXXIV through XLIII are an ethics code incorporated into the Standing Rules. They are not the subject of this book. These rules are as follows:

XXXIV—Public financial disclosure
XXXV—Gifts
XXXVI—Outside earned income
XXXVII—Conflict of interest
XXXVIII—Prohibition of unofficial office accounts
XXXIX—Foreign travel
XL—Franking privilege and radio and television studios
XLI—Political fund activity; definitions
XLII—Employment practices
XLIII—Representation by members

Glossary[1]

Administration bill An informal designation that the bill is part of the president's program.

Amendment A proposal to change part or all of a bill or resolution.

Appropriations bill By tradition, such bills originate in the House. Legislation actually provides funds for programs, usually on an annual basis.

Authorization bill Legislation establishing a program and setting maximum spending limits annually or for the life of the program. Distinguished from appropriations, which actually make money available.

Bills Most legislative proposals before Congress are in the form of bills and are designated as "H.R." (House bill) or "S." (Senate bill), according to the body in which they originate; they are given a number, assigned in the order of introduction, from the beginning of each two-year Congress. "Public bills" deal with general questions and become public laws if approved by Congress and signed by the president. "Private bills" deal with individual matters, such as claims against the government, immigration and naturalization cases, land titles, and so on, and become private laws if approved and signed. Any number of senators may join in introducing a bill. Many bills in reality are committee bills and are introduced under the name of the chairman of the committee or subcommittee as a formality. All appropriation bills fall into this category, as do many other bills, particularly those dealing with complicated and technical subjects. A committee frequently holds hearings on a number of related bills and may agree on one of them or on an entirely new bill.

Bills referred When introduced, a bill is referred to the committee having jurisdiction over the subject covered by the bill. The appropriate reference for bills is spelled out in Senate and House rules. Bills are referred by the

Speaker in the House and the presiding officer in the Senate (in reality, the parliamentarian). Appeals may be made from their decisions.

By request   Legislation submitted by a senator at the request of someone else, such as the administration.

Calendar   The Senate calendar, published daily by the legislative clerk when the Senate is in session, lists all Senate bills and resolutions reported by the Senate committees in the order in which they were reported (that is, order number); it also lists some House-passed bills. It is from this list (which also shows the Senate report number of a bill or resolution, the date when it was reported, and so on) that the majority leader decides which bills will be considered on the Senate floor.

Calendar item number   The reference number for a measure pending on the Senate's legislative calendar and ready for floor consideration.

Cloakroom   There are Republican and Democratic cloakrooms just off the Senate floor at the rear of the chamber, where senators can confer privately. When the Senate is not in good order, the presiding officer will often ask senators to retire to the cloakroom to converse.

Cloture   Method of limiting debate. A cloture petition must be signed by at least sixteen senators before it can be filed in the Senate. Once the cloture petition is filed, one calendar day of the session must elapse before a vote may be taken. Three-fifths of the senators duly elected and sworn (sixty) must vote in the affirmative before cloture can be invoked on most items; for cloture on a proposal to change the Senate rules, two-thirds of those present and voting must vote in favor. Once cloture is invoked, a thirty-hour cap is placed on further consideration, but this cap may be increased by a three-fifths affirmative vote of the senators duly elected and sworn. No senator shall be entitled to speak more than one hour on any pending matter. A senator may yield all or part of his one hour to the majority or minority leader or his designee, who may in turn yield that time to other senators. Any senator who has not had a chance to speak may seek recognition and be guaranteed up to ten minutes to speak. Except by unanimous consent, no amendment can be proposed after cloture is invoked unless it has already been submitted in writing before the beginning of the cloture vote and is germane. No senator can call up more than two amendments for a vote until every other senator has had the opportunity to call up an amendment.

Committee   When a bill is introduced, it is referred to one of the committees of the Senate, which normally holds hearings, rewrites (or "marks up") the bill, and then reports the legislation back to the full Senate for further consideration.

Committee calendars   The calendar, kept by each committee, lists all bills and resolutions referred to that committee and any action taken thereon (hearings, markups, and so on).

Committee process   Bills and resolutions are referred to one of the standing legislative committees where hearings are held, amendments considered, and a report written. Committee hearings are generally open to the public, although some may be closed if they deal with national security matters.

Companion bill   A bill introduced in one house, often identical to legislation submitted in the other.

Concurrent resolution   A concurrent resolution (H.Con. Res. or S.Con. Res.) must be adopted by both houses but does not require the signature of the president and does not have the force of law. Concurrent resolutions generally are used to express the sentiment of the two houses. A concurrent resolution, for example, is used to fix time for adjournment of a Congress. It might also be used to convey the congratulations of Congress to another country on the anniversary of its independence. The concurrent resolution on the budget is another important example.

Congressional Record   The transcript of debate and proceedings in Congress, printed daily when Congress is in session and delivered the following morning. Transcripts of verbatim debate may be corrected by a senator (before printing) in the Reporters Office, room S-219 of the Capitol, but only as to grammar, not as to substance. The *Record* is eventually republished in bound volumes, usually after a session has adjourned.

Continuing resolution   When a fiscal year ends without an appropriation for a department or agency for the following fiscal year having been approved, a continuing resolution is enacted allowing departments to spend at a specific rate, usually what they were spending during the previous year.

Cosponsor   One who joins in sponsoring legislation. Often the sponsor asks colleagues to join as cosponsors; this also tends to give wider support for the measure.

Daily Digest   Final portion of the daily *Congressional Record* summarizing chamber action and committee meetings. At the end of the "Chamber Action" section is the program for the next meeting of the Senate, including time of meeting, bills to be considered, and so on.

Engrossed bill   The final copy of a bill as passed by one chamber, with the text as amended by floor action and certified by the clerk of the House or the secretary of the Senate.

Enrolled bill   The final copy of a bill that has been passed in identical form by both chambers. It is certified by an officer of the house of origin (House clerk or Senate secretary) and then sent on for signatures of the Speaker of the House, the Senate president, and the U.S. president. An enrolled bill is printed on parchment.

Executive business   The Senate, unlike the House, performs certain executive functions, such as the confirmation of nominations and the ratification of treaties. These duties are carried out in executive session as distinguished from legislative session. (Executive session should be distinguished from closed session, when the Senate chamber is closed to all, except senators and selected staff.)

Executive calendar   Published by the executive clerk, this lists all nominations and treaties reported by committees that are pending for action by the Senate as a whole.

Executive communication   Messages from the president and executive agencies to the Speaker of the House and president of the Senate, usually requesting legislation, making a report, or expressing a view on problems and policies. *See also* Presidential messages.

Extension of remarks   Primarily used by the House of Representatives. This portion of the *Record* contains speeches and other material that are not germane to debate under way in the chamber but that the member wants printed as part of the *Record*.

Filibuster   A time-honored Senate tradition, the filibuster is a way of balancing minority rights with the principle of rule by the majority. By threatening a talkathon filibuster, a senator or group of senators can force the majority of senators to amend or even abandon a particular piece of legislation. A filibuster can last for many days and is a tactic of last resort for a determined minority. There are complicated rules for ending a filibuster. *See* Cloture.

Fiscal year   The government's bookkeeping year, which runs from October 1 through September 30, is designated by the calendar year in which it ends. For example, fiscal year 1989, often written FY89, began on October 1, 1988, and ended on September 30, 1989.

Floor manager   A senator, usually representing sponsors of a bill, who attempts to steer it through debate and amendment to a final vote in the chamber. Floor managers are frequently chairmen or ranking majority members of the committee that reported a bill. Managers are responsible for apportioning the time granted supporters of the bill for debating it. The minority leader or the ranking minority member of the committee often apportions time for the minority party's participation in the debate.

Holds   A senator can place a "hold" on a particular piece of legislation by calling the Republican or Democratic cloakroom and stating (and later backing this up with a written notice) that he wants a "hold" placed on a particular bill. He does not have to state why. He may be very opposed to the bill and want to prevent its passage if possible, or he may simply want more time to prepare amendments to it. The majority leader honors generally these "holds" for a reasonable period of time whenever he can. However, "holds" are not in any way official; they are simply a part of the unwritten code of "senatorial courtesy" and can be overridden by the majority leader, who has broad discretion to set the Senate's program. (Note: This practice may change in the 105th Congress.)

Joint resolution   A joint resolution, designated H.J. Res. or S.J. Res., requires the approval of both houses and the signature of the president, just as a bill does, and has the force of law if approved. There is no major difference between a bill and a joint resolution. The latter is generally used in dealing with limited matters, such as a single appropriation for a specific purpose and constitutional amendments. Note, however, that constitutional amendments do not require the president's signature.

Legislative day   The "day" extending from the time either house meets after an adjournment until the time it next adjourns. Because the House normally adjourns from day to day, legislative days and calendar days usually coincide. But in the Senate, a legislative day may, and frequently does, extend over several calendar days.

Markup   In a committee meeting in preparation for floor action, the bill is literally "marked up"; that is, amendments are agreed to, language is changed, and so on. The bill will next be ordered reported.

Morning business   Time in which senators may briefly discuss issues not germane to pending legislation, introduce bills and resolutions, and so on. It is a time for routine legislative housekeeping and can occur any time of the night or day, not just in the morning.

Motion to recommit   A motion to send a bill back to the committee that reported it. Generally, a motion to recommit, if adopted, means the end of floor consideration of the bill unless the motion is accompanied by instructions.

Motion to recommit with instructions   A motion to send a bill back to the committee that reported it, with specific instructions to report it back to the floor, usually within a specified time period and usually with amendments.

Motion to table   A tabling motion, if carried, postpones consideration of a matter before the Senate and usually has the effect of killing it. Tabling of a motion to reconsider Senate action has the effect of confirming that action.

Ordered reported   Approval by a committee of a bill for floor consideration.

Parliamentary inquiry   This is a question about the Senate's rules of procedure. No matter what the pending business of the Senate, a parliamentary inquiry is always in order and takes precedence over any other action of the Senate, but a senator must have the floor to make a parliamentary inquiry.

President of the Senate   The Constitution designates the vice president of the United States as the president, or presiding officer, of the Senate. Normally, the vice president presides over the Senate only if an upcoming vote is expected to be close, because he can vote to break a tie; also, he may want to preside over the Senate when it debates or votes on an important administration policy.

Presidential messages   Policy statements, frequently requesting specific legislation, addressed to one or both houses of Congress. Unlike executive communications, presidential messages are delivered to the Senate in sealed envelopes.

President pro tempore   The president pro tempore is responsible for presiding over the Senate in the absence of the vice president.

Presiding officer   May be any member of the Senate designated by the president pro tempore to preside during Senate sessions. Since 1977, the practice has been that only senators from the majority party preside, normally for one hour at a time.

Printed amendment   An amendment printed in the *Congressional Record*. At the back of the *Congressional Record*, under the Senate's Daily Digest, is an item called "Amendments Submitted." It refers to a page number where printed amendments may be found, organized by the title of the bill they seek to modify. *See* Unprinted amendment.

Quorum call   Method of determining whether a legislating quorum is present in the Senate chamber. Today, this is used mainly as a kind of parliamentary "time-out" while senators meet on and off the Senate floor to decide how to proceed on a particular piece of legislation. Usually, there are several quorum calls on any given day the Senate is in session. It is a routine way of suspending debate without recessing or adjourning the Senate. It is triggered when a senator says, "I suggest the absence of a quorum," and the clerk begins slowly to call the roll of the Senate. Regular business resumes when a senator says, "I ask unanimous consent that further proceedings under the quorum call be dispensed with."

Reading a bill   Under Senate rules, every bill must be read three times. First reading and second reading occur when a bill is introduced; it is given a title and a number and is referred to the appropriate committee. Third reading occurs before final passage. The bill is not "read" from start to finish; instead, the clerk reads the bill title.

Recognition   According to the traditions of the Senate, the majority leader has the right to be recognized first by the presiding officer when the majority leader wishes to speak. After the majority leader rank, in order of precedence, the minority leader, the majority floor manager of legislation the Senate is working on, the minority floor manager, and finally any senator first requesting recognition.

Regular order   This refers to the Senate's returning to the pending business that, for a variety of reasons, has been suspended by unanimous consent.

Relevancy This term is used to describe a standard that requires amendments to relate to the subject of the bill (relevancy is broader than the Senate's germaneness test).

Report The report describes the purpose and scope of a bill, together with supporting reasons. It lists and explains amendments adopted by the committee and usually includes departmental comments on the bill and cost estimates from the Congressional Budget Office. Minority views by those opposing the measure, as well as supplemental views of other members of the committee, may be included.

Reported A bill is deemed reported when it has been released by the committee and has been transmitted to the Senate for floor action. At this time, the bill is listed on the Senate legislative calendar.

Reserving the right to object After a senator makes a unanimous consent request, one or more senators will often say something such as "Reserving the right to object" or "I do not intend to object." This is a way of using a unanimous consent request to gain the floor for some other purpose, such as asking for a clarification of the consent request or asking the majority leader about the schedule of upcoming business.

Resolution A simple resolution, designated H. Res. or S. Res., deals with matters entirely within the prerogatives of one house or the other. It requires neither passage by the other chamber nor approval by the president and does not have the force of law. Most resolutions deal with the rules of one house. They are also used to express the sentiments of a single house, as condolences to the family of a deceased member, or to give "advice" on foreign policy or other executive business.

Roll call vote A vote in which each senator is recorded for or against a bill, amendment, motion, and so on. Such votes are recorded in the *Congressional Record*. Normally, a roll call vote lasts twenty minutes. The clerk calls the entire roll of the Senate once and then reports how senators voted. During the second part of the roll call, the names of individual senators are announced by the clerk in the order they appear. Finally, the completed tally is announced.

Sponsor The senator who introduces legislation, an amendment, a motion, and so on; also known as the chief or prime sponsor.

Time agreement This is a variety of unanimous consent agreement that states a time limit on debate for a specific legislative item and can set out how it will be divided between opposing sides and among competing amendments.

Two-day (or forty-eight-hour) rule Senate rules provide that a report on a bill, resolution, and so on must be available to the members for two days (forty-eight hours, Sundays and legal holidays excepted) prior to its consideration on the Senate floor. A senator can inform the Republican cloakroom that he wants this "two-day rule" enforced and therefore see that legislation is not considered on the floor until forty-eight hours have expired since the report is printed and available.

Unanimous consent   Procedurally, anything can be done in the Senate by unanimous consent. However, it takes the objection of only one Senator present on the floor at the time to prevent a unanimous request from being agreed to. Unanimous consent agreements act as the Senate's "traffic cop" with regard to time of debate, time on amendments, and so on. All pending unanimous consent agreements are printed each day on the first few pages of the Senate calendar.

Unprinted amendment   This is an amendment that, when offered on the Senate floor, has not yet been printed in the *Congressional Record*. *See* Printed amendment.

Voice vote   Vote on pending matter without the senators' votes being recorded. Most Senate actions are taken by voice vote to expedite the Senate's business.

Wrap-up   The period at the end of the Senate's day when the Senate passes noncontroversial bills by voice vote.

Yeas and nays   During debate on a measure, a senator asks for the yeas and nays; if there is a sufficient second, the yeas and nays are then ordered. This means that a definitive vote will necessarily occur at the end of debate, either when there are no further amendments or when all the allotted time for the measure has expired.

Yielding time   When the Senate is considering a measure under a time agreement, the majority and minority floor managers control the time allotted to proponents and opponents. A senator may not speak on the measure until a floor manager yields a specified amount of time. When a senator begins speaking without being yielded time, the presiding officer interrupts by asking, "Who yields time?"

Notes

CHAPTER 1

1. In particular, see U.S. Constitution, art. 1, secs. 3–7.

2. Rule V, para. 2.

3. Rule V, para. 1. The Parliamentarian advises that if a proposal to amend the Standing Rules has been introduced at least one day prior to the time it is moved, he will construe that the notice requirement has been met. Accordingly, there is no need to file an additional notice the day before the rules change will be attempted.

4. Cloture procedure is set out in Rule XXII, para. 2.

5. The seven recodifications took place in 1806, 1820, 1828, 1868, 1877, 1884, and 1979. See U.S. Congress, Senate, *The Senate 1789–1989*, by Robert C. Byrd, vol. 2, S. Doc. 100-20, 100th Cong., 1st sess., 1988, p. 48.

6. Congressional Budget and Impoundment Control Act of 1974, as amended, Section 305.

7. 5 U.S.C. 802(g).

8. These are legislative vehicles that are internal to one house only and are effective when passed by that house. They do not have the force of law. Presidential signature is not required.

9. These are vehicles that can start in either chamber and are effective on passage of both houses. They do not have the force of law. Presidential signature is not required.

10. Stanley Bach, "Fast-Track or Expedited Procedures: Their Purposes, Elements, and Implications," CRS Report No. 98-888, Congressional Research Service, Library of Congress, Washington, D.C., 2001, p. 1.

11. Rule-making statutes often contain automatic or expedited discharge provisions that intrude on a committee's normal prerogative not to report legislation to the floor.

12. Bach, "Fast-Track or Expedited Procedures," p. 12.

13. 42 U.S.C. 10101 et. seq.

14. 42 U.S.C. 10135.

15. Richard Beth, "Statutory Provisions for Calling Up Measures Subject to Expedited Procedures in the Senate," CRS Memorandum, Congressional Research Service, Library of Congress, Washington, D.C., 2002, p. 2.

16. In 1957, Minority Leader William Knowland (R-CA) successfully moved to proceed to civil rights legislation. Majority Leader Lyndon Johnson (D-TX) acquiesced in that strategy and voted in favor of the motion, which was propounded on July 8 and adopted on July 16.

17. In a voice vote, senators vote yea or nay in a chorus, and their individual positions are not recorded.

18. The Congressional Review Act contains expedited procedures to facilitate congressional disapproval of government regulations. Presidential signature is ultimately required to make the disapproval legislation effective.

19. 5 U.S.C. 802.

20. Floyd M. Riddick, Senate Parliamentarian, Oral History Interviews, Senate Historical Office, Washington, D.C., p. 429.

21. Riddick, pp. 162–63.

22. Riddick, p. 429.

23. U.S. Senate, *Riddick's Senate Procedure*, S. Doc. 101-28, 101st Cong., 2nd sess., 1992, p. 994.

24. *Riddick's Senate Procedure*, pp. 428–29.

25. A time agreement is a unanimous consent order that limits time for debate and may impose additional restrictions. For example, such an agreement could limit debate on a bill to four hours, equally divided, and debate on amendments to the bill to one hour each.

26. *Riddick's Senate Procedure*, p. 1356.

27. Rule XX, para. 1.

28. Rule XX, para. 1.

29. Rule XXII, para. 2.

30. Rule XX, para. 2.

31. *Riddick's Senate Procedure*, p. 989.

32. In such a case, even a submitted point of order would not be debatable.

33. *Riddick's Senate Procedure*, p. 992.

34. Such provisions express the Senate's opinion or position on a subject, but they do not carry the force of law.

35. *Riddick's Senate Procedure*, p. 167.

36. *Riddick's Senate Procedure*, p. 147.

37. *Riddick's Senate Procedure*, p. 725.

38. Rule XX, para. 1.

39. Congressional Budget and Impoundment Control Act of 1974, sec. 904.

40. *Riddick's Senate Procedure*, p. 627.

41. A fuller explanation of the parliamentarian's myriad duties can be found in the interview of Floyd M. Riddick, part of the Senate's oral history project. Riddick, pp. 95–99.

42. The words "in relation to" mean a vote on a tabling motion, so in this case a vote to table the appeal would be a vote in relation to the appeal. A motion to table is

nondebatable and is often used against amendments. If agreed to, the motion to table kills the amendment against which it was lodged.

43. In his contribution to the Senate's oral history project, Riddick claimed that in twenty-five years of advising the presiding officer, the Senate only once voted to overturn him on appeal. He also cites an example of Vice President Alben Barkley ignoring the parliamentarian's advice, only to be overturned on appeal. Riddick, pp. 126–28.

44. Riddick, p. 69.

45. Riddick, p. 61.

46. Author's note: I was privileged to be present on the floor to hear Senator Byrd's speech. Being there was happenstance. I had no idea that he was launching such a comprehensive and noteworthy project. As later speeches were delivered, I understood that something important was in development, and I made a point to be present whenever possible.

CHAPTER 2

1. Constitution, art. 1, sec. 3.

2. U.S. Senate, *Riddick's Senate Procedure*, S. Doc. 101-28, 101st Cong., 2nd sess., 1992, p. 66.

3. Constitution, art. 1, sec. 3.

4. Rule I, para. 1. Rule I, para. 3, allows the president pro tempore to name another senator to perform the duties of the chair. Freshman senators are frequently tapped for chair duty. Prior to the 1970s, the parties would sometimes rotate chair duty when one party controlled the vice presidency and the other controlled the White House. Since then, the majority party has supplied all senators needed to occupy the chair.

5. U.S. Congress, Senate, *The Senate 1789–1989*, by Robert C. Byrd, vol. 2, S. Doc. 100-20, 100th Cong., 1st sess., 1988, p. 56.

6. If the Senate has been in continuous session, Rule IV, para. 2, provides that its proceedings will be interrupted at noon for the prayer.

7. Rules VII and VIII. A legislative day begins when the Senate convenes after an adjournment and ends when the Senate next adjourns. If the Senate recesses at the close of business, the legislative day does not change.

8. Such a provision has become a standard feature of daily wrap-up consent orders sequencing activity for the next session day.

9. Customarily, the managers are the chairman and ranking member of the jurisdictional committee or subcommittee.

10. This practice took root during the leadership of Senator Mike Mansfield (D-MT) and has continued. Mansfield served as leader between 1961 and 1977. His predecessor, Lyndon Johnson, would not customarily allow anyone to use the leader's desk.

11. If amendments are proposed, the leaders will offer them on behalf of other senators. Seldom is any senator on the floor at these times other than the two leaders or their designees and the presiding officer.

12. It has become more common for party cloakrooms to "hotline" measures or matters by telephone to determine if there is objection to proceeding to their consideration. If there is objection, a senator or his staff notifies the party cloakroom immediately. Not every measure, matter, or consent proposal is "hotlined," but the practice of doing so is much more common now than in years past.

13. Per Rule XIV, para. 6, consent was required to proceed to the resolution on the day of its introduction.

14. The preamble is a series of "whereas" clauses that establish the predicate for the resolution.

15. Rule XVII requires that each bill and joint resolution be read three times before passage. The readings are done by title twice before referral to committee and then for the third time at the conclusion of the amendment process just before the bill is passed.

16. Later, the order for the yeas and nays was vitiated by unanimous consent, and the amendment was taken into the committee substitute by voice vote. Resistance persisted, however, on allowing a vote on the substitute containing the educational scholarship program, much less moving to passage of the underlying House measure.

17. If the measure is subject to a time agreement, the presiding officer cannot put the question until all time has been used or yielded back.

18. The Republicans' remedy would be to file cloture, which could have delayed resolution for several days, assuming that sixty votes were available to invoke cloture in the first place.

19. The following day, the amendment was accepted by voice vote, meaning that the effort to avoid a roll call succeeded.

20. The educational scholarships provision was inserted in an omnibus appropriations bill that passed at the very end of the session.

21. Rule VII, para. 1.

22. The *Journal* is a minute book of Senate proceedings. Its contents are described at Rule IV, para. 1(c).

23. Rule IV, para. 1(a).

24. Rule III, para. 1(b).

25. A precedent from February 5, 1987, establishes that quorum calls instituted for purposes of delaying a vote on approving the *Journal* can be considered dilatory. A precedent from May 13, 1987, states that for purposes of delaying a vote on approving the *Journal*, a senator's declining to vote and then seeking to explain his reasons for doing so can also be considered dilatory. Under Senate rules, dilatory behavior is out of order only after cloture, but these precedents are exceptions to that policy.

26. Rule VII, para. 1. An example of an executive message can be found in the *Record* of October 31, 2003, at page S13709, making a nomination that was referred to the Committee on the Judiciary. An example of a House message also appeared in the *Record* of that day as follows: "At 10:03 a.m., a message from the House of Representatives, delivered by Mr. Hays, one of its reading clerks, announced that the House has agreed to the report of the committee of conference on the disagreeing votes of the two Houses on the amendment of the Senate to the bill (H.R. 3289) making emergency supplemental appropriations for defense and for the reconstruction of Iraq and Afghanistan for the fiscal year ending September 30, 2004, and for other purposes."

27. Petitions and memorials are communications to the Senate from interested parties, be they units of government, organizations, or individuals. For example, on Friday, October 17, 2003, the Senate received petitions and memorials from the Michigan House of Representatives on low-interest loans for military personnel called to active duty, from the Vermont Senate concerning the Vermont National Guard, and from the city council of Friendswood, Texas, relative to the Corps of Engineers and six other such documents. Petitions and memorials are referred without debate to the committee of predominant jurisdiction. If there is a dispute as to jurisdiction, a motion to refer the petition or memorial to a different committee will be decided without debate. The Senate will receive petitions from foreign governments or citizens when transmitted by the president.

28. Rule VII, para. 1, states that new resolutions shall take priority over resolutions carrying over from a previous day. The older resolutions would be put before the Senate via a process established in Rule XIV, para. 6, known as coming "over under the rule." That procedure is discussed more fully elsewhere in this book.

29. *Riddick's Senate Procedure*, p. 921.

30. Rule VIII.

31. *Riddick's Senate Procedure*, p. 260.

32. This is the so-called Anthony Rule, named for Senator Henry Anthony (R-RI). Initiated in 1870, it was a modest filibuster control device because a single objection could cause a measure on the call to be bypassed. The Senate could vote to keep the measure under consideration, or it could consider at another time. In either case, the Anthony Rule would not operate, and the measure would be fully debatable.

33. Rule VIII, para. 1.

34. Rule XVII, para. 4.

35. Rule XVII, para. 4.

36. Rule XIX, para. 1.

37. On Mondays, the mandatory call of the calendar under Rule VIII precludes the nondebatable motion to proceed during the Morning Hour.

38. *Riddick's Senate Procedure*, p. 1370.

39. *Riddick's Senate Procedure*, p. 1370.

40. *Riddick's Senate Procedure*, p. 664.

41. *Riddick's Senate Procedure*, p. 657.

42. Today, a nondebatable motion could dispense with the reading of the *Journal*. This motion was incorporated into the Standing Rules via a 1986 amendment. In 1978, it was unavailable to the leadership, and waiver of the reading of the *Journal* required unanimous consent.

43. Killing a pending motion to proceed is a consequence of adjourning.

44. Had the motion been made outside the Morning Hour, H.J. Res. 638 would have displaced rather than suspended the prior legislation. That measure would have returned to the calendar of general orders rather than assuming the status of unfinished business.

45. Floyd M. Riddick, Senate Parliamentarian, Oral History Interviews, Senate Historical Office, Washington, D.C., pp. 251–56.

46. Robert A. Caro, *Master of the Senate* (New York: Alfred A. Knopf, 2002), p. 575.

47. Caro, pp. 572–73.

48. Caro, p. 1336.
49. *Congressional Record*, October 27, 2003, p. S13262.
50. *Congressional Record*, October 28, 2003, p. S13353.
51. *Congressional Record*, October 28, 2003, p. S13356.
52. *Congressional Record*, October 29, 2003, p. S13484.
53. Rule XVI, paras. 2 and 4.
54. This motion is sometimes called a motion to proceed to executive session. Nominations and treaties are considered while the Senate is in executive session. When the Senate wishes to return to legislative business, the leader or his designee will move that the Senate return to legislative session, a motion that stands in precisely the same priority. Because these motions are nondebatable, the leader can normally secure consent to move between legislative and executive session.
55. The use of nongermane amendments (see chapter 6) is an essential tool for the minority party to keep the majority leader from using his scheduling prerogative to restrict the range of issues to be considered on the Senate floor.
56. *Riddick's Senate Procedure*, p. 3.
57. *Riddick's Senate Procedure*, p. 7.
58. *Riddick's Senate Procedure*, p. 7.
59. *Riddick's Senate Procedure*, p. 7.
60. *Riddick's Senate Procedure*, p. 6. If the Senate has agreed to a consent order that it recess at the close of business rather than adjourn, then a motion to recess would be in order, and a motion to adjourn would not.
61. *Riddick's Senate Procedure*, p. 14.
62. *Riddick's Senate Procedure*, p. 657.
63. This means that each house must convene at least once every three days.
64. *Riddick's Senate Procedure*, p. 9.
65. Any business that requires a change in the legislative day to ripen, such as measures that Rule XVII mandates cannot be considered on the same legislative day they are reported and can be addressed only by unanimous consent.
66. *Riddick's Senate Procedure*, p. 1083.
67. *Riddick's Senate Procedure*, p. 1087.
68. *Riddick's Senate Procedure*, p. 1087.
69. *Riddick's Senate Procedure*, p. 1087.
70. Otherwise, the only motions in order would be to adjourn or ones to produce a quorum.
71. *Riddick's Senate Procedure*, p. 1081.
72. *Riddick's Senate Procedure*, p. 1086.
73. *Riddick's Senate Procedure*, p. 1086.
74. *Riddick's Senate Procedure*, pp. 837–38.
75. The lengthy debate some two decades ago over the Panama Canal treaties offers a good illustration of this procedure. The leadership brought the treaties before the Senate for a certain amount of time each day, then double tracked to set the treaties aside for consideration of legislative business.
76. *Riddick's Senate Procedure*, pp. 837–38.
77. *Riddick's Senate Procedure*, p. 942.
78. Rule XIX, para. 1(b).

79. Rule XIX, para. 1(a).

80. *Riddick's Senate Procedure*, p. 714.

81. Under Rule XXII, all debatable propositions, such as the motion to amend or the motion to refer, stand in lower priority than the motion to table. A tabling motion can be offered against an amendment even though a cloture motion has been filed on that amendment. See *Riddick's Senate Procedure*, p. 1277.

82. *Riddick's Senate Procedure*, p. 1287.

83. *Riddick's Senate Procedure*, p. 1278.

84. *Riddick's Senate Procedure*, p. 1277.

85. Rule XV, para. 4.

86. *Riddick's Senate Procedure*, p. 1278.

87. *Congressional Record*, December 20, 2001, p. S14049.

88. *Riddick's Senate Procedure*, p. 999.

89. *Riddick's Senate Procedure*, p. 1164.

90. *Riddick's Senate Procedure*, p. 1152.

91. *Riddick's Senate Procedure*, p. 1164.

92. Rule XXII, para. 2.

93. *Riddick's Senate Procedure*, p. 1112.

94. *Riddick's Senate Procedure*, p. 1114.

95. This means an amendment to the text of the instructions (first degree) and an amendment to the amendment (second degree).

96. *Riddick's Senate Procedure*, p. 1153.

97. *Riddick's Senate Procedure*, p. 1111.

98. *Riddick's Senate Procedure*, p. 1111.

99. Shortly thereafter, the Senate found a way out of the energy bill morass and adopted a bipartisan substitute amendment that eased passage of the bill and a conference with the House. In light of those developments, a consent order was entered vitiating the cloture process against Frist's motion.

100. For instance, a committee cannot be asked to report language that would be in the jurisdiction of another committee, and if the Senate is considering a measure under a requirement that all amendments be germane, the instructions cannot require the committee to report an amendment that would be nongermane.

101. *Riddick's Senate Procedure*, p. 1110.

102. This is known as a closed rule.

103. The Senate Committee on Rules and Administration may have a name similar to the House Rules Committee's, but it does not have a like function. Its jurisdiction is more closely parallel to that of the House Committee on Administration.

CHAPTER 3

1. This is also codified at Rule VI, para. 1.

2. U.S. Senate, *Riddick's Senate Procedure*, S. Doc. 101-28, 101st Cong., 2nd sess., 1992, p. 1062.

3. *Riddick's Senate Procedure*, p. 1057.

4. *Riddick's Senate Procedure*, p. 1066.

5. *Riddick's Senate Procedure*, p. 1066.

6. *Riddick's Senate Procedure*, p. 1067.

7. *Riddick's Senate Procedure*, p. 1049. This is unlike a roll call vote, which commences when the first senator answers to his name.

8. Rule VI, para. 3.

9. Rule XIV, para. 3.

10. Pairs represent an arrangement between senators so that a senator who is present withholds his vote to accommodate an absent senator who takes an opposing position. The senator present announces his own position and that of the absentee, and then neither is counted in the roll call tally.

11. The presiding officer is entitled to take notice of the presence of such senators. U.S. Congress, Senate, *The Senate 1789–1989*, by Robert C. Byrd, vol. 2, S. Doc. 100-20, 100th Cong., 1st sess., 1988, p. 110.

12. *Riddick's Senate Procedure*, p. 1057.

13. *Riddick's Senate Procedure*, p. 1038.

14. Rule VI, para. 4.

15. See Senator Robert Byrd's discussion of the quorum provisions in the Constitution and in Rule VI in the *Congressional Record*, February 23, 1988, p. 2041.

16. Rule VI, para. 4.

17. *Riddick's Senate Procedure*, pp. 217–21.

18. *Congressional Record*, February 23, 1988, p. 2040.

19. Byrd, pp. 158–59. Senator Byrd notes that the sergeant at arms arrested Packwood, who went to the Capitol under his own power but insisted on being carried on the floor to demonstrate that he had not returned to the chamber voluntarily.

20. Byrd, pp. 286–88.

21. Rule VI, para. 4.

22. An exhaustive list of precedents relating to these categories may be found in *Riddick's Senate Procedure* at pp. 1043–45.

23. *Riddick's Senate Procedure*, p. 1075.

24. A list of precedents related to what does not constitute business for purposes of further quorum calls may be found in *Riddick's Senate Procedure*, pp. 1045–46.

25. Rule XII, para. 4.

26. The requirement that a senator stand and address the presiding officer dates back to the 1789 Senate Rules, originally at Rule III.

27. Rule XIX, para. 1 (a).

28. See Byrd, p. 56, for a discussion about Senate debate norms.

29. Don Oberdorfer, *Senator Mansfield* (Washington, D.C.: Smithsonian Institution Press, 2003), p. 170.

30. *Riddick's Senate Procedure*, pp. 775–78.

31. A demand for the regular order will bring a halt to speeches that masquerade as questions.

32. Rule XIX, paras. 2 and 3.

33. A senator cannot be interrupted to make a point of order, but a demand for the regular order would call into immediate question the potential violation of debate

rules. Floyd M. Riddick, Senate Parliamentarian, Oral History Interviews, Senate Historical Office, Washington, D.C., p. 428.

34. Rule XIX, para. 4.

35. Named for Senator John Pastore (D-RI), this provision is codified at Rule XIX, para. 1(b).

36. After cloture has been invoked, debate is also required to be germane. See *Riddick's Senate Procedure*, p. 310.

37. *Congressional Record*, November 7, 2003, p. S14229.

38. Rule XIX, para. 1(a).

39. Stanley Bach, "Filibusters and Cloture in the Senate," CRS Document No. RL 30360, Congressional Research Service, Library of Congress, Washington, D.C., 2001, p. 4.

40. *Riddick's Senate Procedure*, p. 783. This test requires application of common sense to the question of what constitutes a speech. Merely securing recognition for some purpose but not uttering substantive remarks would not qualify as a speech under such a test.

41. *Riddick's Senate Procedure*, pp. 781–85.

42. *Riddick's Senate Procedure*, p. 782.

43. *Riddick's Senate Procedure*, p. 1278.

44. *Riddick's Senate Procedure*, p. 1278. This means that the amendment cannot be reoffered in identical form.

45. The provisions of the cloture rule are located at Rule XXII, para. 2.

46. When the cloture rule was first adopted in 1917, there were ninety-six senators. The sixteen needed to sign a cloture motion was one-sixth of that total.

47. *Riddick's Senate Procedure*, p. 321.

48. *Congressional Record*, October 20, 2003, p. S12885.

49. *Riddick's Senate Procedure*, p. 330.

50. Apart from the requirements of the cloture rule, amendments need not be filed in advance.

51. Rule XXII, para. 2.

52. "Germaneness" has a special meaning in Senate procedure, as distinguished from a lay definition. A discussion of the Senate's germaneness standard is found later in this book.

53. Indeed, during a famous 1977 filibuster on a natural gas deregulation bill, Majority Leader Byrd called up thirty-three procedurally defective amendments that had been filed by other senators so that they might be ruled out of order.

54. *Riddick's Senate Procedure*, p. 286.

55. *Riddick's Senate Procedure*, p. 1038.

56. *Riddick's Senate Procedure*, p. 1324.

57. For amendments to be restricted when time has expired, the order must specify that is the case. For instance, the order might say that a vote will occur at 5:00 P.M. on adoption of a committee substitute and that no amendments to the substitute other than those then actually pending would be in order.

58. Charles Francis Adams, ed., *Memoirs of John Quincy Adams*, vol. 1 (Philadelphia, 1874), p. 365, quoted in Joseph Cooper, *The Previous Question: Its Standing as*

a Precedent for Cloture in the United States Senate, S. Doc. 87-104, 87th Cong., 2nd sess. (Washington, D.C.: U.S. Government Printing Office, 1962), p. 4.

59. Sarah A. Binder and Steven S. Smith, *Politics or Principle? Filibustering in the United States Senate* (Washington, D.C.: Brookings Institution Press, 1997), p. 39.

60. Early filibusters had also included extended debate in 1841 on the appointment of Senate printers.

61. Franklin L. Burdette, *Filibustering in the Senate* (Princeton, N.J.: Princeton University Press, 1940), p. 23.

62. Burdette, p. 24.

63. Byrd, p. 116.

64. Burdette, p. 25.

65. Burdette, p. 56.

66. Burdette, p. 57.

67. Before 1937, Congress would convene on the first Monday in December of the odd-numbered year following an election. It would remain in session until August or September of the election year (the so-called long session). Congress would reconvene in the December immediately following the election until its adjournment in the odd-numbered March that followed (the so-called short session). Twenty-seven special sessions have been convened in response to a presidential call, sometimes because there was a need for legislation during months that Congress otherwise would not sit. For instance, the famous Hundred Days New Deal legislation was passed during a special session called by President Franklin D. Roosevelt. Since the Twentieth Amendment, special sessions called by the president have been rare. The last such special session was a postconvention session called on July 26, 1948, by President Harry Truman.

68. *Congressional Record*, 65th Cong., special session, March 5, 1917, p. 11.

69. *Congressional Record*, 65th Cong., special session, March 5, 1917, p. 11.

70. On March 10, 1949, Majority Leader Scott Lucas (D-IL) filed a cloture motion on a motion to proceed to a bill. Senator Richard Russell (D-GA) made a point of order that the cloture motion was not in order. Notwithstanding the parliamentarian's advice that Russell was correct, Barkley ruled against Russell. Russell appealed the ruling, and by a vote of 50–46, the Senate did not sustain the chair. See a discussion of this moment in Riddick, pp. 126–28.

71. *Congressional Record*, 83rd Cong., 1st sess., January 6, 1953, p. 11.

72. Riddick was a proponent of the "continuing body" theory. In his oral history, he made the following case for the Senate as a continuing body: "That was the intent of the fathers of the Constitution when they provided that only one-third of the Senators would come up for election every two years. It made the Senate have a two-thirds membership at all times, under all circumstances. As they said, the Senate was an everlasting institution, that there was no break. Supreme Court decisions have been cited to that effect; cases concerned with committees citing people for contempt when the Senate was not in session; the Supreme Court has held more than once that the Senate is a continuing body." Riddick, p. 132.

73. *Congressional Record*, 85th Congress, 1st sess., January 4, 1957, pp. 178–79.

74. *Congressional Record*, 86th Cong., 1st sess., January 8, 1959, p. 96.

75. *Congressional Record*, 86th Cong., 1st sess., January 8, 1959, p. 102.

76. Johnson's provision is now codified at Rule V, para. 2. It states, "The rules of the Senate shall continue from one Congress to the next Congress unless they are changed as provided in these rules."

77. In that Congress, Majority Leader Mansfield chaired the Rules Committee. Not since then has a majority leader concurrently served as a committee chairman.

78. Quoted in Riddick, p. 178.

79. In effect, the vote would be on whether to substitute the procedures set out in McGovern's motion for the Rule XXII cloture process.

80. Mansfield was one of the fifty-one senators who voted for cloture, claiming that he favored the goal of cloture by three-fifths present but only through the regular order. Accordingly, he supported Holland's appeal. Earlier in his Senate career, Mansfield supported Anderson's efforts to reform the rules through extraordinary means. He cosponsored Anderson's rules change proposals in 1953 and 1957 but opposed such strategies once he became leader.

81. Riddick notes that Humphrey ruled that Holland's appeal was not debatable because it arose in connection with cloture. Thus, says Riddick, Humphrey applied one part of Rule XXII (that appeals under cloture are not debatable) while ignoring another (at the time, that cloture required a two-thirds vote of senators present). Riddick, pp. 198–99.

82. Quoted in *Riddick's Senate Procedure*, p. 203.

83. *Riddick's Senate Procedure*, p. 205.

84. *Riddick's Senate Procedure*, pp. 135–39.

85. In general, Senate rules are not self-enforcing. For instance, the presiding officer has no authority to rule amendments out of order except in response to a point of order from the floor.

86. When the floor is open, the majority leader has priority of recognition over all other senators. In addition, the minority leader, the majority bill manager, and the minority bill manager, in that sequence, follow the leader in enjoying preferential recognition over other senators.

87. Amendments in the first degree would have to be filed by 1:00 P.M. of the day between the moment the cloture motion was entered and the day it ripened. Amendments in the second degree would have to be filed no later than one hour before the cloture vote was taken.

88. Without this provision, the Pearson motion would have been debatable indefinitely, subject to the Rule XXII cloture process.

89. The notion that the Senate is a continuing body arose during debate on the 1917 rules change and was central to debates every time advocates of filibuster reform attempted to go outside the rules in order to effect rules changes. Here, Mansfield is referring to a provision in Johnson's rules change compromise.

90. The presiding officer never decides constitutional points of order and must always submit them to the Senate.

91. In his oral history, Riddick characterizes Pearson's approach as akin to a previous question motion. Riddick goes on to note that, under general parliamentary law, adoption of a previous question motion requires a two-thirds vote. Pearson has supplied a procedure that did not exist under the Senate rules or under general parliamentary law.

Through his self-executing motion, he would in essence impose the previous question by a simple majority. *Riddick's Senate Procedure*, pp. 212–13.

92. The essence of Vice President Nixon's 1957 advisory opinion was that the Senate need not be governed by entrenched rules if it wanted to use extraordinary procedures at the beginning of a Congress to change those rules. Once the Senate operated under the old rules, it acquiesced to them, and for the remainder of the Congress, rules changes could be made only pursuant to those rules. Byrd argues here that a majority at any given moment must choose not to be bound by these restraints and could use extraordinary means to change the rules at any time.

93. Adjournment of the Senate kills a pending motion to proceed. See *Riddick's Senate Procedure*, p. 657. The Equal Rights Amendment case study previously examined also illustrates this point.

94. If the Senate were following the terms of the Mondale motion, neither Allen's motion nor any debate thereon would be in order.

95. *Congressional Record*, February 25, 1975, p. 4209.

96. Before the roll call was instituted, Allen sought recognition. A parliamentary inquiry would have been in order at that moment had Allen been recognized. Rockefeller later apologized for any discourtesy to Allen or to the Senate.

97. Long is the first senator to broach this compromise openly.

98. Byrd wishes to create a new legislative day so that S. Res. 93, now on the calendar, could be taken up during the Morning Hour on nondebatable motion.

99. Rule XIV, para. 6. Motions coming over under the rule are the last item in the litany of Morning Business set out in Rule VII. Had the Morning Hour proceeded smoothly enough for S. Res. 93 to be reached, Byrd could have laid down a cloture motion against it.

100. *Congressional Record*, March 5, 1975, p. 5251.

101. Also subsumed within this motion is a motion to return from executive business to legislative business. This motion is often described as a movement from executive session to legislative session or vice versa.

102. *Riddick's Senate Procedure*, p. 761.

103. *Riddick's Senate Procedure*, p. 761.

104. Rule VIII, para. 2.

105. Rule VII, para. 2.

106. *Riddick's Senate Procedure*, p. 762.

107. *Riddick's Senate Procedure*, p. 763.

108. Rule XX, paras. 1 and 2.

109. Rule XXII, para. 2. Under Rule XX, any issue that the presiding officer submits to the Senate can be debated, but the cited language of Rule XXII overrides this general provision.

110. Rule XX, para. 1.

111. Rule XXII, para. 2.

112. Rule XX, para. 1.

113. Rule XVI, para. 4.

114. Rule VII, para. 3.

115. Rule VI, para. 4.
116. Rule XIX, paras. 1 and 4.

CHAPTER 4

1. For example, the Committee on Banking, Housing, and Urban Affairs requires that two-thirds of all senators cosponsor commemorative coin legislation before it will act on such measures.

2. The rule also contains limitations on subcommittee memberships.

3. A detailed history of the process and rationale for these reforms can be found in Floyd M. Riddick, Senate Parliamentarian, Oral History Interviews, Senate Historical Office, Washington, D.C., pp. 391–424.

4. Pursuant to Rule XXV, para. 1.

5. See, for example, S. Res. 18, 108th Congress, making majority party appointments.

6. Rule XXIV, para. 1, states, "On demand of any Senator, a separate vote shall be had on the appointment of the chairman of any such committee and on the appointment of the other members thereof." The last senator who attempted to amend a committee membership resolution was Wayne Morse of Oregon. Morse entered the 83rd Congress as an independent, having left the Republican Party before the Congress convened, but continued to vote with the Republicans to organize. Neither party gave Morse committee assignments. The senator futilely attempted to use Rule XXIV at the beginning of that Congress to secure assignments for himself.

7. See, for example, S. Res. 50, authorizing expenditures for the Committee on Foreign Relations, submitted by Chairman Richard Lugar (R-IN), *Congressional Record*, February 10, 2003, p. S2123.

8. Rule XXVI, para. 9.

9. For a comprehensive review of Rule XXVI requirements, see Stanley Bach, "Legislative Activity in Committee: The Impact of Senate Rules," Report No. 95-9 S, 1994, Congressional Research Service, Library of Congress, Washington, D.C.

10. Rule XXVI, para. 1.

11. Rule XXVI, para. 2.

12. Rule XXVI, para. 3. The Committee on Appropriations is exempted from this requirement. This provision also states that a meeting may be called on petition of three of the committee members, filed with the committee clerk. If within three calendar days after this request has been filed the chairman has not called a meeting to be held within seven days, a majority of the committee is empowered to call a special meeting.

13. Rule XXVI, para. 4(a). The Appropriations and Budget Committees are exempt from this requirement.

14. Rule XXVI, para. 4(b). The Appropriations Committee is exempt from this requirement.

15. Rule XXVI, para. 4(d).

16. Rule XXVI, para. 5(a). The Appropriations and Budget committees are exempt from this requirement.

17. *Congressional Record*, October 15, 2003, p. 12631.

18. Rule XXVI, para. 7(a)(1) and (2). For this purpose, the conduct of business included holding a markup but not a hearing.

19. Rule XXVI, para. 7(a)(3).

20. Rule XXVI, para. 7(a)(1).

21. Some committees do not permit proxies at all. Others permit them, but only to allow a senator to record his position. A proxy cannot be used to satisfy the reporting requirements of Rule XXVI.

22. Rule XXVI, para. 7(a)(3) See also Rule XVII, para. 3, which provides that the proper reporting of a measure under Rule XVII, para. 7(a)(3), obviates any point of order that could be raised against a faulty hearing procedure pursuant to Rule XXVI, para. 4.

23. Thomas P. Carr, "Reporting a Measure from a Senate Committee," Report No. 98-246 GOV, Congressional Research Service, Library of Congress, Washington, D.C., 2001, pp. 1–2.

24. Rule XXVI, para. 10(b).

25. Rule XXVI, para. 10(b).

26. Rule XXVI, para. 7(c).

27. Rule XXVI, para. 11(a).

28. Rule XXVI, para. 11(b).

29. Rule XXVI, para. 12. This is known as the Cordon Rule.

30. The Appropriations Committee is not subject to these requirements.

31. Rule XXVI, para. 7(c).

32. Rule XV, para. 5.

33. Rule XV, para. 5.

34. Rule XVII, para. 4.

35. Rule XVII, para. 5.

36. Rule XVII, para. 5. A one-house legislative veto is unconstitutional, but the rule has not been updated to reflect that. The two-day rule would be waived relative to a two-house legislative veto, which, under the Constitution, would also require presentment to the president.

37. *Congressional Record*, July 7, 2003, p. S8893.

CHAPTER 5

1. Rule XIV, para. 1, stipulates that if objection is heard to the introduction of a measure, the introduction shall be postponed for one legislative day.

2. Committee reports can also be filed under the same Standing Order.

3. Jurisdictional divisions are set out in Senate Rule XXV. Sometimes these questions are not clear-cut. In his oral history, Riddick describes several examples of how the interests of committee chairmen, in either acquiring or setting aside jurisdiction, influenced the referral process. U.S. Senate, *Riddick's Senate Procedure*, S. Doc. 101-28, 101st Cong., 2nd sess., 1992, pp. 439–41.

4. Rule XVII, para. 1.

5. The motion to commit cannot be made while a motion to proceed is pending because the measure to which it relates is not yet pending before the Senate.

6. *Riddick's Senate Procedure*, p. 1153.

7. Rule XVII, para. 2.

8. The two readings are deemed to occur and are not done aloud, unless there will be an effort to use Rule XIV to bypass referral, a process discussed later in this chapter.

9. *Riddick's Senate Procedure*, p. 256.

10. Rule XIV, para. 4.

11. The reading is done by title. The entire text is not read.

12. Rule XIV, para. 4.

13. *Congressional Record*, October 31, 2003, p. S13735.

14. Joint resolutions are sometimes used to pass continuing resolution appropriations measures and receive the same treatment as bills. They are also the vehicles for constitutional amendments.

15. Rule XIV, para. 6.

16. A legislative day commences when the Senate reconvenes following an adjournment of whatever duration and continues until the Senate next adjourns.

17. Rule XIV, para. 6. A newly introduced resolution will take priority over a resolution coming "over under the rule."

18. *Riddick's Senate Procedure*, p. 961.

19. *Riddick's Senate Procedure*, p. 959.

20. Stanley Bach, "Minority Rights and Senate Procedures," CRS Report No. RL 30850, Congressional Research Service, Library of Congress, Washington, D.C., 2001, p. 9.

21. Rule XIV, para. 8.

22. Rule XIV, para. 8.

23. *Congressional Record*, July 29, 2003, p. S10166.

24. Bach, p. 19.

25. Proponents argue that public disclosure would promote accountability. Opponents contend that it would also promote posturing and harden positions that might be more difficult to untangle.

26. This assumes that the one- and two-day rule layover requirements have been met or, if not, no point of order will be raised. Once a measure is pending, it is too late subsequently to make such a point of order.

27. Richard S. Beth, "Motions to Proceed to Consider in the Senate: Who Offers Them?" Report No. RS21255, Congressional Research Service, Library of Congress, Washington, D.C., 2002, p. 3.

28. A "motion to proceed" is also called a "motion to consider."

29. Rule VIII. Note that the rule provides that motions to proceed to resolutions to amend the Standing Rules are always debatable.

30. Examples of such vehicles would include measures considered under provisions of the 1974 Congressional Budget and Impoundment Control Act, such as budget resolutions and budget reconciliation bills.

31. See *Riddick's Senate Procedure*, p. 761.

32. *Riddick's Senate Procedure*, pp. 664, 1036.

33. If the motion were made inside the Morning Hour, what had been the unfinished business would not be displaced and indeed would recur when the Morning Hour concluded. The unfinished business can be displaced only when the Senate votes, outside the Morning Hour, to consider a different nonprivileged vehicle. *Riddick's Senate Procedure*, p. 666.

34. *Riddick's Senate Procedure*, p. 679.

35. *Riddick's Senate Procedure*, p. 657.

36. *Riddick's Senate Procedure*, p. 658.

37. *Riddick's Senate Procedure*, p. 668.

CHAPTER 6

1. U.S. Senate, *Riddick's Senate Procedure*, S. Doc. 101-28, 101st Cong., 2nd sess., 1992, p. 33.

2. *Riddick's Senate Procedure*, p. 35.

3. *Riddick's Senate Procedure*, p. 59.

4. *Riddick's Senate Procedure*, p. 113.

5. *Riddick's Senate Procedure*, p. 30.

6. *Riddick's Senate Procedure*, p. 116.

7. *Riddick's Senate Procedure*, p. 76. The most complex of the amendment tree diagrams depicts eleven amendments pending at once. None of these amendments is in the third degree.

8. For reasons set forth in the section titled "Principles of Precedence," second- and first-degree amendments to the text proposed to be stricken by the substitute will be voted on before amendments to the substitute itself.

9. *Riddick's Senate Procedure*, p. 115.

10. *Riddick's Senate Procedure*, p. 41–42.

11. *Congressional Record*, October 30, 2003, p. S13608.

12. *Riddick's Senate Procedure*, p. 73.

13. Rule XV, para. 3. *Riddick's Senate Procedure*, p. 76. For example, if a bill is pending and Senator A moves to strike Title III, the question before the Senate is whether Title III shall remain in the bill or be stricken. This principle permits Senator B to propose an amendment to the language that Senator A proposes to strike, to improve that language before the Senate must decide to strike it entirely.

14. Such an amendment would be possible theoretically, but it is not permitted. One can use the Principles of Precedence to explain or justify the positioning of amendments on the charts, but they cannot be used to expand the number of amendments that are possible.

15. Rule XV, para. 2. See also *Riddick's Senate Procedure*, p. 119.

16. *Riddick's Senate Procedure*, p. 119.

17. *Riddick's Senate Procedure*, p. 121.

18. *Riddick's Senate Procedure*, p. 121.

19. *Riddick's Senate Procedure*, p. 123.
20. *Riddick's Senate Procedure*, p. 295.
21. *Riddick's Senate Procedure*, p. 65.
22. *Riddick's Senate Procedure*, p. 55. Rule XV, para. 3, governs the division of amendments.
23. If an amendment has multiple parts, one of which is to strike and insert, that portion can be divided for a separate vote from the other parts, but it is not possible to divide within the strike-and-insert portion.
24. *Riddick's Senate Procedure*, p. 811.
25. *Riddick's Senate Procedure*, p. 809.
26. *Riddick's Senate Procedure*, p. 56.
27. *Riddick's Senate Procedure*, p. 287.
28. *Riddick's Senate Procedure*, p. 811.
29. *Riddick's Senate Procedure*, p. 810.
30. *Riddick's Senate Procedure*, pp. 807–8.
31. The amendment in the first degree would have been disposed of with prejudice—that is, it could not be offered again in identical form. The second-degree amendment, which was taken down because the underlying amendment was killed, could be reoffered subsequently without change.
32. U.S. Congress, Senate, *The Senate 1789–1989*, by Robert C. Byrd, vol. 2, S. Doc. 100-20, 100th Cong., 1st sess., 1988, p. 57.
33. Rule XV, para. 3.
34. Rule XXII, para. 2.
35. Rule XVI, para. 4.
36. For example, under the Congressional Budget and Impoundment Control Act of 1974, all amendments to budget reconciliation bills must be germane.
37. For example, the Nuclear Waste Policy Act of 1982 made no provision for Senate amendments to the Yucca Mountain nuclear waste repository resolution (S.J. Res.34, 107th Congress), and so, given the expedited nature of the consideration process, amendments were construed to be barred.
38. Sense of the Senate amendments proposed from the floor are not germane per se and are subject to the same germaneness tests as would apply to legally binding amendments.
39. *Riddick's Senate Procedure*, p. 884.
40. Rule XVI, para. 4.
41. *Riddick's Senate Procedure*, p. 165.
42. Rule XVI, para. 4, states that "all questions of relevancy of amendments under this rule, when raised, shall be submitted to the Senate and be decided without debate."
43. *Riddick's Senate Procedure*, p. 167.
44. *Riddick's Senate Procedure*, p. 168.
45. *Congressional Record*, May 17, 2000, pp. 4062–65.
46. Rule XVI, para. 4.
47. Rule XVI, paras. 2 and 4.
48. Rule XVI, para. 4.

CHAPTER 7

1. Article 1, sec. 3.
2. Article 1, sec. 5.
3. Article 2, sec. 2.
4. Article 1, sec. 7
5. Article 5.
6. For example, the Rule XXII requirement for sixty votes to invoke cloture.
7. For example, the budget enforcement points of order found in the 1974 Budget Act.
8. Some scholars have argued that any expansion of the supermajority list would be unconstitutional. See, for example, the argument of Lloyd Cutler, former counsel to President Clinton, raising questions about the constitutionality of the cloture rule. Joint Committee on the Organization of Congress, Floor Deliberations and Scheduling Hearing, May 18, 1993, pp. 21, 24.
9. Rule XXII, para. 2.
10. U.S. Senate, *Riddick's Senate Procedure*, S. Doc. 101-28, 101st Cong., 2nd sess., 1992, p. 1045.
11. *Riddick's Senate Procedure*, p. 1404.
12. *Congressional Record*, July 31, 2003, p. 10870.
13. *Riddick's Senate Procedure*, p. 1405.
14. This would connote a requirement for one-fifth of a presumptive quorum, that is, eleven members. In some cases, the Senate actually sticks to this requirement, but it is much more common to order the yeas and nays with a smaller second if there is a bipartisan understanding to do so.
15. *Riddick's Senate Procedure*, p. 1416.
16. *Riddick's Senate Procedure*, p. 1397.
17. Rule XII, para. 1.
18. *Congressional Record*, June 10, 2003, p. 7576.
19. *Riddick's Senate Procedure*, p. 968.
20. *Riddick's Senate Procedure*, p. 968.
21. *Riddick's Senate Procedure*, p. 970. Rule XII, para. 2, requires that if a senator declines to vote, he must state his reasons, and the Senate will determine without debate whether he should be excused.
22. Rule XII, para. 1. Original Senate Rule XI stated, "When the yeas and nays shall be called by one-fifth of the members present, each member called upon shall, unless for special reasons he be excused by the Senate, declare, openly and without debate, his assent or dissent to the question."
23. Rule XII, para. 2.
24. Rule XII, para. 3.
25. The Morning Hour is the first two-hour period after the Senate convenes on a new legislative day. Other than on Mondays, a motion to proceed to any measure on the calendar of business is nondebatable.
26. In 1986, Rule IV was amended to permit the *Journal* to be approved on a nondebatable motion.

27. Pursuant to Rule XXII, dilatory procedures are out of order after cloture is invoked. The rules do not speak to dilatory behavior precloture, so this precedent broke new ground. Whether the precedent could be expanded to declare other proceedings dilatory before cloture remains to be seen.

28. Rule XIII, para. 1, governs reconsideration of legislative measures.

29. A senator who declined to vote because he was paired is eligible to move to reconsider.

30. A simple majority carries a motion to reconsider, even though the underlying proposition requires a supermajority vote. Reconsidering a cloture vote would need a simple majority, even though invoking cloture would require a three-fifths vote.

31. It is not in order to move to reconsider the vote to table a motion to reconsider. See *Riddick's Senate Procedure*, p. 1145.

32. Rule XIII, para. 1.

33. *Riddick's Senate Procedure*, p. 1132.

34. *Riddick's Senate Procedure*, p. 1134.

35. For example, a motion to proceed to reconsideration of a cloture vote would not be debatable because the underlying cloture motion is not debatable.

36. *Riddick's Senate Procedure*, p. 1134.

37. Rule XIII, para. 2.

CHAPTER 8

1. The priority of motions prior to the stage of disagreement is set forth in U.S. Senate, *Riddick's Senate Procedure*, S. Doc. 101-28, 101st Cong., 2nd sess., 1992, pp. 127–28.

2. The motion to concur may be superseded with a motion to concur with an amendment. In other words, under this process, the bicameral deal cannot be protected from floor amendments unless the amending possibilities have been exhausted.

3. *Riddick's Senate Procedure*, p. 130.

4. Rule IX, para. 1.

5. Rule VII, para. 3.

6. *Riddick's Senate Procedure*, p. 129.

7. If even one senator objects, these motions could each be filibustered, leading to highly burdensome delays in arranging for conference.

8. *Riddick's Senate Procedure*, p. 456.

9. The chair normally appoints conferees, but the McCarran motion illustrates that the power of appointment vests in the Senate, if the Senate chooses to exercise it.

10. *Congressional Record*, April 5, 1950, p. 4802.

11. Following the stage of disagreement, if the Senate wishes to change course and concur in the House position, with or without an amendment, it must first conclude the stage of disagreement. It does so by receding either from its disagreement to House language or from its insistence on Senate language.

12. *Washington Post*, October 19, 2003, p. 1.

13. If cloture were invoked on the motion to appoint conferees, then only amendments to the list that were actually pending at the conclusion of thirty hours postcloture could be considered, at most two such amendments. Also, amendments to the list could be tabled, meaning that debate on the amendments might not occur, but a filibuster by roll call could.

14. Following the stage of disagreement, if the Senate wishes to change course and concur in the House position, with or without an amendment, it must first conclude the stage of disagreement. It does so by receding either from its disagreement to House language or from its insistence on Senate language.

15. *Riddick's Senate Procedure*, p. 479.

16. Instructions that would command the conferees to take action that would otherwise be beyond their authority, such as instructing them to include nongermane material, would be out of order.

17. *Congressional Record*, June 6, 1990, p. S7436.

18. Cloture is not an effective way to curtail motions to instruct conferees. While each such motion is debatable and thus subject to the cloture process, each cloture petition would end debate on an individual motion to instruct and any amendments proposed to that motion. The process would have to be repeated for each subsequent motion to instruct, which cannot be subsumed under the first cloture motion.

19. A Rule XXVIII point of order exists because on December 15, 2000, the Senate adopted a Standing Order to reaffirm the rule. This Standing Order reversed the so-called FedEx precedent, which was set on October 3, 1996, relative to a Federal Aviation Administration reauthorization conference report. Conferees had included new material amending the Railway Labor Act, impacting on Federal Express. A Rule XXVIII point of order was sustained against the provision, but the presiding officer was overturned on appeal. From that moment until imposition of the Standing Order four years later, Rule XXVIII restrictions on the content of conference reports did not operate. For a discussion of this precedent, which could be revived in a similar dispute over the enforceability of Rule XXVIII, see Paul S. Rundquist, "S. Res. 160: Rule XVI and Reversing the Hutchison and FedEx Precedents," Report No. RS20276, Congressional Research Service, Library of Congress, Washington, D.C., 1999, p. 2.

20. The conferees having been discharged, there is no conference to which the report can be recommitted after the point of order. For the same reason, if the House has already acted, no motion to recommit is possible when the conference report is before the Senate. If the Senate were the first body to act, a motion to recommit could be offered. The motion to recommit could also include instructions to the conferees.

21. *Congressional Record*, October 15, 2003, p. S12632.

22. Rule XVII, para. 4, says that measures must lie over for one legislative day before they may be considered on the floor.

23. Rule XVII, para. 5, says that printed reports must be available for two days (forty-eight hours) before the measure to which they pertain may be considered on the floor.

24. Rule XXII, para. 1.

25. Rule XXVIII, para. 4.

26. *Riddick's Senate Procedure*, p. 487.

27. *Riddick's Senate Procedure*, pp. 485, 489, 491.

28. A concern with using this strategy is that the amendments are debatable and amendable, even with nongermane provisions.

29. The enrollment resolution is also debatable and amendable, so presumably this strategy would not work unless there were a consent order limiting debate and amendments.

30. Stanley Bach, "Conference Committee and Related Procedures: An Introduction," Report No. 96-708 GOV, Congressional Research Service, Library of Congress, Washington, D.C., 1999, p. 7.

31. *Congressional Record*, September 11, 2003, p. S11426.

32. Rule XIV, para. 5.

33. If the amendments are not technical, then the concurrent resolution will be treated like an ordinary resolution and will not be privileged.

34. *Congressional Record*, November 19, 2002, p. S11580.

35. Constitution, article 1, section 7.

36. Constitution, article 1, section 7, states, "If any Bill shall not be returned by the President within ten Days (Sundays excepted) after it shall have been presented to him, the Same shall be a Law, in like Manner as if he had signed it, unless the Congress by their Adjournment prevents its Return, in which Case it shall not be a Law."

37. *Congressional Record*, January 3, 2001, p. S8.

38. Richard Beth, "Presenting Measures to the President for Approval: Possible Delays," CRS Report No. 95-571 GOV, Congressional Research Service, Library of Congress, Washington, D.C., 1996, p. 3.

39. Louis Fisher, "The Pocket Veto: Its Current Status," CRS Report No. RL30909, Congressional Research Service, Library of Congress, Washington, D.C., 2001, pp. 1–23.

40. Article 1, section 7, provides that the House receiving the veto message "shall enter the Objections at large on their Journal, and proceed to reconsider it."

41. *Congressional Record*, April 26, 2003, p. S2910.

42. Article 1, section 7, provides, "If after such Reconsideration two-thirds of that House shall agree to pass the Bill, it shall be sent, together with the Objections, to the other House, by which it shall likewise be reconsidered, and if approved by two-thirds of that House, it shall become a Law."

43. Article 1, section 7, states, "the Votes of both Houses shall be determined by the Yeas and Nays, and the Names of the Persons voting for and against the Bill shall be entered on the Journal of each House respectively."

44. Gary L. Galemore, "The Presidential Veto and Congressional Procedure," CRS Report No. 98-156 GOV, Congressional Research Service, Library of Congress, Washington, D.C., 2001, p. 1.

CHAPTER 9

1. Although the House deems appropriations bills to fall under the revenue clause, they will not consider Senate tax amendments that have been drawn to appropriations

measures. The House will not receive Senate tax provisions unless those amend a revenue vehicle reported from the House Committee on Ways and Means.

2. The practice by which the House refuses to receive a Senate bill because of what the House deems is a violation of the revenue clause is known as "blue slipping." In the Senate, someone could address the revenue clause issue by raising a constitutional point of order. The point of order would be referred to the Senate for decision, would be debatable, and would be resolved by a simple majority vote.

3. U.S. Senate, *Riddick's Senate Procedure*, S. Doc. 101-28, 101st Cong., 2nd sess., 1992, p. 160.

4. Paragraph 7 of Rule XVI provides that if an amendment does not meet these conditions, it must be identified with particularity in the Appropriations Committee's report.

5. *Riddick's Senate Procedure*, p. 153.

6. *Riddick's Senate Procedure*, p. 173.

7. *Riddick's Senate Procedure*, p. 173.

8. Between March 16, 1995, and July 26, 1999, the rule barring legislative amendments to appropriations bills was not enforced. In 1995, Senator Kay Bailey Hutchison (R-TX) offered a legislative amendment to a supplemental appropriations bill. On a point of order, the presiding officer ruled that the amendment violated Rule XVI. Hutchison appealed, and the ruling was reversed. Agreement to S. Res. 160, 106th Congress, restored prior precedents permitting enforcement of the rule. See Paul S. Rundquist, "S. Res. 160: Rule XVI and Reversing the Hutchison and FedEx Precedents," Report No. RS20276, Congressional Research Service, Library of Congress, Washington, D.C., 1999, p. 2.

9. *Riddick's Senate Procedure*, p. 183.

10. *Congressional Record*, October 15, 2003, p. 12630.

11. This peculiar structure, under which questions of germaneness are decided by the Senate without debate rather than by the presiding officer, is unique to Rule XVI. In all other cases, the presiding officer is empowered to decide questions of germaneness, subject to appeal. Indeed, under postcloture procedure, he rules on questions of germaneness without the need for there first being a point of order from the floor.

12. Rule XVI, para. 2.

13. *Congressional Record*, October 16, 2003, pp. 12687–88.

14. For instance, the defense of germaneness would then be available on floor amendments, which could be claimed to be germane to the House bill.

15. This is pursuant to section 303(a) of the Budget Act. This point of order is enforced by a simple majority vote.

16. This is known as a section 302(a) allocation.

17. This is known as a section 302(b) allocation.

18. Bill Heniff Jr., "Budget Resolution Enforcement," Report No. 98-815, Congressional Research Service, Library of Congress, Washington, D.C., 2001, p. 2.

19. James V. Saturno, "The Appropriations Process and the Congressional Budget Act," Report No. 97-947, Congressional Research Service, Library of Congress, Washington, D.C., 1997, p. 6.

20. Budget authority is the legal authority for agencies to enter into obligations, and outlays are the actual disbursement of funds.

21. Section 502 of H.Con. Res. 95, 108th Congress.

22. These points of order have been strengthened and expanded on in the years since 1974 as Congress continues to explore ways to exert fiscal discipline.

23. The 1921 act established the Bureau of the Budget, which later became the Office of Management and Budget.

24. Robert Keith, "A Brief Introduction to the Federal Budget Process," Report No. 96-912 GOV, Congressional Research Service, Library of Congress, Washington, D.C., 1997, p. 7.

25. Keith, p. 9.

26. Bill Heniff Jr., "Allocations and Subdivisions in the Congressional Budget Process," Report No. RS20144, Congressional Research Service, Library of Congress, Washington, D.C., 2001, p. 1.

27. Section 301(a) of the Budget Act stipulates the basic content requirements for a budget resolution.

28. For example, section 505 of the fiscal year 2004 budget resolution conference report extends PAYGO rules through fiscal year 2008. These rules, which are enforced through a sixty-vote point of order, require tax reductions or entitlement spending beyond that assumed in the budget resolution to be offset with tax increases or entitlement cuts.

29. Authority to include reconciliation instructions is found at section 301(b)(2) of the Budget Act.

30. The point of order would lie under section 313(b)(1)(B), a portion of the act known as the Byrd Rule.

31. A reconciliation bill is legislation containing the response of one or more committees to budget resolution reconciliation instructions. If multiple committees are instructed, they report to the Budget Committee, which then reports to the full Senate, and the reconciliation bill is placed on the calendar of business. If only one committee is instructed, it reports its reconciliation bill directly to the calendar. See section 310(b) of the act.

32. Keith, p. 11.

33. The House did not include such provisions in its version of the budget resolution.

34. Section 305(b) of the Budget Act sets forth debate time limits and amendment germaneness requirements.

35. Extended discussion of these concepts can be found in material earlier set forth on the amendment process.

36. Section 305(b)(6).

37. Rule V, para. 1, provides for a motion to suspend the rules following one day's notice in writing, a procedure that is very seldom used.

38. The waiver is a preemptive maneuver. Once a ruling is made, a senator could appeal, again with the same voting burden as with the waiver motion.

39. The Byrd Rule bars extraneous provisions from reconciliation bills.

40. *Congressional Record*, November 24, 2003, p. 15698.

41. In contrast, Rule XXII governing cloture provides for a limitation on overall consideration, which includes time consumed in debate, but also on quorum calls, roll call votes, and so on.

42. Statutory rules, like those contained in the Budget Act, are generally interpreted as if they were part of a unanimous consent order. Those orders have been construed to permit continuing amendments after debate time has elapsed, unless the consent order contains a time certain to vote.

43. Faced with the absurdity of voting on a rapid-fire sequence of amendments with no debate, the Senate has customarily consented to very brief debate periods prior to each vote, such as two minutes, equally divided.

44. Section 305(c) establishes procedures for consideration of conference reports and amendments between houses.

45. This is true for the same reason that there is no debate on a motion to consider a budget resolution. In both cases, the Budget Act is silent on debate. The presiding officer construes that no debate is in order because to conclude the opposite would undermine the expedited nature of consideration on the budget resolution or reconciliation bill.

46. For example, an amendment could be offered to strike a revenue increase, even though the effect of doing so would be to worsen the deficit, and the amendment would not have to be offset to ameliorate its effects.

47. The committee could not have taken 20 percent of the aggregate for additional tax cuts because that would have caused the $350 billion aggregate ceiling to be exceeded.

48. Under the Byrd Rule, at section 313(b)(1)(B), if a committee is not in compliance, then a point of order can be asserted against any provision it reports that increases spending or decreases revenue.

49. Section 310(d)(2) states that it shall not be in order to consider an amendment to a reconciliation bill that would either decrease budget outlay reductions or reduce federal revenue increases beyond the instructions provided in the budget resolution for the fiscal years it covers. This rule does not apply if the spending increases or revenue cuts are offset, except that a motion to strike is always in order.

50. *Congressional Record*, October 24, 1985, p. 14032, as quoted in Robert Keith, "Budget Reconciliation Procedures: The Senate's 'Byrd Rule,'" Report No. RL30862, Congressional Research Service, Library of Congress, Washington, D.C., 2002, pp. 2–3.

51. Keith, "Budget Reconciliation Procedures," pp. 4–5.

52. For this purpose, provisions having no budgetary effect are those that cannot be scored. Provisions that have no net budgetary impact because of offsets are not extraneous. See Keith, "Budget Reconciliation Procedures," p. 6.

53. Budget resolutions typically cover either five- or ten-year windows. In a ten-year resolution, a tax cut would have to be sunset after the tenth year because continuing it in force past that time would mean that the fiscal position of the government would be diminished in the eleventh year, a violation of the Byrd Rule. The Bush tax cuts of 2001 were sunset for exactly this reason. To avoid the sunset, proponents would have to have sixty votes to waive the rule or sixty votes to invoke cloture on a nonreconciliation vehicle, a burden they could not meet.

54. This means changes in the Old Age Survivors and Disability program in Title II of the Social Security Act and not other Social Security programs, such as Medicare. Keith, "Budget Reconciliation Procedures," p. 6.

55. For example, a provision to reform medical malpractice laws by imposing liability caps will have an impact on Medicare costs, but its impact extends far beyond the Medicare program. The primary purpose of the provision is not its impact on the federal treasury. Because of the Byrd Rule, reconciliation cannot be used to enact it.

56. Congressional Budget Act, section 313(d)(2).

57. Most likely, the House bill, as no Byrd Rule point of order can be asserted against original House language.

58. Keith, "Budget Reconciliation Procedures," p. 1.

CHAPTER 10

1. It is common for a senator, while in legislative session, to ask unanimous consent to speak or act "as in executive session" or to seek consent while in executive session to speak or act "as in legislative session."

2. Rule XXII, para. 1.

3. U.S. Senate, *Riddick's Senate Procedure*, S. Doc. 101-28, 101st Cong., 2nd sess., 1992, pp. 837–38.

4. Rule XXXI, para. 1.

5. Rule XXXI, para. 1.

6. If the Senate were already in executive session, then the motion to consider a particular nomination would be debatable, as would a motion to consider a treaty. It is extremely likely, however, that consent would be granted to consider that nominee. If there were objection and the prospect loomed that the motion to consider would actually be debated, a majority leader could avoid the problem by offering a nondebatable motion to return to legislative business. Once there, he could make a nondebatable motion to return to executive business to consider that specific nomination.

7. The most noteworthy filibuster of a nominee thus far is the 2003 filibuster of Miguel Estrada to be a judge on the District of Columbia Court of Appeals. Seven unsuccessful cloture votes were taken before Estrada requested President George W. Bush to withdraw his name from further consideration.

8. *Congressional Record*, October 17, 2003, p. S12855.

9. Rule XXXI, para. 3.

10. Rule XXXI, para. 3.

11. *Riddick's Senate Procedure*, p. 948.

12. Rule XXXI, para. 5.

13. *Congressional Record*, December 20, 2001, p. S14049.

14. Rule XXXI, para. 6.

15. Rule XXX, para. 2.

16. Constitution, article 2, section 2: "The President shall have the Power to fill up all Vacancies that may happen during the Recess of the Senate, by granting Commissions which shall expire at the End of their next Session."

17. Henry B. Hogue, "Recess Appointments: Frequently Asked Questions," CRS Report RS21308, Congressional Research Service, Library of Congress, Washington, D.C., 2002, p. 2.

18. Hogue, p. 3.

19. 5 U.S.C., sec. 5503.

20. Hogue, p. 5.

21. Treaty documents received by the Senate are deemed secret until the Senate votes to remove the "injunction of secrecy" from them. Usually, consent is granted to do this at the beginning of Senate proceedings, but it may occur at any stage of the process. The requirement that treaty documents remain secret until the injunction of secrecy is removed is found in Rule XXX, para. 1(a).

22. *Congressional Record*, September 2, 2003, p. 10987.

23. Rule XXX, para. 1(b), governs procedures to be observed once the treaty is reported.

24. *Riddick's Senate Procedure*, p. 1301.

25. *Riddick's Senate Procedure*, p. 1295.

26. Rule XXX, para. 1(c), sets out procedures for presentation of the resolution of ratifications and any amendments to the resolution.

27. *Riddick's Senate Procedure*, p. 1295.

28. Most of the time, unanimous consent is granted to take the treaty through all parliamentary steps up to the resolution of ratification, obviating a formal process of amendments to the treaty itself.

29. *Congressional Record*, July 31, 2003, p. S10870.

30. U.S. Congress, Senate, *The Senate 1789–1989*, by Robert C. Byrd, vol. 2, S. Doc. 100-20, 100th Cong., 1st sess., 1988, p. 22.

31. Rule XXX, para. 1(d).

32. Article 2, section 2, of the Constitution sets forth the president's power to make treaties with advice and consent of the Senate, provided that two-thirds of senators present concur. Rule XXX, para. 1(d), carries forward this voting requirement.

33. Rule XXX, para. 2.

34. Byrd, p. 19.

35. *Riddick's Senate Procedure*, p. 277.

36. *Riddick's Senate Procedure*, pp. 277–78.

37. This list includes "the Secretary of the Senate and the Assistant Secretary, the Principal Legislative Clerk, the Parliamentarian, the Executive Clerk, the Minute and Journal Clerk, the Sergeant at Arms, the Secretaries to the Majority and the Minority, and such other officers as the Presiding Officer shall think necessary."

38. Rule XXIX, para. 5.

39. Rule XXIX, para. 5.

40. Rule XXXI, para. 2.

41. Rule XXXI, para. 2, p. 280.

42. Article 1, section 3.

43. Article 2, section 4.

44. Elizabeth B. Bazan, "Continuation of an Impeachment Proceeding or an Impeachment Investigation from One Congress to the Next Congress," memorandum, Congressional Research Service, Library of Congress, Washington, D.C., 1998.

45. United States Senate, 99th Cong., 2nd sess., Document 99-33.
46. Impeachment Rule I.
47. Impeachment Rule II.
48. Impeachment Rule II.
49. Impeachment Rule III.
50. Impeachment Rule III.
51. Impeachment Rule IV.
52. Impeachment Rule VII.
53. See *Nixon v. United States*, 506 U.S. 224 (1993), and also discussion in Elizabeth B. Bazan, "Impeachment: An Overview of Constitutional Provisions, Procedure and Practice," CRS Report No. 98-186A, Library of Congress, Washington, D.C., 1998.
54. Rule IV, para. 1(d).
55. Impeachment Rule XVI.
56. Impeachment Rule XIX.
57. Impeachment Rule XIX.
58. Impeachment Rule XX.
59. Impeachment Rule V.
60. The rules could also have been suspended by unanimous consent. Because consent could not be achieved, proponents of open deliberations used the Rule V suspension procedure.
61. Impeachment Rule XIII.
62. Impeachment Rule XXII.
63. Impeachment Rule XXIII.
64. Impeachment Rule XXIV.
65. Impeachment Rule XXIII.
66. Impeachment Rule XXIII.
67. Article 1, section 3. Judge Alcee Hastings was impeached in 1989 but not barred from elective office. He was subsequently elected to the U.S. House of Representatives. By contrast, Judge Robert Archibald was impeached and convicted in 1913 and was barred from public office on adoption of a motion following his conviction.
68. Bazan, "Impeachment."
69. Bazan, "Impeachment."
70. Article 1, section 5.

GLOSSARY

1. Provided with permission of the Senate Republican Policy Committee.

Selected Bibliography

Bach, Stanley. "Conference Committee and Related Procedures: An Introduction." Report No. 96-708 GOV., Congressional Research Service, Library of Congress, Washington, D.C., 1999.

———. "Fast-track or Expedited Procedures: Their Purposes, Elements, and Implications." CRS Report No. 98-888, Congressional Research Service, Library of Congress, Washington, D.C., 2001.

———. "Filibusters and Cloture in the Senate." CRS Document No. RL 30360, Congressional Research Service, Library of Congress, Washington, D.C., 2001.

———. "Legislative Activity in Committee: The Impact of Senate Rules." Report No. 95-9 S, Congressional Research Service, Library of Congress, Washington, D.C., 1994.

———. "Minority Rights and Senate Procedures." CRS Report No. RL 30850, Congressional Research Service, Library of Congress, Washington, D.C., 2001.

Bazan, Elizabeth B. "Impeachment: An Overview of Constitutional Provisions, Procedure and Practice." Report No. 98-186A, Congressional Research Service, Library of Congress, Washington, D.C., 1998.

———. Memorandum. "Continuation of an Impeachment Proceeding or an Impeachment Investigation from One Congress to the Next Congress." Congressional Research Service, Library of Congress, Washington, D.C.

Bell, Lauren Cohen. *Warring Factions: Interest Groups, Money, and the New Politics of Senate Confirmation.* Columbus: Ohio State University Press, 2002.

Beth, Richard S. "Motions to Proceed to Consider in the Senate: Who Offers Them?" Report No. RS21255, Congressional Research Service, Library of Congress, Washington, D.C., 2002.

———. "Presenting Measures to the President for Approval: Possible Delays." CRS Report No. 95-571 GOV, Congressional Research Service, Library of Congress, Washington, D.C., 1996.

———. "Statutory Provisions for Calling Up Measures Subject to Expedited Procedures in the Senate." CRS Memorandum, Congressional Research Service, Library of Congress, Washington, D.C., 2002.

Binder, Sarah A., and Steven S. Smith. *Politics or Principle? Filibustering in the United States Senate*. Washington, D.C.: Brookings Institution, 1997.

Burdette, Franklin L. *Filibustering in the Senate*. Princeton, N.J.: Princeton University Press, 1940.

Caro, Robert A. *Master of the Senate*. New York: Random House, 2002.

Carr, Thomas P. "Reporting a Measure from a Senate Committee." Report No. 98-246 GOV, Congressional Research Service, Library of Congress, Washington, D.C., 2001.

Cooper, Joseph. *The Previous Question: Its Standing as a Precedent for Cloture in the United States Senate*. S. Doc. 87-104, 87th Cong. 2nd sess. Washington, D.C.: Government Printing Office, 1962.

Evans, L. "Floor Decision Making in the U.S. Senate." Paper. APSA Meeting. Washington. August 31–September 3, 2000.

Fisher, Louis. "The Pocket Veto: Its Current Status." CRS Report No. RL30909, Congressional Research Service, Library of Congress, Washington, D.C., 2001.

Galemore, Gary L. "The Presidential Veto and Congressional Procedure." CRS Report No. 98-156 GOV, Congressional Research Service, Library of Congress, Washington, D.C., 2001.

Gamm, G., and S. S. Smith. "Evolution of Floor Management in the U.S. Senate." Paper. MPSA Meeting, April 23–25, 1998.

Heniff, Bill, Jr. "Allocations and Subdivisions in the Congressional Budget Process." Report No. RS2, Congressional Research Service, Library of Congress, Washington, D.C.

———. "Budget Resolution Enforcement," Congressional Research Service, Library of Congress, Washington, D.C., 2001.

Hogue, Henry B. "Recess Appointments: Frequently Asked Questions." CRS Report RS21308, Congressional Research Service, Library of Congress, Washington, D.C., 2002.

Keith, Robert. "A Brief Introduction to the Federal Budget Process." Report No. 96-912 GOV, Congressional Research Service, Library of Congress, Washington, D.C.

———. "Budget Reconciliation Procedures: The Senate's 'Byrd Rule.'" Report No. RL30862, Congressional Research Service, Library of Congress, Washington, D.C., 2002.

Riddick, Floyd M. Senate Parliamentarian, Oral History Interviews. Washington, D.C.: Senate Historical Office.

Rundquist, Paul S. "S. Res. 160: Rule XVI and Reversing the Hutchison and FedEx Precedents." Report No. RS20276, Congressional Research Service, Library of Congress, Washington, D.C., 1999.

Saturno, James V. "The Appropriations Process and the Congressional Budget Act." Report No. 97-947, Congressional Research Service, Library of Congress, Washington, D.C., 1997.

Schiller, W. "Strategic Leadership in Congress: The Use of Senate Rules to Shape Intra-Chamber and Inter-Chamber Legislative Behavior." Paper. APSA Meeting, Washington, D.C., August 31–September 3, 2000.

U.S. Congress, Senate. *The Senate 1789-1989*, by Robert C. Byrd, vol. 2. S. Doc.100-20 100th Cong., 1st sess., 1988.

U.S. Senate. *Riddick's Senate Procedure*. Senate Document No. 101-28. 101st Congress, 2nd Session, 1992.

Index

GAYLORD S

About the Author

Martin B. Gold is an attorney in private practice in Washington, D.C. In 1972 he began Senate service in the office of Senator Mark O. Hatfield (R-OR) and subsequently worked under Senator Hartfield's sponsorship at the Senate Select Committee on Intelligence and the Senate Committee on Rules and Administration. In 1979 he joined the staff of Senate Minority Leader Howard H. Baker Jr. and concluded his tenure at the Senate in 1982 as counsel to Majority Leader Baker. In 2003, he served Senate Majority Leader William H. Frist as counsel and floor advisor.

Mr. Gold first published *Senate Procedure and Practice: An Introductory Manual* in 1981 and revised that work seven times during the following twenty years. In addition, he is coauthor of *The Book on Congress*, published in 1992.

Mr. Gold has spoken in numerous domestic and international venues on Senate procedure and on American politics and government. He lives in Washington, D.C., with his wife, Celeste.